Praise for
Twenty-Percent Soldiers

"The Dellickers' engaging account of life in the National Guard ⸱ fitting complement to the brave men and women who serve part-time in the US military and the families who support them. The ideal of the 'citizen-soldier' taking up arms and returning to civilian life when the battle is won is as old as our republic and remains true today. Susan and Kevin's story is a poignant reminder that our freedom still depends on 'twenty-percent soldiers' who volunteer to protect and defend our nation when duty calls."

> —Tom Ridge
> 43rd Governor of Pennsylvania, First US Secretary of Homeland Security

"This book by Susan and Kevin Dellicker is important for many reasons. It tells a story that needs to be told about the role of the National Guard in a world changed by the events of September 11, 2001, from the perspective of a Guardsman, and perhaps even more importantly, from the perspective of his spouse. The stories told are delightful, exciting, human, and patriotic. As you turn the pages you will have a laugh and then shortly after that you will shed a tear. Ultimately, you will be proud to be an American and proud of the men and women who serve our country and the family members who support those who serve in uniform."

> —John L. Gronski
> Major General, US Army (Retired)

"AN AMAZING MUST READ. The Dellickers offer an awesome story of two ordinary people who juggle thousands of crystal balls. They keep all the crystal balls in the air through daily life and deployments to war. *Twenty-Percent Soldiers* is an extraordinary view into the life of a citizen-solider and his supportive wife and family."

> —Jessica Garfola Wright
> Major General, US Army (Retired), Former Under Secretary of Defense for Personnel and Readiness, 50th Adjutant General of Pennsylvania, 2020 Inductee into the US Army Women's Foundation Hall of Fame

"As a writer/journalist who has twice been on assignment in Afghanistan, including time spent with the Pennsylvania National Guard, and who frequently writes about the military, *Twenty-Percent Soldiers* resonates on many levels . . .

"This is a memoir with a strong love story at its core, not only the love of Kevin and Susan Dellicker for each other and their three boys, but the love of country and the sacrifices made to protect it. *Twenty-Percent Soldiers* is also a history book that chronicles twenty years of war from the perspective of the 'citizen-soldiers' of the National Guard, during one of the most critical times in our country's history. And it is a testament to Christian faith and the strength such faith can bring to a marriage, a family, and a warrior.

"Strongly written and a smooth read, *Twenty-Percent Soldiers* will leave you with a deep appreciation for the service of our men and women of the National Guard, as well as the realization of what it means to wear our country's uniform."

—Pamela Varkony
Award-Winning Journalist and Writer, Pearl S. Buck International Woman of Influence

"This is the best portrayal that I have read of the joys, trials, and tribulations of being a citizen-soldier family . . . the twenty percenters! I was honored to have served with Kevin. I wish that I had gotten to know Susan and the boys . . . but through their life-story in this book, I feel that I do now. Change the dates, times, and names, and this story of Kevin and Susan could just as easily have been the story of Wilbur and Amy or any one of hundreds of thousands of National Guard families. Well done, Susan and Kevin . . . for God, Family, and Country."

—Wilbur E. Wolf III
Brigadier General, US Army (Retired)

"The Dellicker family journey is at the same time unique and universally American. A very sincere, engaging page-turner about choosing and achieving important missions of life."

—Chris Bravacos
Communications Consultant and Chief Executive Officer

"This book is an excellent read on the very unique role of citizen-soldiers in the National Guard. Being a 'part-time soldier' and full-time civilian really is doing two full-time jobs at the same time. The authors do a great job bringing the challenges and rewards that come with being both civilians and military members/family into sharp focus.

"Told with humor and humility, with discussions about service in both the Army and Air Force, the challenges of being a military mom with three small and active sons, and the tremendous support provided by their family, friends and personal faith, this is a must read for anyone who cares about our military service members and their families. It is the part-time citizen-soldier who has parts of their lives in both worlds, the military and civilian."

—Wesley E. Craig
Major General, US Army (Retired), 34th Commanding General, 28th Division, 51st Adjutant General of Pennsylvania

"You will be drawn into this book as the Dellickers provide a detailed account of the struggles, sacrifices, hard work and commitment our National Guard soldiers dedicate to protecting our country. This is a truly inspirational tale from an ordinary family that has done extraordinary things. The Dellickers pull back the curtain on the life of a Guardsman. But until I read this book, I underestimated the level of commitment, dedication, perseverance, and passion needed to balance the life of a soldier, a spouse, and a parent."

—Marty Nothstein
Olympic Gold Medalist, Author of The Price of Gold: The Toll and Triumph of One Man's Olympic Dream

"*Twenty-Percent Soldiers* is the first book I've read that captures so well the heartfelt journey of a National Guard family. Kevin and Susan Dellicker's life, and those of other military families, should not stay a secret. It may technically be a part-time job, but in *Twenty-Percent Soldiers*, Kevin and Susan Dellicker show us National Guard service is a full-time commitment, not only for a soldier, but his wife and children, too. Anyone wanting to understand the joys, challenges and perils facing National Guard families should read *Twenty-Percent Soldiers*."

—Jeanette Krebs
Former Opinions Editor, The Patriot-News/Pennlive

"This book brings to light the many struggles a typical Guardsman family faces, particularly at home. Kevin's and Susan's account of the balancing act of family, civilian job, and military will show that being a 'weekend warrior' is not for the meek. They intertwine real life experiences, including the good, bad, and ugly, with such finesse that on one page you will be laughing and then turn the page and realize you need to stop the tears of sorrow. All Guardsmen struggle with their commitments, and this book will show you firsthand why the struggle is real."

—Sharon A. Hedges
Colonel, US Air Force (Retired)

"*Twenty-Percent Soldiers* is a raw dose of reality about the strength, dignity, and sacrifice of our National Guard and Reserve families. The perfect story of striving to achieve family-work-military balance with an inside glimpse into the unique Special Operations Command mission of the world's only Commando Solo weapon system and the Guard unit that employs it. A journey into the thrills, challenges, depression, heartache, and resolute faith of professional citizen-soldiers and their families, as well as driving home the importance of delivering support resources to these families in communities where they live!

"A must-read for all military leaders to understand the tremendous knowledge and skills available in the Guard and Reserves while offering a glimpse into the struggles they experience abruptly transitioning from civilian to military. A must-read for teachers/supporters/therapists/friends/members connected to military reservists, their children, friends, neighbors, parents and in-laws to best connect, understand the struggles, and support them as they continue to support the most noble cause of service to our community, state, and nation. Thank you to all who have done so!"

—Kathleen Fabrizi
Executive Director of the Pennsylvania National Guard Associations, Veteran, Mother, and Military Spouse

"Twenty-Percent Soldiers is a brutally honest account of the challenging lives faced by members of the National Guard and their families. We owe them all a great debt of respect, gratitude and honor when oftentimes we have them go it alone. Increasingly, our state and nation rely on them completely; while we continue to underfund their units and family support while treating them as half-citizens and half-soldiers. Frankly, I can't wait to share this book with family and friends as well as policy makers in Harrisburg and Washington."

—Kelly Lewis
Esquire, Former Pennsylvania State Representative, Civilian Lobbyist, Pennsylvania National Guard Associations

"Twenty-Percent Soldiers is an engaging, well-written depiction of today's part-time Guardsman/Reservist, told from the perspective of the service member, his wife and family. It lays out the challenges and sacrifices that today's Guardsman/Reservist faces, and the perseverance needed to commit to a part-time military career. The book provides an insider's insight into service as a member of a National Guard that is now utilized as an operational component of the total military, a Guard that provides much more to the nation's readiness, and defense, than they receive in support, funding, or recognition.

"Every citizen should read this book to gain an understanding of the requirements/challenges of serving in today's all-volunteer Guard and Reserve. Every employer should read this book to gain a perspective and better appreciation of the patriotic duty, to our country, undertaken by those who volunteer to serve in the National Guard and Reserve. Long gone are the days of the weekend warrior. The men and women in today's Guard, and Reserve, are the very best of America, willing to put their lives on the line to defend our freedom, our values, and our American way of life."

—James Astor
Colonel, US Air Force (Retired)

Twenty-Percent Soldiers

by Susan and Kevin Dellicker

Cover photo courtesy of Jodi Chandler Photography.

Published by

◤ köehlerbooks™

3705 Shore Drive
Virginia Beach, VA 23455
800–435–4811
www.koehlerbooks.com

Twenty Percent Soldiers

our secret life in the National Guard

SUSAN AND KEVIN DELLICKER

VIRGINIA BEACH
CAPE CHARLES

To all the soldiers, airmen and families of the National Guard.

TABLE OF CONTENTS

DISCLAIMER

THIS MANUSCRIPT AND SUPPLEMENTAL photographs submitted for prepublication security review are CLEARED AS AMENDED for public release by the Defense Office of Prepublication and Security Review, Department of Defense.

Except for public officials and military generals, the full names of military members and private citizens are used with prior written permission. Otherwise, individuals are identified by rank and partial name only, or by a pseudonym, to protect their privacy and safeguard the identity of anyone assigned to a sensitive military unit.

The views expressed in this publication are those of the authors and do not necessarily reflect the official policy or position of the Department of Defense or the United States government. The public release clearance of this publication by the Department of Defense does not imply Department of Defense endorsement or factual accuracy of the material.

FOREWORD

THIS IS THE STORY of a National Guardsman and his wife serving our country together for almost two decades of war. It was written collaboratively by us, Susan and Kevin Dellicker, to describe our experiences in the Pennsylvania National Guard as part-time contributors to the Global War on Terrorism.

During this time, we have occupied a complicated space somewhere between military and civilian life without really feeling at home in either. Yet our story is not unique. There are thousands of other Guard and Reserve families just like ours across the nation. This is their story too.

To most of our neighbors, we are typical civilians. We own a small business and work regular jobs. We live in rural Pennsylvania and spend most of our free time watching our teenage boys play sports and hanging out with our friends. We appear to live a normal, middle-class American life. And we do. But we live a secret life too.

Kevin is an intelligence officer in the 193rd Special Operations Wing, the most deployed unit in the Air National Guard. Susan is a military wife working behind the scenes. Together, we've supported four overseas deployments, ten stateside missions, twenty-two formal schools, twenty-four training exercises, and 1,549 days on orders. Through it all, we've been on some kind of military status for just about *20 percent* of our life together. It's a part-time job with a full-time commitment for the entire family.

Our purpose in writing this book is threefold. First, we hope to reassure other Guard and Reserve families that they are not alone. As generations of "citizen-soldiers" have successfully balanced civilian and military life, so too can modern reservists. Although it can be daunting at times, our story is proof that part-time soldiers and their families still can survive and thrive, even in a state of perpetual war.

Second, we hope that our friends and neighbors can better understand what the National Guard does and its importance to our country. We don't just put on uniforms and "play Army" once a month, as we've heard it described. We have a unique responsibility for homeland defense and critical role in overseas missions. And, it's not just civilians that have misunderstandings. Despite 250 years of integration, much of our full-time force remains uninformed about the vital contributions of the National Guard to our past military victories and present combat operations.

Finally, we want to raise awareness of the family support challenges unique to the part-time force. While blessed by the generous gratitude of ordinary Americans, Guardsmen and their families do not receive the same level of institutional support as their full-time counterparts. That's primarily because most active-duty families are concentrated near large military bases with abundant resources, while most Guard families are dispersed in communities with no bases at all. Perhaps this book will inspire a policymaker to fix this problem and provide Guard and Reserve families the resources they deserve.

Being part of the National Guard comes with more than its fair share of challenges. But we are not victims. We are pleased to carry on the tradition of the citizen-soldier. As a military weapon, the Guard is a potent force multiplier, one that no other country can emulate or defeat. As a cultural force, the Guard is our most effective bridge between the military and civilians. It unites us in the shared values of integrity, service, and patriotism. And, in these times of seemingly boundless strife, that's something all Americans can still believe in.

National Guardsmen and their families should not have to serve in secret. Perhaps this account will shine some light on this uniquely American institution, the part-time soldiers and airmen who report for duty, and the families who serve full-time right beside them. We hope you find our story mostly interesting, sometimes funny, and always sincere.

God bless,

Susan & Kevin Dellicker

INTRODUCTION: I DIDN'T ASK FOR THIS

TOILET BRUSH.

Wastepaper basket.

Paper towel holder.

These were just a few of the items on my list for my shopping trip to the Kmart that morning. Kevin and I had just moved into our new home near Kutztown, Pennsylvania the week before. I went to Kmart because it was the only store I knew how to find.

As I was checking out, the woman in line in front of me told the cashier that a plane had flown into one of the World Trade Center towers.

What a terrible accident, I thought.

I bought my household items and drove home.

Out of curiosity, I turned on the TV to see what was going on with the plane crash. By then, the second plane had hit tower number two. This was no accident.

I watched my son Will toddle across the floor; I went over, scooped him up, and with a tear in my eye, gave him a tight squeeze. I held him, as long as a fourteen-month-old will let you before they squirm away. He went on playing on the living room floor as I sat glued to the TV.

Soon, I had watched this terrible event unfold long enough. I knew that my life had just changed drastically.

Today, I had become a wartime military wife.

Would Kevin be safe?

Would he be homesick?

Would he be near the action or away from the front lines?

Would he be home in time for the new baby? [I guess I forgot to mention that I was six months pregnant with our second son.]

What I didn't know, and could not comprehend, was that this new role as a wartime military wife would last eighteen years. Kevin's temporary service as a National Guardsman would become a permanent obligation for our entire family.

I didn't ask for this.

But I accepted it, sometimes with grace and class and sometimes kicking and screaming.

This is our account of how we built a marriage and raised three sons as a part-time military family in a permanent state of war.

CHAPTER ONE: A DAY OF RECKONING

I WAS SITTING IN a bar in Albany, New York, in 1995. We were watching March Madness basketball on TV and eating buffalo wings at the Hill Street Cafe. My friends and I were talking about our future plans and I told them I wanted to join the military. "Someday, but not right now."

My friend Murph chuckled and rolled his eyes.

"Kevin," he said. "You're never joining the military. You've missed your chance."

Murph had heard me talk about joining the service before. In fact, I had been saying it for years. I was going to be a military man, just like my father and grandfather. I wanted to serve my country in uniform. But there was never a convenient time.

First I skipped a Navy ROTC opportunity because I wanted to go to college without the extra commitment. After graduating, I passed on Marine Corps Officer Candidate School so I could get a master's degree. Then I declined a chance to join the Air Force because I had gotten a new job in New York. Now, I had a raise and a promotion, and life was good. I definitely was going to join the military someday. Just not today.

"You're too old," he snickered.

Who was I kidding? Murph's blunt words hit me like a ton of bricks. After I left the bar, I thought about them all night. Murph was right. I was all talk and no action.

At twenty-four years old, I wasn't really too old to join the military, although I was already much older than a typical recruit. The fact is, I was too comfortable with my civilian life. I needed to stop lying to myself. The next day I went to the local recruiter to enlist in the Army National Guard.

My dad thought I was nuts. My father, retired Colonel Bill Dellicker, had been a Navy fighter pilot in Vietnam for six years and an officer in the Air National Guard for another twenty-nine. He had given me the same advice dozens of times. "If you are going to join the military, make sure you are an officer." Instead, I decided to enlist in the infantry.

I suppose this was some kind of strange way to rebel against my dad. I admired him more than any other man and always wanted to be like him. But I didn't want to be his clone. So instead of being an officer aviator, I became the thing most opposite of that I could imagine and still be in the service, an enlisted grunt.

In joining the military, I decided to go part-time in the Army National Guard instead of full time on active duty. My father had attended weekend meetings and annual training exercises for most of my childhood, so I was familiar with the concept of part-time service. I figured the Guard would let me have the best of both worlds- military and civilian, just like the TV commercials. How hard could it be?

It wasn't just my father who thought I made an unusual choice. Some of my friends figured I was making a terrible decision and urged me to reconsider. Others thought I was wasting my education, going on a vacation, or running away from something. Most people were supportive but puzzled about why a seemingly normal guy with a college education and a good job would enlist in the infantry. If I hadn't acted so quickly, I might have talked myself out of it like I had done before. But this time, I just did it.

I had arrived in Albany through a circuitous route. Three years prior, I had been a student at Penn State University, finishing up undergraduate degrees in history and environmental resource management. The first degree was for enjoyment. The second was to get a job. I was a bona fide tree-hugger and wanted to be a park ranger or something like that.

After graduating, I got a job offer as an environmental consultant in Fairfax, Virginia, but it didn't start for another six months. In the meantime, I applied for a graduate program at Syracuse University and earned a scholarship. I decided to forgo the environmental job in Virginia and get my master's degree in public administration instead.

While at Syracuse, I met the girl I thought I would marry. It wasn't Susan. She was a law student who had another year to go, so when I graduated, my primary goal was to stay close to Syracuse. Then when she finished law school, we could move somewhere together and start a life.

I found out about this one-year fellowship program in Albany, New York, which seemed to be a great stopgap position. It was an internship with the state legislature with no obligations after it ended. I could gain experience without looking like a job-hopper, then leave the job with no strings attached. Plus, it was only a two-hour drive to Syracuse, so I could visit my girlfriend every weekend.

The fellowship was structured to be nonpartisan research and policy work. When you applied, you didn't know which office you would be supporting or whether your boss would be a Democrat or Republican. Based on my background and their requirements, I was assigned to the office of the Senate majority leader, who happened to be a Republican. I would work on economic and environmental policy issues, which seemed to be a good match to my education.

That was September of 1994, and the nation was about to experience a wave election, putting Republicans in office across the country. In Washington, this was the era of Newt Gingrich and the so-called "Contract for America," which delivered a Republican majority in Congress for the first time in decades. In Albany, it meant the election of George Pataki, the first Republican governor since the era of Nelson Rockefeller, twenty years prior.

Although I had nothing to do with the election and didn't know anything about New York politics, the aftermath had important implications for my job. The Senate majority leader was a lukewarm supporter of the new governor and got forced out of his leadership role soon after the election. Several of his closest aides either quit or were fired, and other staffers in the office took jobs in the Pataki administration.

By the end of November, I was one of a handful of people left in the office. The new Senate majority leader needed warm bodies to fill all the open positions, so he hired me out of my internship into a full-time role. I don't think I ever even met the senator before I got the job. Within two months, I had gone from being a newbie intern with no political connections to a full-time staffer in the office of a high-ranking legislator.

Meanwhile, my relationship with the Syracuse law student ended abruptly. What a strange turn of events. I had arrived in Albany for a temporary job and a permanent relationship. Now I had a permanent job and no relationship. Maybe joining the Army was my way of running away after all.

When I enlisted, I suppose I didn't consider much what my employer would think. I told my boss in May that I would be leaving for basic training in October, which was plenty of notice. I knew that a state senator could not possibly criticize a staff member for departing for military duty. I also knew that federal law requires employers to allow their employees to enter military status and then return to their jobs without penalty. While this is a critical legal protection for Guardsmen, the back-and-forth of military service can be very difficult for employers and fellow workers to manage. This is often overlooked when describing the impact of part-time military service on people's lives.

I didn't interact much with the senators and had no personal relationships with them, so I didn't really care what they thought. But I did care what my colleagues thought, and I felt bad about sticking them with extra work, especially my good friends Pam and Bob. Our busiest time was during budget season, which stretched from mid-January to August. I felt better about leaving my colleagues because I would go during our slowest period and be back before February, an ideal time to be gone.

My direct boss was the majority leader's top lawyer. Tim. He was friendly and smart but also an intense workaholic. After I told him about my commitment, he took a drag on his cigarette and thought for a minute. He said that as long as I would be back in time to work on the budget by February, he didn't mind if I was gone during the fall. After he gave me his blessing, I went on my way.

On October 16, 1995, I left for Fort Benning, Georgia. Even though I had been living away from home for seven years, I had never experienced the lack of freedom you get at basic training. I suppose it's like being in jail, except I hear you get to watch TV in jail.

Right out of the gate, I hit an unforeseen snag. I got stuck in the dreaded 30th Adjutant General (AG) reception battalion. The 30th AG may be the worst place in the Army. Anyone who has ever been through Army Infantry School knows what I am talking about and probably is shuddering in revulsion just thinking about it.

The 30th AG is supposed to be the place at Fort Benning where recruits arrive to get their shots, uniforms, and haircuts before proceeding to actual basic training. Its real purpose, however, is to test your ability to withstand hopeless boredom for an extended period. One private described it as hell except with more heat casualties and less sleep. Purgatory is probably a better metaphor.

You are not allowed to do anything at the 30th AG except wait around to get out of the place. Meanwhile, you are constantly getting screamed at for nothing. Some of the screaming is from drill sergeants, which is unpleasant but expected. Much of it comes from grumpy civilians, which is puzzling. The worst is getting screamed at by other recruits who arrived at the 30th AG two days before you did and now think they are General Patton.

I found out that a hurricane had come through a few weeks prior and delayed all the training schedules around Fort Benning. Hundreds of recruits were jammed into this human warehouse, sleeping, eating, and waiting. Sleeping, eating, and waiting. Eventually, even the Patton kids became demoralized and fell into line. Sleeping, eating, and waiting.

After about two weeks, I finally got out of that place and made it to real basic training. They loaded us onto cattle trucks and deposited us on Sand Hill, where we would live for the next few months. We experienced the so-called "shark attack," where the drill sergeants welcome the recruits like you see in the movies, but most of us didn't mind. We were just happy to be out of the 30th AG.

In my new training platoon, I was not like the other young men in several respects. First, I was older. Almost all my fellow trainees were eighteen or nineteen and right out of high school. Second, I had a white-collar job. There was only one other guy in the platoon who had worked in an office prior to enlisting, and only a handful had a college education. At one point, I remember teaching a bunch of the kids how to tie a necktie.

Because of my age and education, the drill sergeants made me "platoon guide," or "PG," as they would say. This meant that when one of the young guys messed up, I got punished for it. I was like the head janitor, the house mom, and the security guard combined. It's a crappy job, but it teaches you a lot about leadership. If you can get a bunch of teenage boys to do something they don't want to do with precision and enthusiasm, you can pretty much do anything in the civilian world.

I quickly learned that book smarts mean nothing in the infantry. These kids may have been young and inexperienced, but they were motivated and hardworking. Plus, they were smart, common sense smart, which is something a lot of the fancy fellows in Albany were not.

For three months, I experienced all the sleep deprivation, physical hardships, and mental pressures of 11-Bravo (11B) training at Fort Benning. For all the non-soldiers reading this, 11B is the Army Military Occupational Specialty (MOS) code for light infantry soldiers. Infantry basic training was one of the best times of my life.

One of the transformative experiences for me at Fort Benning involved my relationship with God. I had been raised a Christian and had attended various churches throughout my life. But despite all those years of church attendance, I was no choirboy. I was still very immature in my faith.

For an Army recruit, Sunday mornings presented a straightforward choice: you could either stay behind in the barracks with the drill sergeants or go to church. Especially during the first few weeks of basic training, most soldiers would have chosen getting their teeth pulled over staying in the barracks for any reason, let alone risking an encounter with the drill sergeant. Almost everybody went to church.

Inside the Sand Hill chapel at Fort Benning, the first thing you saw was the enormous stained-glass window of an infantryman, outfitted with his M-16 rifle, kneeling in prayer. Soldiers come and go, but that iconic image has endured for at least three generations. Thousands of infantrymen have paused to consider what he represents.

Our chaplain had been a member of the infantry before becoming a minister. I don't remember his name, but he was a paratrooper and went to combat during the first Gulf War. He commanded respect before he even spoke. But his demeanor was gentle, his words were convincing, and his presence was comforting to a bunch of homesick and scared young men.

At Fort Benning, I realized that I had a lot to learn about God, religion, and myself. For the first time, I read the New Testament all the way through from Matthew to Revelation. I witnessed dozens of men learn about God, become baptized, and commit their lives to Jesus. And it was the first time I really talked about God with other people outside of church. I realized that going to church and "acting religious" were not the same as having a relationship with God.

In some respects, infantry basic training was the godliest experience of my life up to that point, and I know that others in my battalion felt the same way. That may seem strange at first, but it makes perfect sense. Every day, we were learning either how to kill people or avoid being killed. We didn't often think of it in such stark terms, but during those rare moments when the drill sergeants weren't screaming at us, we came to realize that we were a group of young men being educated in death. If a curriculum like that doesn't force a person to contemplate his mortality and his moral responsibilities toward others, then he's probably a sadist that should never have his finger on a trigger.

Nobody forced their religion on anybody at Fort Benning. But I found my Army counterparts and instructors more spiritual than any other population of citizens I had previously known. Thank God for that. American soldiers always have fought for something larger than themselves. From my experience, that tradition continues in the modern military, despite some organized efforts to stamp it out.

So does the tradition of professionalism. At basic training, I learned what a real American soldier is like, especially in the noncommissioned officer (NCO) corps. Our drill sergeants were among the most impressive individuals I have encountered in any part of my life. Almost everyone was a combat veteran, most from the first Gulf War in Iraq. They did not just talk about hardship and service; they had lived it. In their military bearing, technical knowledge, and leadership abilities, these men provided an example of manhood to emulate.

Plus, they had a way with words. For me, the most memorable line from basic training was from Sergeant First Class McKinney, the senior drill sergeant for Alpha Company, 2-54 Infantry Brigade. To paraphrase, he told us recruits, "You are here to protect those who cannot defend themselves and those who will not defend themselves."

I had often thought about the first part of his statement. It was the second part that gave me the shivers. Until Murph's good-natured ribbing at Hill Street Cafe earlier that year, I was on the way to becoming one of those people so aptly described in the latter half of Sergeant First Class McKinney's statement.

Don't get me wrong. There are plenty of great ways to serve your country besides the armed forces. Millions of people who want to serve can't pass the physical. Many more have alternative commitments to work, family, or faith that contribute substantially to our nation. I have no patience for misguided veterans who disparage, disrespect, or denigrate non-veterans just because they never wore the uniform. For lots of good reasons, military service is just not something that most people do.

But somebody must. And I was proud to stand with Sergeant First Class McKinney. I could feel my military service quickly becoming part of my identity.

In basic training, there was no difference between the National Guard and the active duty. The term "active duty" generally describes full-time servicemen and -women who join the military and then spend the duration of their enlistment in full-time service to their country. These are the so-called "regulars" of American military history and the soldiers, sailors, airmen, Marines, and Coasties (people in the Coast Guard) who make up the bulk of the modern US military.

In contrast to the active duty, the National Guard is part of the reserve component, informally known as "the reserves." This component encompasses the Reserves (with a capital "R"), which includes all service branches, and the National Guard, which only includes the Army and Air Force. It primarily consists of servicemen and -women who are part-time members of the US armed forces. I know it's complicated. This is one reason why so many people inside and outside the service can't figure out who's who in the American military.

Fortunately, nobody knew or cared about your status at basic training. Whether you were active duty or reserves, full-time or part-time didn't matter. We were all just soldiers. In fact, it wasn't until the very end of basic training that most people figured out your status at all. That's when the drill sergeants announced the follow-on assignments for all the graduating trainees. The active-duty guys went all over the place. And the reserve guys went home.

It was kind of romantic hearing all the places that the active-duty soldiers were going. My battle buddy was excited to be going to the 25th Infantry Division in Hawaii. Another guy went to Korea, which was the closest thing to a combat zone at the time. Another guy went to Fort Bragg, North Carolina, which is where he grew up. That was a nice surprise for his family. One fortunate soldier got selected for Army Airborne School and a chance to become a Ranger. I was a bit envious of that opportunity.

I got released from active duty on Friday, February 2, 1996. I flew home to my parents, had a quick visit, and picked up the new truck I had purchased with the money I had saved during basic training. Then I drove home to Albany.

I can't remember for sure, but think I was back at work in the New York State Senate that following Monday morning.

CHAPTER TWO: GUARDSMAN WHIPLASH

THE NEXT FEW MONTHS were my first experience with what Susan and I would later call "Guardsman Whiplash." That's a sudden change in direction from a military setting to civilian life without adequate transition. It's culture shock in your own environment. It affects both Guardsmen and their families, and it also can affect coworkers, as I would quickly come to realize.

When I returned from basic training, I felt like I had been a part of something special, a tradition of service going back to ancient times. I was in a brotherhood only fellow soldiers could truly understand. I felt like I could relate to my father better, and my grandfather too. I was proud to be a soldier.

I also connected with a new group of people, a bunch of guys very different from those I had been around since high school. At Penn State, Syracuse, and Albany, I had had plenty of good friends, and they were all unique and different. But most of them were white people from the mid-Atlantic region with middle-class backgrounds.

Not so in the Army. The infantry was diverse, blue-collar, and gritty. There were lots of guys from the South who came from proud but poor families. My battle buddy was a Jamaican with a thick accent and something to prove. There were street-smart inner-city kids and redneck country bumpkins. It was an awesome, amazing group of people working together for a common purpose—to defend their country by taking up arms.

Back in Albany, I told all my funny basic training stories and described all the cool stuff I had done. I told them how I mistakenly shot the bunker with my M-16 after my night-sights failed and how my drill sergeant yelled at me while pummeling me on the head with a stick. "What are you trying to do, shoot snakes?" he had screamed.

I talked about how I was issued "birth control" glasses and never wore them because they were so ugly. I bragged that I had earned "expert" in hand grenade throwing, learned to set up Claymore mines, and qualified to fire the dragon anti-tank missile. I told them about puking on my commander during a company run: he hadn't even noticed the vomit on the back of his legs, but he did wonder why guys were slipping and falling out of formation behind him. I talked about the coyotes we had heard and the cadences we had sung, and how cold it was in Georgia in January. I described pugil stick fighting and bayonet stabbing, the crazy-eyed guy from Minnesota, and the funny "Yooper" from Michigan.

I wanted to tell everybody about all my experiences, but nobody could relate. I had already become that boring old guy at the diner who never stopped telling his war stories. Except I was still young and had never gone to war. Eventually, I guess, I just stopped talking about it, but I never really got back to my pre-Army mindset. Something was different. Although I was no longer on active duty, I didn't feel like a civilian either.

I picked up right where I left off in my senate job. I had a new apartment downtown, a new Ford F-150 4X4 pickup truck, and a new confidence in my leadership abilities. I was going to make the best of my time in Albany, even if it didn't feel like home. During the next year and a half, I immersed myself in my work, both military and civilian.

For my National Guard commitment, I had to travel once a month to my duty station in Kutztown, Pennsylvania. I could have chosen something closer to Albany, but I wanted to return to Pennsylvania eventually, and Kutztown was near my parents' house. It gave me a good reason once a month to visit them while I came to town for drill. The four-hour drive each way was kind of a pain, but it was no big deal in my nice new truck.

I was a member of Charlie Company, 1-111th Infantry Regiment (1-111 INF or 1-111th), a subordinate unit to the 28th Infantry Division (28th ID or 28th). These were storied units with a long history of service. The 111th was named the "Associators" by its founder Benjamin Franklin in 1747 and fought alongside George Washington in the Revolutionary War. I got a lot of crap for wearing the Associators unit crest on my left sleeve during basic training because it looked like an Army Ranger Battalion insignia. In fact, our regiment had earned that special crest before the Ranger Battalions even existed. It was the longest continually serving unit in the United States Army.

The 28th Infantry Division, deemed the Iron Division by General Pershing because of the soldiers' tenacity during World War I, has a bright red Keystone patch as its combat service identification badge. German soldiers, seeing this insignia on the uniforms during World War II, nicknamed the unit the "Bloody Bucket." The 28th is arguably best known for its service during the Battle of the Bulge in World War II. However, the Iron Division has been deeply involved with every major conflict, except for Vietnam, since the American Civil War.

The soldiers in Charlie Company were not quite as diverse as the guys in basic training—most were from eastern Pennsylvania—but they were just as blue-collar. It was refreshing to have a core group of friends and colleagues from the military so different from the people in my civilian job. They all knew about the 30th AG and the shark attack and could elaborate on all my stupid basic training stories. It was like returning to a safe and familiar place every month with a bunch of old friends, even though I had just met everybody. I didn't know the individuals, but I knew the type. We were infantrymen.

And we were Guardsmen. When the weekend was over, we went back to our real jobs, the ones that paid the bills.

My civilian career was going well, and I was gaining lots of responsibility in the New York State Senate. In fact, I gained too much responsibility for a young staffer with limited life experiences, as I would later learn. But at the time, it was quite an exciting job. I was managing legislation and developing budgets that dealt with environmental and economic development policies. Since these two issues were key parts of Governor Pataki's agenda, I was often at the negotiating table with much more experienced people. As a twenty-six-year-old kid, I was negotiating billion-dollar budgets.

It's insane, really, that someone with such limited life experiences could have that kind of influence. Yes, I had a good education. But besides a bunch of summer gigs as a laborer and bartender, my position in the senate was my first full-time job. I had no relevant experience, only book smarts. And although Army infantry school provides lots of leadership training and practical experience, it doesn't exactly qualify you to make statewide environmental policy.

Nonetheless, I had broad authority to review and comment on legislation before it had a chance to pass, and I often knew more about what was going on than the senators themselves. I had a lot of power for a kid, which, I came to learn, is typical for legislatures across the country.

The most interesting work I did in Albany came during negotiations on something called the Clean Air/Clean Water Environmental Bond Act. New York voters had approved borrowing $1.75 billion to fund a whole bunch of environmental projects around the state. I, along with a small group of young staffers (and a few older ones too), had to figure out how to spend it. To my surprise and chagrin, one of my novel ideas made it into the legislation.

For several years, upstate Republicans representing rural communities tried to pass legislation allowing farmers to eradicate so-called "nuisance beavers" that were building dams and flooding their fields. And each year, downstate Democrats representing New York City blocked the bills to protect their beloved state animal. At one Bond Act negotiating session, I flippantly proposed that we spend the new money on "non-lethal beaver control mechanisms."

In other words, instead of just shooting problem rodents, the state would finance special construction projects to divert beaver dam ponds to nearby rivers. This would satisfy angry farmers and beaver-lovers alike while saving the lovable, furry creatures.

I was joking. But the guy from New York City loved the idea. He pitched it to some downstate legislators, and they liked it too. In the end, the legislation allocated up to $15 million for "dam safety projects" that would allow my non-lethal beaver control diversions to become reality. For the next few years, Albany would be spending taxpayer money on water slides for beaver families across upstate New York.

To make matters worse, my friends at the negotiating table told the activist lady from the beaver protection society that the dam safety projects were my idea. She was so grateful that she presented me with a massive framed picture of a beaver along with a handwritten signed thank-you note. For the next year, I was finding beaver paperweights on my desk, getting beaver stuffed animals for birthday presents, and washing my hands with beaver-shaped soap that I received from my colleagues.

While I enjoyed my job in the senate and made some very good friends, Albany wasn't exactly the most exciting place for a single guy in his twenties. After that legislative session in 1997, I was already looking for ways to move along.

Meanwhile, I was in a routine with the Pennsylvania National Guard. Once a month on Friday evenings after work, I would drive four hours and either stay with my parents or go straight to drill. Then I would stay at my parents' again on Sunday evening before getting up really early on Monday morning and driving to work on time in Albany.

"Drill" is what Guardsmen and Reservists call their regular training meetings at their base or armory. We don't actually "drill," as in practice military drill and ceremony like Baron von Steuben did in Valley Forge. We don't twirl rifles or march around a parade field. Instead, we "drill" to stay proficient in our military specialties. For me, that meant infantry training.

Drill at Charlie Company was a blast. Usually, we either went to Fort Dix in New Jersey or Fort Indiantown Gap in Pennsylvania, where we practiced small unit tactics or fired weapons on a range. Sometimes, we just stayed in Kutztown and did land navigation in a local park. Regardless, the outdoor physical activity was a welcome diversion from the indoor office work I did all day long in my civilian job.

Besides infantry skills, I learned lots of other interesting and important things on drill weekends, like how to play Spades. That was our card game of choice. My friend Sergeant John was the best, and he would always bail me out when I made stupid mistakes.

I also learned to smoke cigars. Most of the guys were hooked on cigarettes, and I never was tempted to try one. But the cigars smelled good, and I needed something to keep the bugs away in the field. Master Sergeant Bob, our crusty old supply sergeant, always had a box of White Owls with him and was generous in handing them out. They probably had more sawdust than tobacco inside, but I enjoyed them nonetheless.

We also learned how to play Kevlar bowling. Our combat helmets were made from the heavy protective material, designed to stop bullets and shrapnel from destroying our skulls. We called the helmets our "Kevlars." We did Kevlar bowling at the end of a training exercise, when everything was cleaned up and we were getting ready to go home, usually up in the wooden bays at Fort Pickett or Fort Indiantown Gap or wherever.

You'd stack a bunch of beer cans like bowling pins and then run and dive Kevlar-first into them to see how many you knocked over. Platoon Sergeant Gary was the champion Kevlar bowler until he knocked out his front tooth while bowling a strike. We stopped bowling after that.

Although I was trained as light infantry, our unit had M-113 Armored Personnel Carriers (APCs), aluminum boxes on tracks that could fit an infantry squad of about ten people inside. They had a fifty-caliber machine gun mounted on top and could travel about forty miles per hour. They were designed to transport infantry troops into battle.

Unfortunately, the ones we had were mostly leftover pieces of junk from Vietnam. The aluminum was so thin that high-caliber bullets could go right through the sides. They also lacked advanced communications systems and sensors that other modern Army vehicles had. Since the rest of the mechanized infantry was training with state-of-the-art Bradley Fighting Vehicles, our out-of-date M-113s weren't a part of anybody's war plans.

Soon, I started to realize that even though we all had the same initial training as the active duty and wore the same uniforms, our resources were second-class. As Master Sergeant Bob used to say, "They'll call up the Boy Scouts before they call up the Pennsylvania Army National Guard." In the pre-9/11 Army Guard, I wondered if he was right.

Sometimes, just thinking about this got me irritated. I didn't go through all that hard work at Fort Benning to train on outdated equipment back at my unit. But we didn't necessarily need to have all the best equipment. That's because back then, our role was "strategic reserve." In other words, we were supposed to supplement the active duty in case of World War III. When I thought about it that way, I didn't mind so much that we had old APCs. We were still playing an important part in our nation's defense.

Fortunately, Charlie Company's leadership was good at playing the hand they were dealt. With or without the proper resources, our leaders made the training relevant, kept the troops engaged, and did their best to make it fun. I learned important lessons about Guard resourcefulness and a positive attitude during my first years in the Kutztown infantry unit, bouncing around in those aluminum cans.

Those lessons were on full display during our two-week "annual training" exercises, which occurred during the summer at various

Army bases on the east coast. In my four years at Charlie Company, we went twice to Fort Stewart, Georgia, once to Fort Pickett, Virginia, and once to Fort Indiantown Gap, right down the road near Lebanon, Pennsylvania. You didn't need much to get good infantry training. Mostly, you would go out into the field with your rucksack and M-16 rifle and practice your tactics, techniques, and procedures (TTPs).

But we did have those M-113s, and the Army expected us to use them, even if they weren't integrated with any overall battle plan. So somebody in leadership came up with a clever idea. We would use our outdated equipment to practice maneuvers as an opposing force (OPFOR) against other Army units that had modern gear. That way, we could get good infantry training, be productive in our use of the M-113s and help others become more proficient with their Bradley Fighting Vehicles.

It was a simple concept, but it was an incredible boost for morale. Instead of complaining about training on outdated equipment, we felt like we were contributing something to the modern Army. Plus, we became underdogs, striving to defeat a superior force with inferior weapons. That motivated our group of Charlie Company Guardsman to be the best OPFOR we could be, and we had a great experience in the field.

Generally, we used MILES gear to conduct these training exercises. MILES stands for *Multiple Integrated Laser Engagement System,* and it consists of a series of sensors and transmitters attached to military equipment. It's laser tag for Army soldiers.

If you get shot by an M-16 with a MILES laser attached, the harness you are wearing beeps loudly for all to hear. The system is connected to people, tanks, even aircraft, and calibrated for the particular weapon or target. So, for example, if you shoot your MILES-enabled M-16 at a tank with MILES sensors, it won't do anything because a real M-16 round wouldn't damage a main battle tank. But if a tank shoots its main gun at a field of soldiers, all their MILES gear would beep because they all would be dead.

I remember one MILES exercise at Fort Stewart. Our infantry squad was supposed to go on a scouting mission to find the enemy's location and report back to the main body. The "enemy" was another Guard unit from Georgia, working with active duty evaluators to determine proficiency. We only had one M-113, and we were moving at night when we unexpectedly encountered the entire enemy platoon. Our scouting mission became a movement-to-contact as we dismounted to engage the Bradleys. After a couple of hours in a simulated firefight, our rag-tag squadron had destroyed all four Bradleys with anti-tank weapons and escaped unscathed.

It was the kind of memorable team-building experience that we often had in the infantry and exemplified the type of work we did in the field. We didn't have the best equipment, but we made the most of our training. Our part-time grunts were proud to be in the infantry and enjoyed the camaraderie of the Guard. Plus, when the training was over, we got to go home.

For me, that meant going back to Albany, and I was overdue for a change. The monthly drives from New York to Pennsylvania had gone from pleasant escapes to boring drudgery. And after the initial excitement of legislative work, that too was becoming routine. Mostly, I had no ties to New York, and Albany just wasn't where I wanted to be.

I started looking for ways out of town. Many of my friends still lived in Pennsylvania. I enjoyed my Kutztown unit, and most of my family was still there, so I set out to find a job in Harrisburg. After all, my only real work experience outside of the infantry was in state government.

I started making calls and sending resumes, but I quickly learned an important, difficult lesson about working for politicians. If they didn't know you, they probably wouldn't hire you. They probably wouldn't even take your calls. Despite my good record in New York, I had zero political connections in Pennsylvania, and I couldn't even land an interview for assistant dogcatcher.

I was indignant. I had a master's degree from a top graduate program and was working at the highest level of state government in the biggest northeastern state. I was successfully navigating nasty politicians and playing hardball every day, gaining tons of relevant experience negotiating deals and analyzing policy. Plus, I had saved the beavers. Yet I couldn't even get a return phone call from anybody in Harrisburg.

One day, during the summer of 1996, I just decided to drive to Pennsylvania unannounced and make my case in person. I was going to knock on doors until somebody read my resume and told me face to face that I was unqualified. Yes, I had a chip on my shoulder.

I went to the Harrisburg campaign office of presidential candidate Bob Dole. The office was staffing up for the general election, and I figured they could use an experienced policy analyst. I went into the office and met this guy named Keith, who said he was the number two guy for the Pennsylvania campaign. He was snarky and told me to go away.

When I asked if I could speak with the number one guy, he let it slip that his boss would be back sometime soon. So I just sat there in the reception area, earning several eye rolls, multiple deep sighs, and a couple of sarcastic comments from Keith, who had already decided I was just a distracting annoyance. But I had been to the 30th AG, so I could sit and do nothing for days. Plus, I found his snotty demeanor mildly amusing.

Eventually, his boss arrived. His name was Patrick. I introduced myself and told him about my background and desire to come home to Pennsylvania. He only seemed to be half-listening while he stared at my face.

Then he said something strange. He asked if I had seen President George H.W. Bush speak at Penn State in 1992. Yes, I told him. I had been there. I had helped to set up chairs as part of a volunteer student group.

"That's where I've seen you before," he said. "I was working for his campaign back then, and you helped me get things organized. You did a good job. You're hired."

Keith couldn't believe it.

After Pat had jarred my memory, I remembered meeting him too. I recall thinking how strange it was that my academic record and professional experience weren't the deciding factors, but an afternoon stacking chairs in State College had seemingly made the difference. Oh, well, I got the job regardless. Pat would become a great boss.

I drove back to Albany to inform Tim that I would be taking a three-month leave of absence from my Senate job to work for the Dole campaign in Pennsylvania. Since I was working for another Republican and gaining campaign experience during another slow time in the legislative year, he was happy to oblige again. I guess he was used to me coming and going by now.

Getting involved in politics is much different in the Guard than on active duty. In the regular Army, servicemen and -women are forbidden from engaging in politics because of their full-time status in the service of civilian authorities. Active-duty soldiers can vote and express private preferences, but they cannot attend political events in uniform, offer endorsements, or otherwise do anything political. This tradition is rooted in constitutional law and reflects deeply held beliefs, especially among the officer corps.

In the Guard, most of our lives are spent out of uniform. Therefore, forbidding our political activity in our non-military lives would be impractical, inappropriate, and illegal. The National Guard has hundreds of elected officials serving in its ranks from township supervisors to members of Congress. It makes sense because Guardsmen tend to have strong leadership skills and stay in the same community for a long time.

Nonetheless, many military officers, especially those on active duty, don't recognize the distinction and frown upon any political behavior at all. I think these attitudes are gradually changing, and not necessarily for the better. Washington now seems full of hyperpolitical military officers and wannabe politician generals falling all over themselves to get on CNN. Regardless, I was always extra careful to keep my Guard service separate from my political work.

The Dole campaign was fun. I sublet an apartment in Harrisburg for three months while I worked around the clock. We drove to rural towns and talked about the Second Amendment. I went to fancy dinners in Philadelphia and met celebrities and wealthy donors. I got to see almost every county in Pennsylvania and met lots of interesting people.

That summer was also the first time after basic training that my military obligations interfered with my civilian job. My time as a paid campaign staffer was only a few months long, and I was expected to be available 24-7. Soon after I took the position, the campaign organized an important event with the candidate's family somewhere in central Pennsylvania. I was expected to be there, but I couldn't. It was a drill weekend. I could have probably asked to perform a makeup drill at an alternate time and place, but I figured the same thing would happen in September, and again in October and November. I told the campaign I couldn't make it.

Keith rolled his eyes. Pat wasn't happy either, but he understood. Besides, what were they going to do, fire me for attending required military service? Eventually, I would take my first makeup drill in November for a last-minute campaign stop by the candidate himself. That was also the time I got my first dent in my new pickup truck.

I was setting up for a rally at the Philadelphia Airport on the day before the election. Most people didn't know it, but Bob Dole could not use his right hand. He had injured it in combat during World War II, making it nonfunctional and deformed. To avoid awkward handshakes, Mr. Dole would hold a pen or something in his right hand so that people would shake his other hand. His handicap also required some special accommodations to make his campaign events more comfortable, including a specially fitted podium from which he preferred to deliver all his important speeches.

On that day in November, some people from the Washington staff started yelling about Bob Dole's podium. I didn't know what they were talking about, but it sure seemed important because everybody was upset about it. As I later learned, the candidate was about to arrive for a big event, and nobody could find his special podium. Eventually, somebody figured out it was still on the candidate's airplane, parked somewhere in the Philadelphia airport. Since I was the only guy with a pickup truck, they told me to drive across the apron to his campaign jet, unload the podium into the back of my truck, and hurry back to set it up.

This was pre-9/11, so security was nothing like it is today. But I was still a bit unnerved to be speeding across the flight line to the Bob Dole campaign aircraft. I was hoping somebody had informed the airport police, so they didn't think I was some kind of terrorist attacking the candidate.

I made it to the plane, where two big guys were waiting for me with the podium in a big metal box. It kind of looked like one of those cases for a coffin. They had me back up to the jet right below the cargo door. Then they just tossed the box off the plane into the back of my truck, about a ten-foot drop.

Bang! That box must have weighed at least 100 pounds. It smashed into the back of my truck, bounced it up and down, and put a huge dent in the bed. "Be careful!" I yelled, but all the guys cared about was that I got that podium to Bob Dole in time for his speech. I took off down the flight line. That would be the last occasion I would speed down the apron of a major international airport in my pickup.

Later that day, I met Bob Dole himself for the first and only time. I wanted to say something funny about his podium and my truck, but I just thanked him for his military service.

Mr. Dole ended up losing badly to President Bill Clinton in the election, but I will always remember him as a class act, and the guy responsible for the dent in my truck bed, which still exists to this day.

After the election, I returned to Albany with a fat Rolodex

of contacts I made in Pennsylvania and more experience doing something different. I knew it was just a matter of time before I would make a move back to Pennsylvania. I continued to drill in Kutztown and completed another legislative term in Albany. By the fall, I was in contact with different people in Harrisburg and finally got some job interviews.

Around Thanksgiving of 1997, I accepted a position with the popular Pennsylvania governor Tom Ridge. I was going to be an economic and technology policy analyst. It was a good job with a nice pay raise. I also noticed that while the people around me were still young, there were a lot more adults in my new office than in New York. I packed up and left Albany in December and started my new career in Harrisburg after the new year. I was excited about the change.

CHAPTER THREE: CHIMPLES

FOR ME, GETTING TO Harrisburg was an absolute fluke.

I was finishing up graduate school in Cincinnati with a master's degree in German literature. Originally, I had thought I wanted to be a university professor, but over time, I had realized I just wasn't suited for a life in academia—too much narrow focus and ivory-tower pretentiousness. Unfortunately, there weren't a lot of job openings outside universities for experts in nineteenth-century Saxon authors.

Meanwhile, I was dating a man who was in law school, and we got very serious. He asked me to marry, and I accepted his proposal. My fiancée was offered a paid internship in Harrisburg, Pennsylvania, so I started to look for a summer job there to be with him. I wanted something temporary because his internship was only for the summer.

My job search was a quick success. I lined up a promising temporary internship of my own with the state Department of Environmental Protection doing community relations work. I guess they thought German literature was sort of like a communications degree. I was thankful for the opportunity.

But my personal life was in shambles. I realized almost immediately that I had made a mistake getting engaged, and I was confused about what to do. In April, I called off the engagement, but by then, I had already accepted the internship in Harrisburg. Now, I was facing a temporary job in a strange town that I would never have considered if not for a relationship with a man I no longer dated. Ugh.

I had no better plan, so I took the internship. After a few months working in state headquarters, I got an offer for a permanent position as a community relations coordinator in the South-Central regional office, which was also in Harrisburg. By the end of the summer, my former fiancée had left, and I had stayed. I was grateful for a good job and a fresh start.

So Susan and I were in the same cheesy movie. We just didn't know it yet.

In March of 1998, just three months after moving from Albany to Harrisburg, I attended a St. Patrick's Day party at an Italian restaurant named Angelina's, thrown by a friend named Steve, on Friday the thirteenth. It was one of the first warm days of spring, so I drove my motorcycle with my new neighbor Brian, who lived a couple of houses down in my apartment complex.

That was when I saw Susan.

She was flitting around the bar, moving from person to person with a smile so bright it caused dimples on her cheeks—I called them chimples. She had beautiful brown eyes and looked so confident and at ease, I was drawn to her immediately.

So were all the other guys in the place, it seemed. Brian was smitten, and he darted across the room to meet her. She was there on a date with somebody else, but as soon as he slipped away, another guy would move in. Susan was flirty but seemed genuine, and I don't even think she realized that all those guys were hitting on her.

I tried to play it cool. I introduced myself by butting in on Brian and then seized an opening. I heard Susan say she was from Beaver, a small town near Pittsburgh. I told her that today was her lucky day because I was an expert on beavers. She blushed and giggled and flashed her chimples, and I knew right then that I wanted to marry her.

I didn't talk to her long that night; her date came back around, and Brian was still in hot pursuit. But I got her name and the office where she worked, which was all I needed to track her down. Later that week, I left a message for her at work to call Rod Dent from Beaver, Pennsylvania. Yes, that was horrible, but it worked. She called me back.

My confidence was soaring. I figured if she returned an awful message like that, I was a shoo-in. But when I asked her out, she simply said no. I got no explanation and no indication that she would change her mind.

I was discouraged but not defeated. I waited a few days and left a message on her work answering machine. This time, I left her the phone numbers of my grandmothers, Elisabeth and Phoebe. I figured they would be good references for Susan to check. They could attest to my high moral character and charming personality.

Moving to Harrisburg was a good choice. There were a lot of fun young professionals, and I had a lot of good friends and acquaintances. We canoed and camped, had parties, and grew up together. I enjoyed being single, and after my bad engagement experience, I was in no rush to settle down.

About two years after I arrived in Harrisburg, I was invited by a guy I was going out with to a St. Patrick's Day party at a local restaurant and bar. On the way there, he announced he had some "networking" to do, so I would be on my own much of the time. Oh, brother. I wouldn't know many people at the party, but I wasn't going to let my politicking date ruin my evening. I decided to be outgoing and flirty—not a big stretch for me.

One guy, in particular, got my attention. He was wearing a beautiful leather Harley jacket and had the twinkliest eyes I'd ever seen. When I saw him, the rest of the room didn't matter anymore. I could only clearly focus on him, and I hung on every word he said.

He had a terrific sense of humor, and while we talked, I made sure he knew how to get in touch with me without actually giving him my number. I was thrilled when he called Monday at the office. He asked me out. I said no. Not because I didn't want to go out with him, but because I wanted to completely end it with the guy I had gone to the party with, and he was out of town for a few days.

There was something really different about this guy. His name was Kevin Dellicker, and he worked for Governor Ridge. He called again to ask me out. This time he left both his grandmothers' phone numbers as character references. I figured that any man who knows his grandmas' phone numbers by heart was a good person. I didn't need to actually call them—they would only gush about him.

Susan never did call my grandparents, which was kind of disappointing. They would have provided glowing recommendations. But the ploy worked. About a week later, she called me back and accepted my invitation to dinner. I found out later that she was using the time to break up with her current date, the guy I had seen with her at the party two weeks prior. From that point on, marriage was a foregone conclusion. She couldn't resist.

I didn't have any knowledge of or exposure to the military before I met Kevin. Well, I had had a friend in the Reserves in college who was activated in support of Desert Storm and was gone in twenty-four hours. Other than that, I only knew about the military from movies and books.

My first impression of the military was that it was an interesting part-time job. Kevin went one weekend a month to Kutztown, which was a little more than an hour away. He went out in the woods around the area or went to Fort Dix for an exercise. He was able to visit his family when he went to drill because they lived nearby. And it gave me a weekend to do what I wanted without Kevin.

He got a tremendous opportunity to go to England for two weeks and saw Belgium and Germany. By all accounts, it was a fantastic trip. He went on his two-week training in Georgia and seemed to enjoy spending time outdoors. Boy, was I naïve.

Susan knew nothing about the military. Her grandfather, James Frank, had been an army chaplain in the Pacific Theater during World War II. He had experienced some of the fiercest fighting of the war but didn't talk much about his service. He had seen horrible things in the Pacific theater and didn't want to recount those memories to his innocent granddaughter.

Her father, Curtis Frank, was registered for the draft in Vietnam but never got the call. She had a few friends in the military, but the National Guard was entirely new to her. For the first year, the Guard mostly meant me leaving periodically for training and the introduction of a group of colorful friends that she would soon get to know pretty well. Otherwise, life in the Guard pre-9/11 was rather manageable.

Soon after we met, in the spring of 1998, I got selected to represent the Pennsylvania National Guard on a military exchange with the Territorial Army of the United Kingdom (UK), England's version of the Reserves. Basically, two noncommissioned officers from the UK would come and train with our Guard unit, and then two NCOs from Kutztown would go and train with them overseas. It was quite an honor to be selected, and I was very excited about such an interesting opportunity.

For our part of the exchange, we headed to Fort Stewart, Georgia, for two weeks of training with other Army National Guard units. My commute from Harrisburg to Kutztown was much shorter now, only about an hour and a half, and I arrived on a Friday afternoon to get ready to go. The plan was to leave that evening and drive all night before arriving near the base the next day.

I assumed everything was in order for the two British soldiers, but a couple of hours went by, and they hadn't arrived. When I asked Master Sergeant Bob if somebody had already gone to pick them up at the airport, his cigar almost fell out of his mouth. We had completely forgotten about them.

"No worries," said Sergeant Mike. Sergeant Mike was about fifty years old and still an E-5, which was my pay grade after just a few years of service. Nobody really knew what he did in the infantry, but he was one of the most beloved benefactors of the unit. He lived in Reading and owned a funeral business, among other things, and everybody assumed he was loaded. Whether he was rich or not, I don't know, but he was certainly generous to the unit and the guys who served.

Sergeant Mike told me to wait for a few minutes while he arranged transportation. I hung out anxiously with Staff Sergeant Rich, the other American soldier from Charlie Company who was going on the exchange, imagining the payback we would receive in England for leaving our counterparts stranded at the airport.

The next thing we knew, Sergeant Mike pulled up in a stretch limousine. It was a long, black Cadillac, full of chrome and all decked out. It was his funeral home vehicle. No, it wasn't a hearse, but knowing Sergeant Mike, he probably used it to haul plenty of dead bodies.

Anyway, Sergeant Mike, Staff Sergeant Rich, and I drove to the airport to pick up these two infantry grunts from England in this shiny, black limousine. We were a few minutes late, but they didn't notice with all that chrome in their eyes. We told them that the Pennsylvania Army National Guard always transported its infantry soldiers like this.

Sergeant Mike proceeded to take these two guys on a road trip that could have been made into a movie with Zach Galifianakis and Vince Vaughn. He treated them to steak dinners at fancy restaurants, diversions to tourist sites along the way, and an overnight stay in a nice hotel. They both had a blast, and Sergeant Mike paid every dime, not just for them, but for Staff Sergeant Rich and me too.

When we arrived in Georgia two days later, we rolled in with our unit and went straight to the field. It was a typical two weeks of Army training—hot, dirty, and extremely physical, but also very worthwhile and fun. On the way home, I took the normal bus so that somebody else could experience the limo. Sergeant Mike gave the

British guys the same royal treatment, showing them Parris Island, Washington, D.C., and Gettysburg along the way. They got some great infantry training, but they also had a fantastic tour up and down the East Coast.

The British soldiers were extremely grateful, and they returned the favor when Staff Sergeant Rich and I went to England a few weeks later. We arrived in London and proceeded to the White Cliffs of Dover, then across the English Channel into France, on through Luxembourg and Belgium to their training location. There, we got to fire all kinds of different British infantry weapons, go out into the field with the Territorial Army, and generally experience military life with English infantry grunts.

I can't say for sure, but based on my experience with the Territorial Army, maybe infantry grunts across the world are pretty much the same. They had different names, accents, and uniforms, but otherwise, they were just like my fellow soldiers in the Pennsylvania Army National Guard. These were blue-collar, hardworking guys, full of common sense and devoted to a higher calling. Just like every soldier I ever met, they would do anything for their buddies. And they knew how to have a good time.

In the evenings when we were not in the field, the Brits held elaborate dinners with pomp and circumstance. We had to wear neckties on occasion. I had a hard time keeping up with all the beer-drinking, and they stayed up until the early hours before waking up at dawn and doing it all again.

In the field, the biggest difference was where we trained. At home in the US, we train on huge army bases, fenced in and separated from the civilian population. At least in Belgium, where we were conducting this NATO exercise, we just walked right through people's backyards. And when it was time to sleep, we laid down in somebody's field or pasture and set up camp.

I guess the Europeans don't have as much space as we do back home and are used to this kind of thing. They certainly don't have the Second Amendment. I can't imagine how gun-toting rural Americans would react if a bunch of government workers started traipsing through their farms at night.

I remember a difficult road march through the woods of Belgium. It was very hot, and guys were dehydrated and tired. We had gotten little sleep and were moving long distances very fast. I was impressed by the high level of intensity and realistic training environment.

Then all of a sudden, everybody just stopped their tactical movement.

"What are we doing?" I asked.

"Time for tea," said the sergeant.

I thought they were joking, but they were completely serious. The British infantry guys pulled out little cans of Sterno along with these military-issued metal kits for brewing tea in the field. When they were done with their tea, they used the tea bags like mini-scouring pads to clean their kits before packing up and moving along.

The English might be among the best in the world at realistic small-unit combat training, but they are not going to miss their afternoon tea. Winston Churchill would be proud.

During the middle weekend of our two-week exchange, the Brits took us to Trier, Germany, a beautiful medieval city on the Moselle River Valley surrounded by grapevines, farms, and forests. I got to spend plenty of time with my British infantry counterparts sampling local food and drinking German beer.

Generally, I found the British infantry soldiers less educated than my Pennsylvania counterparts, and they had a lot of erroneous ideas about American culture, mostly from watching television shows like *Cops* and *The Simpsons*. But just when I was about to conclude that this was a ruffian group, one of the guys found out about a free concert in the main square with some opera singer, and everybody wanted to go. They were incredulous that I didn't know who the singer was, but I tagged along and heard a lovely concert. There I was, with my college degrees and white-collar lifestyle, not appreciating the opera music nearly as much as that group of British infantry grunts with impressions about America shaped by *The Jerry Springer Show*.

Back in Belgium, we saw first-hand the impact of the US Army and the 28th Infantry Division on the European countryside. We were doing our training in the same area that the 28th ID had fought fifty years prior. Many of the towns and villages had monuments with the red "bloody bucket" Keystone badge commemorating their liberation from the Nazis by forces from the Pennsylvania National Guard. We also got to see the monument for the Battle of the Bulge and lots of other memorials that reminded us of the part-time infantrymen before us.

One thing was noticeably different about this trip from my previous training exercises. I missed Susan. I remember being in the heart of beautiful European countryside, calling her on a payphone and acting like a homesick little boy. I wondered what she thought about that. I was experiencing amazing things, and I wanted her to be a part of them.

On the way home, I was able to spend an extra day in London, and the Brits arranged a special tour of the Tower of London for Staff Sergeant Rich and me. We met a representative from their regiment at the gate, who escorted us into a section of the fort off-limits to the general public. We toured their private museum of artifacts and had a special lunch with the unit's leaders. It was an incredible ending to a military experience that I will never forget. But I was anxious to get home and excited to get on with my new life with Susan. I could see my priorities starting to change.

Back at my civilian job, I was getting into a routine. It was the fall of 1998, and Governor Tom Ridge was running for reelection. He was a former enlisted infantry soldier himself, having earned a Bronze Star with "V" for valor for combat achievement in Vietnam. Governor Ridge was popular among people of all political persuasions, and the economy was humming along. Nobody from the opposing party wanted to run against him, so the Democrats ended up nominating a relatively unknown state representative as their token candidate. Governor Ridge ended up winning 57 percent of the vote.

Later that year, I experienced the highlight of my state government career. After his landslide reelection, Governor Ridge set out to reform Pennsylvania's tax system. The Commonwealth's tax burden was high relative to other states, and the governor had campaigned on a platform of tax cuts for economic growth. I was one of the staffers selected to help put his new program in place.

We convened an interagency and interdisciplinary task force that evaluated more than a dozen different personal and business taxes in Pennsylvania compared to all the other states in the nation. Then we were charged with making recommendations for improvement. We used tools of policy analysis and statistics to evaluate which potential tax changes would have the biggest impact on job creation and economic growth in the Commonwealth. Our group worked hard for several months, and I delivered the final report to my boss, the director of policy, just before Christmas in 1998.

Governor Ridge used a collaborative process for making many of his most important decisions. His cabinet, consisting of about a dozen senior leaders, would sit around a big conference room table in his Harrisburg office. Behind it, his supporting staff would sit in a big square around the outside of the room to answer questions and make additional presentations. Mostly, it was the senior staff that did the talking, but the governor would regularly ask the other participants for their input too. He made us feel like part of the team.

For the tax discussion, my boss let me present our findings in front of the governor and his entire senior staff. I had to follow the budget secretary, who had just made a case for a more limited tax cut program, arguing against my position, making the case that the Commonwealth could not afford anything more.

For at least half an hour, I went through my slides and charts in a carefully rehearsed PowerPoint presentation. The room was largely quiet, with the governor and all his staff listening intently. Periodically, one of the task force members would add a comment or elaborate on a topic, but mostly it was my presentation to deliver.

When I was finished, the staff started to argue among themselves about the presentation. Some people were worried about cutting taxes too deeply. Others were concerned about not cutting enough. The communications staffers fussed over how to explain such a complex subject to the public; the political advisors fretted about the winners and the losers of tax reform. I was asked some tough questions, and my friend Tom from the Revenue Department was there to help me out. At one point, the conversation got heated. Through it all, Governor Ridge hardly said a word.

Eventually, everybody had expressed all that was on their minds, and the discussion had run its course. After a brief pause, the governor spoke and addressed me directly. To paraphrase, he said, "I wish every Pennsylvanian could have heard your presentation."

And that was it. He thanked me and walked out. I really didn't know what he had meant.

A few days later, I found out. Governor Ridge included almost every recommendation from my presentation in his budget proposal. It became the foundation of the largest tax cut in state history, a boost for job creation, and a signature achievement of Governor Tom Ridge's time in office. It was exciting for a twenty-eight-year-old staffer to experience, and I told Susan all about it. She was happy for me too.

CHAPTER FOUR: COMMITMENT

EVERYTHING SEEMED TO BE going my way, especially my relationship with Susan. She accompanied me to two very different Christmas parties that year.

The first was at the Kutztown Armory. Among the stacked weapons, stored equipment, and dirty vehicles, Susan ate warm ring bologna and drank Yuengling beer on draught from a plastic cup. She got to hang out with all my infantry buddies, and they treated her like a queen. Afterward, we all went out for beer and wings.

The other was at the governor's mansion. There, she ate fancy brie cheese and sipped wine from a crystal glass. She got to meet the governor, too. When I introduced her as my girlfriend, he replied, "No duh." I guess this was Susan's first experience with a different kind of Guardsman whiplash. She seemed to enjoy it.

Kevin and I had been dating for about nine months when he called me to tell me to pack two bags—one for cold weather and one for warm weather. He was surprising me with a weekend getaway. I was thrilled! Especially because earlier in the week, he had been asking me about my ring size. I remember calling my aunt Ro and squealing like a little girl that this was the weekend he was going to propose.

Well, he picked me up and told me to grab the warm-weather bag, and off to the Philadelphia Airport we went. I found out when he got there that we were headed to Jacksonville, Florida, to spend the weekend in nearby St. Augustine.

It was amazingly beautiful, and I loved sightseeing and eating out, but as the weekend progressed, I was getting more and more excited about his proposal. It didn't come, and it didn't happen, and I started to get agitated. I know he thought I was being grumpy, but I had hyped the whole idea of my engagement so much in mind that I couldn't quite get over the reality that he wasn't going to ask me to marry him.

Eventually, I confided in him and explained my agitated demeanor. I told him you don't ask a girl for her ring size and then take her away on a wonderful trip and not propose.

I had subscribed to one of those cheap airfare email alerts that were popular at the time and bought last-minute tickets to Florida for a ninety-nine-dollar round trip. I booked the flights on a Wednesday, and I think we left that Friday. I just wanted a quick break from the cold weather—I had no idea Susan expected something more.

Besides, I already had alternative plans. I had decided to pop the question several months prior and was planning an elaborate event for mid-February at the same restaurant where we had our first date. I bought her diamond online, had it set at the local jewelry store, ordered a special bouquet of black-eyed Susan flowers, and made reservations for Saturday evening of Valentine's Day weekend. Everything was in order.

That Friday, I went to the gym and drove around town to pick up the ring and the flowers. But when I got back to my apartment, Susan was waiting there with a surprise. She said she was going to cook me dinner.

The problem was that it was twenty degrees outside, and the flowers were going to freeze, but I couldn't get them in past Susan. I figured I could sneak out at some point while she was in the kitchen and hide them somewhere, so I proceeded to get a shower while Susan started in the kitchen. My buddy Chad had brought over a deer roast earlier, and she was going to try cooking wild game for the first time.

Suddenly, the fire alarm started beeping, and smoke filled the room. Susan had caught the garlic bread on fire in the oven, and the flames were getting high. I ran out of the shower wrapped in a towel and tried to put out the fire with one hand, so my towel wouldn't fall off. Eventually, I succeeded, but the roast was toast, the floor was soaking wet, and Susan was crying.

I'm not sure why, but I guess I took this as some kind of sign that now was the time. I threw on some clothes, walked out to the truck, got the ring and the flowers, and asked her to marry me. Through the smoke and the smell of burnt garlic toast, she said yes. It was eleven months from our meeting at Angelina's. We set the date for July, just five months later. Why wait?

Meanwhile, my work on Governor Ridge's staff remained challenging and rewarding. After focusing on the tax issues, I had been assigned to work on several technology projects related to the internet. The governor was interested in making Pennsylvania a leader in the emerging field of electronic government, and he gave his team a long leash to experiment with new ideas. Some of them didn't work out, but a lot of them did. Pennsylvania earned "first-in-the-nation" status with many different innovations in the late 1990s, and I was involved with several of them.

One of the projects almost resulted in a new job. A Pittsburgh-based company called Freemarkets.com created an e-commerce tool to conduct reverse online auctions. Companies needing to buy materials could invite suppliers to participate in a real-time process for selling their goods. Each time one company proposed a price, other companies could beat that price until the time expired. It was another innovative way companies were using the internet to become more productive.

We decided to be the first state to use such a tool for bidding requirements, and I got to organize the process. We chose aluminum for license plates as our first auction item and held a press conference on the day of the affair. The state secretary of general services, a burly former Marine named Gary Crowell, stood up and gave a bold and inspirational speech about how this online experiment was another important step toward bringing Pennsylvania into the Internet Age. Then after hearty applause from an audience of about two-dozen stakeholders, he walked away from the podium and privately barked into my ear, "This better work."

It did, and we saved a bunch of taxpayer money. Later, when I visited Freemarkets' company headquarters, I got an offer to be a part of their emerging team. The pay was low, but they would give me equity in the company. I declined.

A few months later, I watched their stock soar almost 700 percent on the first day of their initial public offering. Gulp. I might have been a wealthy man. Oh well. I missed that opportunity. I think their stock crashed later anyway in the dot-com bust.

Back in Harrisburg, I kept working on other interesting and innovative technology projects, like enabling electronic signatures, reviewing broadband policies, and establishing some of the first e-government websites in the world.

My favorite project was called "PA Open for Business." It was designed as a web-based one-stop-shop for entrepreneurs, and I was the project leader. The idea was simple. Instead of submitting the same information multiple times via paper to different agencies, the prospective entrepreneur would answer a series of simple questions online and hit "Submit." Then the information would populate the forms automatically, saving time and money. It's the same concept that *TurboTax* and similar services now use to fill out your income tax forms. When the project was complete, PA Open for Business was named one of the 50 best innovations in state government for that year by a national trade magazine.

Things were going very well for Susan and me. She was enjoying her new teaching position, and I was gaining experience in my civilian job. Both of us had accepted my military commitment as an important but manageable part of our lives. With a wedding just around the corner, we weren't seeking out any other major changes. We were pretty content with what we had.

Then I got a letter out of the blue from the 193rd Special Operations Wing (193rd SOW or 193rd), an Air National Guard unit in Harrisburg. Several years prior, when I had been exploring all kinds of options for a military career, I had sent a cover letter and resume to the unit inquiring about various job opportunities. I had never heard back and had forgotten about it. My resume had made it to the intelligence section, though, and the form letter I received said they were hiring new officers. It asked if I would like to apply.

I talked it over with Susan, and she was very encouraging. I must admit I was a bit surprised about that. If I got the job, we would have to move to Texas for a year. That would be very disruptive to her career. But she didn't seem to mind. Maybe she thought it would be an adventure. Maybe she just figured she would get a different job in Texas. Regardless, this would have to be my decision. There would be no veto from Susan to make up my mind for me.

I was torn. My initial enlistment was winding down, and I liked the infantry. I was about to re-enlist and get promoted to staff sergeant as a squad leader. Most of the NCOs I knew said being an infantry squad leader was the best job in the Army. I was excited to gain that leadership experience. But there were a few nagging questions about my career in the Army that this unsolicited letter from the Air Force forced me to confront.

First, the infantry is a young man's career field. Even though I was in excellent shape, I was almost thirty years old and not getting any younger. While it was fun to sleep on the ground and train in the field, the work was physically demanding. I had started to notice that a twenty-eight-year-old body took longer to heal after bruising its knees and elbows low-crawling through the mud than it had when I wrestled in high school.

Second, I wondered what it would be like to experience new and different things in the armed forces. That trip to Europe got me thinking about the amazing possibilities of military service and all the places you could go. I liked the Army National Guard and enjoyed my training exercises. But I was starting to make repeat trips to the same military bases on the East Coast. I worked very hard at this part-time job and knew that I was part of the Army's overall strategic deterrent force. Yet I couldn't help but wonder if that two-week exchange with the British Army would be the highlight of my military career.

Finally, I had never fully reconciled my father's comments about being an officer with the path I had chosen. No doubt, being an enlisted grunt in the infantry was an experience I could never have replicated if I had jumped right into military service as an officer. Most of the good officers I knew in the Army Guard had spent time as enlisted soldiers first, and soldiers generally had more respect for the prior-enlisted officers. But I wondered what kind of impact I could have as an officer in the Air National Guard.

I had considered going to Officer Candidate School (OCS) in the Army. However, I had had a bad experience during an orientation weekend, getting myself and my unit in some hot water.

At the time, the Pennsylvania Army Guard had its own OCS program. It consisted of weekend drills and annual training over about eighteen months. These would lead to a Guard commission as a second lieutenant. I heard about this opportunity and attended a special weekend program for prospective cadets.

By this point in my career, I was already a graduate of the Platoon Leader's Development Course (PLDC), the Army's introductory leadership course for NCOs. I had a fantastic experience at PLDC, almost as good as my infantry training at Fort Benning. Like the drill sergeants at basic training, the instructors at PLDC were all seasoned NCOs with extensive experience in the Army. They led by example.

In OCS, the training cadre was dominated by rookie lieutenants and captains, who had just received their commissions a few years earlier. Most of them hadn't deployed anywhere. I was older than some of them, had a better education than most, and had more work experience than almost all. In some cases, I even had more time in military service. Instead of leading by example, some of them seemed to have something to prove.

Everything about that introductory weekend seemed in stark contrast to what I had experienced from my NCOs at basic training, in PLDC, and in my unit. The officer instructors couldn't call cadence without messing up. They were in worse physical shape than most of the potential recruits. They made us sing stupid songs and endure hazing-type rituals. I felt like I was pledging a college fraternity instead of receiving military training.

I was so disappointed with my experience that I wrote a letter explaining in detail all the ways this amateur officer cadre was inferior to the professional NCO corps that I learned from elsewhere. I wrote that if this is what a soldier must experience to become an officer, I was proud to be an NCO for the rest of my life. I sent the letter to the commandant, the lead instructor, and a bunch of other people related to the program. It got their attention.

At drill the following weekend, my company commander said he got chewed out by a lieutenant colonel because I had usurped the chain of command. My squad leader disciplined me for not informing my boss. But in private, both agreed with the substance of the letter. I had acted foolishly by embarrassing my unit and getting my supervisors in trouble, but I decided that being an NCO was where I wanted to be.

Later, I heard that state leaders fixed that program and turned it into a model commissioning school. But at the time, I wanted no part of it. I decided I would finish my career as a sergeant in the Army National Guard.

But I hadn't considered the Air National Guard. They sent prospective officers to a full-time officer training program called the Academy of Military Science (AMS) in Tennessee, instead of a part-time program on weekends. Plus, I would have the opportunity to learn an exciting new career, intelligence. That was always a subject of interest. Mostly, I would be joining a unit with a real-world operational mission. I knew that the 193rd Special Operations Wing was the most deployed unit in the entire Air National Guard, and its affiliation with Air Force Special Operations Command ensured its ongoing relevancy. I decided to give it a try.

My interview at the Wing was interesting. I met Captain Eric McKissick, the full-time leader of the intelligence section. He was with Lieutenant Colonel James McGovern, who was the part-time section chief, and Captain K., a C-130 navigator in the Wing. They asked me some questions about leadership, needled me a bit about being in the Army, and then gave me a problem to solve with a map they had spread out over the table.

I looked at the map and chuckled. I had done a lot of map-reading and land navigation during my time with the infantry, but we had worked 100 meters at a time. This navigational chart had an entire continent on it. I think my calculations were off by about a thousand miles, but they must have given me the benefit of the doubt. I got hired a couple of weeks later. I was leaving the NCO corps in the infantry to become an intelligence officer in the Air Force.

To this day, Susan still reminds me that when she agreed to marry me, I was just an infantry grunt.

"Naïve" is the best word to describe me at the time when Kevin announced he wanted to join the Air Force. I was thinking a lot about our new life together, but I wasn't sure what I was getting myself into. This was pre 9/11, so the Army Guard was rarely deployed, and I felt pretty confident that Kevin was safe. It was just a part-time job he seemed to enjoy and friends with whom he had a special bond because they served our country.

I never really considered how dangerous his Army job would be if he went to war. He would be on the ground kicking in doors. But I was so ill-informed, I glossed over all of that in my mind.

So when Kevin announced he would become an intelligence analyst in the Air Force, I thought it sounded more like an office job, and I figured that meant he would be even more out of harm's way. I knew it came with about a year of school, but from my perspective as a young, single woman, that didn't sound very difficult.

As Kevin was making his career change in the military, I was making my own career move as a teacher. I enjoyed my job at the Department of Environmental Protection, but I knew that I wanted to end up in the classroom. My father had been a high school teacher for thirty years, and my brother had recently gotten his certification too. Including my sister-in-law and aunt, I had an entire family of teachers for inspiration. When I saw a part-time teaching position advertised at the Harrisburg Academy, I decided it was time to quit my job in communications and take a leap of faith in education.

Since Harrisburg Academy is a private school, I didn't need a formal certification to get started. While I taught high school classes there, I took college classes at Millersville University to get my teaching certificate. It was risky to quit a good-paying job with the state for an uncertain future in education, but I knew that I was making the right decision. I wanted to teach.

After a year at the Harrisburg Academy, I finished my education classes and prepared for student teaching. Then I found out about a full-time opening at Central Dauphin East High School. It was a better-paying job with great benefits, right down the road from our apartment. Even though I didn't have my certification yet, the district allowed me to count my student teaching as full-time employment. It was an ideal situation for advancing my educational career.

Our career moves weren't the biggest changes upon us. As Susan wrapped up her work for the state agency, I did one final training exercise with the Army at Fort Indiantown Gap in June of 1999. Then we got married the following weekend over the Fourth of July. By October, Susan was pregnant. Now we would be sharing our new experiences with a baby too.

For the first time since basic training, my military service meant more than one weekend a month and two weeks a year. I would start going to drills in the Air National Guard by November. Then I had seven weeks of training in Knoxville, Tennessee, to get my commission and nine months of follow-up training in San Angelo, Texas, to become qualified in the intelligence career field. I would need to take a long leave of absence from my job, and Susan might have to quit her teaching job outright.

Air Force AMS was okay but not nearly as worthwhile as infantry basic training. Like the officer cadre at Army OCS, all my instructors at AMS were junior Air Force officers. Unlike my Army OCS experience, they were highly professional. Mostly, it was an academic experience, a lot of studying and taking tests. There was very little strenuous physical activity. I think I got out of shape while there.

The leadership training was decent. We had a few field training exercises and a lot of time management work. There were a lot of smart people in my class, including a funny maintenance officer named Will and a feisty C-130 pilot candidate named Dawn. Dawn was also part of the 193rd Special Operations Wing, and I would end up deploying with her a few years later. Will ended up completing a twenty-year career in the Louisiana National Guard and is now retired with a fishing boat in the Gulf of Mexico.

There were lots of great people at AMS, but mostly I was glad when it was over. I graduated in May of 2000, and Susan was there in a blue dress with white polka dots. She was very pregnant. My mom and dad helped Susan pin on my new second lieutenant bars, and I received my first salute as an officer.

Kevin and I didn't forget about our friends in the infantry. We kept in touch and saw them often. One time, when I was very pregnant, we went to the wedding of Kevin's former platoon leader at the Valley Forge Military Academy outside of Philadelphia. There were a couple of hours between ceremony and reception, and some guys from the Kutztown infantry unit were there without dates. We all decided to go get something to eat where everyone (except me, of course) could also have a couple of drinks.

One of the guys said, "How about Hooters?"

"Sure," I said, and we all ended up there—Kevin, me, and a bunch of single guys in Army dress uniforms.

They all flirted with the waitresses, and I vouched for them being good guys. We ate wings, which was great because I was always hungry during that pregnancy. We took pictures with the Hooters girls, and I even snuck into one of the photographs.

CHAPTER FIVE: ON OUR OWN

THINGS WERE MOVING VERY fast. Just a year after getting married, we had our first son, Willard Curtis. We named him after both of our dads. In September, Kevin was scheduled to go to intelligence school in Texas for a year. I was able to take maternity leave and accompany Kevin to Texas instead of us being apart for nine months. It was an abrupt halt to my first full-time teaching job, but I wanted to be a stay-at-home mom even more than I wanted to be a teacher. Plus, the trip to Texas would be our first big adventure as a family.

In August, we packed up all our things and headed southwest. The trip to Texas may have been the highlight of the year. It took us a week and a half to drive from Harrisburg, Pennsylvania, to San Angelo, Texas. We packed up our lives and sent the majority of our belongings to storage because we would have a small two-bedroom apartment off base. The rest of our belongings either were shipped to Texas or were in our Jeep Cherokee. Everything we needed for a newborn was strapped in a canvas carrier on the roof of the Jeep.

Our first stop in August was in Beaver at my parent's house near Pittsburgh. They wanted to see and show off their first grandbaby to their family and friends before we moved him to Texas for the year. They had a wonderful party for us and spent time just holding and doting on the one-month-old Will. He was a delightful baby—he was happy all the time and loved to be loved.

The only drawback was that he ate constantly. I was exhausted breastfeeding this baby, who was seemingly never full. It was a two-hour cycle. He would eat, we would change him, and he would sleep for an hour and a half. Then we started over. Day and night.

The trip to Texas took so long because we had to pause every two hours to feed and change him. It was a sweltering August, so we would try to find air-conditioned places to stop. In Illinois, we visited the Lincoln homestead and watched a film about Lincoln's early life. We stopped in the Archway in St. Louis and fed him there. Sometimes there wasn't any air conditioning, and both Will and I would be dripping with sweat by the time he was done eating.

We stopped in Santa Claus, Indiana, the Walnut Bowl store near Branson, Missouri, and a random cave somewhere in Arkansas. Later, our pediatrician would yell at us for exposing Will to airborne rabies, which I didn't know was a real thing. He never got rabies. We stayed at military bases along the way wherever we could because they were clean and cheap. Around Dyess Air Force Base, Texas, we couldn't find a hotel room because it was the first day of dove hunting.

Near Fort Sill Oklahoma, we pulled over in a state park and somehow ended up in the middle of a herd of buffalo. Two of the males started fighting, and I was terrified we were going to be tipped over or worse. In the end, we didn't get head-butted, and Will never took any notice. He just continued to eat.

The temperatures were around 100 degrees most of the way. I stayed hydrated with slushies from wherever we could find them. The sugar kept my energy up, and the ice kept my temperature down.

Our adventure ended on Friday, September 2, when we pulled into Goodfellow Air Force Base to check in for school, or so we thought. We got there early, but the base was already closing for the Labor Day weekend. I dropped off Susan and Will at the base hotel and went to check in at intelligence school. I handed in my paperwork and figured it would only be a minute before I could rejoin Susan and get settled in for the weekend. Instead, the conversation went something like this.

"Here are my orders and arrival paperwork, ma'am. Where do I report on Tuesday for the first day of class?"

"Let me check," said the civilian clerk. "Oh, I'm sorry, your security clearance paperwork did not go through."

"Okay," I said, figuring there was a minor mistake, or I could start school on Wednesday. I had been in the military long enough to expect paperwork SNAFUs and bureaucratic holdups.

"You can go home and return in two months."

The most amazing part of this exchange is that she didn't see anything wrong with this advice. I explained that I was a part-time Air National Guardsman and had left my job and apartment to come to this training and that all my stuff was in storage, so there was no place to go back to. I also explained that my wife had left her job too, and was in the base hotel caring for my six-week-old son right now.

"I'm sorry, there's nothing we can do."

I wanted to throw a chair through the window, but instead, I called my boss at the 193rd. He had no idea what was going on and started making a bunch of phone calls to get answers. But by now, it was the afternoon before a holiday weekend, and nobody was at their desks. Nothing was resolved before the end of the day, and the last words we had to go on were "There's nothing we can do."

So we went to dinner.

Susan, Will, and I ate at a Mexican restaurant that night called *Mejor Que Nada*, which means "Better than Nothing" in Spanish. That's exactly how we felt. We had no choice but to wait out the weekend and try again on Tuesday to see if we could resolve this fiasco.

I don't remember all the details about how it played out, but while my unit and I were working through official military channels, Susan was trying a back door. Somehow, she found out who the individual was that processed Air National Guard security paperwork in Virginia and got through to her desk.

Susan explained our situation and appealed to her sensibilities as a woman, convincing her to walk the paperwork around desk-to-desk until it was completed and returned to San Angelo. What my supervisors and I were told could take two weeks, Susan accomplished in about two hours. Crisis averted.

By Wednesday, I was in class, Susan was content in the hotel with the baby, and some very nice young airman was getting an award for outstanding customer service. Susan had written a long thank-you note to her boss explaining the important role her small gesture had played in our lives.

The crazy epilogue to this story is what might have happened if Susan had not been so resourceful. Incredibly, neither the airmen processing the paperwork nor the civilians delivering the message found this treatment unusual. Such is life in the active-duty Air Force, I suppose. If the paperwork wasn't ready, you just sat around on charge of quarters (CQ) duty, making copies and receiving full pay, until it was.

But we were not in the active duty; we were in the National Guard. And the Air Force didn't seem to know the difference. Thank goodness my wife was able to explain our situation to a real person who took the time to listen, instead of just annoying a bureaucrat who didn't care. We wondered how many Guardsmen found themselves in the same situation, and how many simply went home. One family is too many.

Despite our rough start, we settled into San Angelo without any further trouble. We got an apartment off base, and I started to learn about my new Air Force Specialty Code (AFSC 14N). For nine months, I learned all about the intelligence career field in a rigorous and extremely worthwhile course.

Intelligence is the study of your enemy. Our job as Air Force intelligence officers was to learn about the weapons, tactics, and capabilities of our adversaries so that we could best counter each threat. This required an interdisciplinary approach that included mathematics, history, physics, languages, economics, political science, and engineering. We learned about various collection methods employed by US intelligence agencies, all kinds of foreign and domestic weapons systems, and how to synthesize and analyze information.

My favorite subject was international affairs, which I had studied in college and graduate school. Many of the instructors had spent time all over the world, so they taught with authority. I loved hearing about all the different religions, cultures, and places they had experienced with the military and wondered if I would ever get to see such sights.

I also became proficient in preparing and delivering military briefings; I enjoyed public speaking. The classes were challenging, the people were interesting, and I liked everything about intelligence school.

Kevin worked every day in the schoolhouse SCIF from seven-thirty in the morning to three-thirty in the afternoon. I always thought it was a SKIFF, but it actually stands for Sensitive Compartmented Information Facility (SCIF). Anyway, he was in this secure building all day long, and except for emergencies, I had no way of contacting him while he was there.

Thank heavens Kevin brought his motorcycle and rode it to work most mornings because it meant I had the Jeep to use. I would care for and play with Will all day except for a morning hour at the gym. I didn't know anyone else. So it was just the two of us.

While Kevin had a group of like-minded colleagues to spend time with and get to know, I was isolated and not exactly sure where or how to make friends. I did get some relief when a woman at the gym invited me to Community Bible Study, a national organization made up of local women. I was able to study the Book of Revelation with them and found mental stimulation and spiritual support. What a godsend.

The other relationship that saved me from going crazy was our new friends, Jeffrey and Elizabeth. They were our next-door neighbors off-base in an apartment complex called Encino Park. Everybody called it Inferno Park, for reasons obvious to anybody who ever spent any time in West Texas during the summer.

Jeffrey and Elizabeth were from Lubbock and had twin girls about a year older than Will. Kevin called them the "meep-meep" twins because they seemed to speak to each other in a mysterious language that sounded like something from the Muppets. Jeffrey took Kevin wild pig hunting on his grandfather's ranch and introduced us to premium Tequila. Elizabeth was a stay-at-home mom like me who kept me company while Kevin was at work.

We became wonderful friends. She was always there for me when I didn't know what I was doing. Although I loved the freedom of raising Will far away from family, I sometimes needed on-the-spot advice and guidance from somebody with experience. I had no one to turn to in that regard except Elizabeth.

One morning, Will pulled himself up to standing with a kitchen chair, which promptly fell over on top of him. He got a nasty cut on his head that looked like it needed stitches. While he was crying, I was panicking. I went to Elizabeth for a second opinion, and she agreed that I should go to the emergency room.

But she didn't stop there; Elizabeth held Will for ten minutes while I ran home to brush my teeth and get dressed. Because this all happened before eight in the morning, Kevin knew nothing of the event until he got back from work that afternoon. Luckily, Will didn't need stitches, and I held it together.

Besides enjoying his classes, Kevin also loved Texas and San Angelo in particular. But I was feeling isolated. It was a three-hour drive to anywhere, and I got bored peering out the window looking for the roadrunner that would sometimes hop around our yard. The shopping in San Angelo wasn't the best, and online shopping wasn't a thing yet. If it wasn't at the Wal-Mart, getting something I wanted for Will wasn't always possible.

Learning to keep secrets was a big part of our intelligence training. We studied the different classification requirements for sensitive information, how to keep it secure, and how to properly disseminate it to military operators and civilian planners. We also discussed why we have secrets in the first place. We don't want our enemies to know what we intend to do, when we plan to do it, or how we collect intelligence against them. And we certainly don't want them to have access to sensitive technologies. It's all pretty straightforward.

To be successful in keeping these secrets, you must follow strict protocols and protect information systems, but mostly you have to keep your mouth shut. That's one reason why I am so dumbfounded by all the leaks and breaches coming out of Washington these days. If a rank-and-file analyst is careless with classified information, it can ruin his career. If he deliberately shares it, he can go to jail. But if a Washington insider blabs to the *New York Times,* he gets a book deal and a spot on the best talk show. They may be flip with secrets inside the Beltway, but we took them very seriously at Goodfellow Air Force Base. And we still do in the Air National Guard.

During training, almost all the study materials in the SCIF were classified SECRET or TOP SECRET, so we weren't allowed to take anything home. That meant we had to study hard to meet our academic requirements within short timeframes; the SCIF was rarely open late, and the material was often difficult. At times, it was intense. The good news was that I almost always had my weekends and evenings free to spend with Susan and Will.

We took advantage of our free time to explore Texas. San Angelo is a charming little town, the largest city in the US without an interstate highway. Surrounded by cotton fields, cattle ranches, and mesquite scrub, the people, the scenery, and the wildlife are vintage Texas. In the evenings, we went for walks around our apartment complex. The warm weather was a nice change from our normally frigid Pennsylvania winters.

About once a week, we went out to eat cheap, and without many national restaurant chains in town, the local choices were outstanding. Our favorite Mexican place was the Corner Stop, which sold breakfast burritos in paper bags on weekend mornings. The best steakhouse was Lowake's, an establishment outside of town that served pound-and-a-half hunks of beef. And our favorite barbecue joint was a combined restaurant and fishing bait shop with pictures of Dale Earnhardt all over it. The owners told us Earnhardt himself stopped there once a year to eat barbecue after hunting nearby with a local rancher.

On the weekends, we took day trips to interesting places nearby. We went to the Rattlesnake Roundup in Stillwater, where we ate fried reptiles and shopped for clear, acrylic toilet seats with encased rattlesnakes inside. We visited Enchanted Rock in Fredericksburg and walked among the beautiful bluebonnet flowers. And we made several trips to New Braunfels and Luckenbach in the Hill Country, which reminded us of the rolling hills of eastern Pennsylvania.

We also made weekend trips when we could, to San Antonio, Austin, El Paso, and Lubbock. Often, we stayed at military bases to save money. Sometimes, we camped. Our most memorable trip was to Big Bend National Park with Jeffrey and Elizabeth.

We had never heard of Big Bend before, but we were excited to visit this little-known national park. Jeffrey and Elizabeth left the meep-meep twins with a babysitter, which should have been a red flag for Susan and me. Anyway, we made the six-hour drive through the barren Texas desert until we reached the Rio Grande valley about noon. We set up camp in a beautiful, mountainous park full of colorful rock formations, stark alpine scenery, and amazing birds and wildlife. It was February, but it was in the mid-seventies as we hiked the trails in shorts and t-shirts with Will in our portable baby backpack.

That night, we learned about weather changes in the desert. By midnight, the temperature had dropped about forty degrees, and we only had lightweight sleeping bags to deal with the freezing weather. Susan and I huddled with Will between the blankets to stay warm. Neither of us slept much at all. We figured we were the worst parents in the world, but Will didn't seem to mind. He was up early playing in the frosty dirt. He wanted to eat.

When we weren't spending time with Jeffrey and Elizabeth, we were playing mom and dad to the rest of the people in my intelligence class. At twenty-nine years old, I was the old man. Almost all the rest of my twenty or so classmates were fresh out of the Air Force Academy. Only one was married, and none had children. And since all the single airmen on active duty had to stay on base, coming to our apartment to hang out was a welcome break from the Goodfellow routine.

We had visitors all the time, and they loved hanging out with Susan and Will. He got passed around like a pet or something. He was always sitting on somebody's lap, smiling, giggling, and doing tricks. I remember him sitting on my buddy Marv's lap all night watching the World Series. Will especially liked hanging out with Donk, this huge former pararescueman (PJ) in my class nicknamed after that character in *Crocodile Dundee*. Will also enjoyed making faces at all the young ladies in the class, who totally doted on him.

For the first and only time in our lives, Susan and I experienced active duty. For me, it was great. I was taking an interesting class with interesting people doing something I enjoyed. I could go to the gym every day, had plenty of free time, and enjoyed the amenities of a fully functional Air Force base. I loved Texas, and San Angelo was the perfect home base to explore the whole state.

But it wasn't all positive for Susan. A few months into our trip, she was feeling homesick and alone. She liked shopping and nice restaurants and culture, and the Home Depot, Dale Earnhardt barbecue joint, and Fort Concho Museum weren't quite doing the trick. Family members came to visit and lifted her spirits, but after they left, she felt even more homesick. While I was away learning new things and being challenged by my academics, Susan was at home in the apartment with the baby. By Thanksgiving, Susan had full-blown symptoms of depression.

I felt like it was my fault.

Later, I learned that Susan had been prone to bouts of depression since she was a young girl; they just didn't know what it was back then. Morbidly, it made me feel better to know that she had experienced these feelings before she met me, as if this was evidence of my innocence in the matter. But thinking those kinds of thoughts just made me feel more selfish and stupid and guilty.

I should have seen it coming. The move, the baby, the isolation, and the strange surroundings all contributed to the onset of her symptoms. So I might not have caused her underlying depression, but I certainly helped provide the triggers. For that reason, I still felt responsible. I wanted to cure her of her depression, not exacerbate her problems. I wonder how many other husbands have felt the same way. Helpless and blameworthy.

Fortunately, we were on active duty and had access to all the resources of a fully functioning Air Force base. I received exceptional treatment from the military doctors and counselors, who recognized my symptoms and helped us understand what was happening. And if I ever needed extra help, the base had an extensive family support infrastructure to help military spouses and their children.

I also got outstanding support from my friend Elizabeth. She was there to provide encouragement, watch the baby, and generally be my companion when Kevin was in the SCIF. I don't know if Elizabeth knows how important she was to me during that rough period in my life.

Postpartum depression affects more than three million women each year in the US. We both knew about this condition; we just never thought it would affect our family. I improved quickly, but the lingering effects lasted for the duration of our time in Texas.

By the spring, we were both ready to go back home. Susan and I treasured our active-duty experience for different reasons, but it wasn't who we were. We were anxious to return to friends and family, and I was starting to miss my regular job. So in May of 2001, we said goodbye to our Texas friends and made our way back to Pennsylvania.

We were in another transition. My job in Harrisburg was great, but it was fleeting. Governor Ridge was well into his second term and soon would be out of office. That meant that soon I might be out of a job.

Meanwhile, Susan's parents retired and were moving from Beaver, about forty-five minutes north of Pittsburgh, to Conneaut Lake, about forty-five minutes south of Erie. We had considered relocating to the Pittsburgh area, but that didn't make as much sense without Susan's parents nearby. And although Erie is a beautiful place, we thought jobs would be harder to find, and winters would be brutal. I'm not sure, but Susan's mom and dad may be the only human beings on the planet who moved to a place with more snow and longer winters for their retirement.

We decided to try my hometown of Allentown, a mid-sized city about sixty miles north of Philadelphia and ninety miles west of New York City. Susan's only demand was to pledge for eternity that I would root for the Steelers and against the Eagles. For some people in Southeastern Pennsylvania, that would have been a deal-breaker. But I am a much bigger baseball fan than football fan, and she made no such demands about the Phillies. I agreed and got off easy.

The plan was to move in with my parents for the summer until we found a home for our new and growing family. We had just found out Susan was pregnant again and were excited to buy our first house somewhere in the Lehigh Valley, which includes Allentown and the surrounding areas of Bethlehem and Easton.

My parents, Trudie and Bill, were gracious hosts and happy to spend time with their first grandson after almost a year away. But living with your parents is never easy, and everybody involved was anxious for us to move along. Besides, I had returned to my state job in Harrisburg and was commuting ninety miles each way. That was a drag, but I couldn't look for a house and a job at the same time. First things first.

We looked at several homes in the area through the summer, all outside my hometown. I didn't want to return to the same school district where I had graduated. I just thought that would be too weird for everyone involved. Nonetheless, after we made offers on two houses away from my hometown that both fell through, we were getting impatient.

Eventually, we made an offer on a four-bedroom colonial on a one-acre lot in my old school district, Northwestern Lehigh. At the end of a cul-de-sac surrounded by woods and cornfields, it looked to us like the perfect location to raise a family.

We closed on the house the Friday before Labor Day. Kevin made an immediate first impression on our neighbors, and not the one we wanted. After we signed all the paperwork, and everybody left, Kevin made a big burn pile out back with cardboard boxes and junk from the move. Since we were living in the country, I guess he figured nobody cared if we burned a bunch of scrap paper.

He lit the fire, and within minutes, flaming pieces of cardboard were flying high into the air outside of our backyard. We didn't have any grass to burn, but the farmer next door did. The flying cardboard caught the hayfield on fire.

I would have called the fire company, but we didn't have a phone. Instead, Kevin grabbed the hose our builder had left behind and started running frantically to put out the fire. What he couldn't reach with the garden hose, I doused with a bucket. When we couldn't get a bucket fast enough, we stomped the fire with our shoes. Eventually, we got it under control. Except for a few burnt patches of hay, the singed hair on Kevin's legs, and the melted rubber soles of our shoes, there were no casualties.

We didn't know it, but our whole neighborhood was watching the entire time. They were all having a backyard cookout a few doors down, and we provided the entertainment. My good friend Rebecca later told me that they all would have pitched in if they thought the fire was getting out of control, but they were having way too much fun watching Kevin and me run around like Benny Hill. Such was our first impression.

It would be a while before we had a proper introduction to our neighbors. Most of our belongings were still in military storage, and we learned that it would be almost a month before they would be delivered. So for the next couple of weeks, we split time sleeping at my parents' house in beds and the new home in sleeping bags. In the meantime, I could switch focus and start looking for a new job near Allentown instead of driving back and forth to Harrisburg.

A three-hour commute gives you plenty of time to think. Susan and I had chosen for our wedding song, "Ordinary People" by Clay Walker. The lyrics say, "The greatest gift that I could ever wish for you and me is a life as ordinary as can be."

So far, our life had not been very ordinary. In four years, we had met, fallen in love, gotten married, had a baby, and started expecting another. Along the way, Susan and I had traveled through twenty-two states, lived in eight apartments, and had five different jobs. Plus, I kept going back and forth to military duty and dragging her along.

To put it mildly, it had been a whirlwind tour. Most of our adventures had been fun, and we had made some amazing memories, but we needed a break. It was time to give Susan the ordinary life I had promised.

CHAPTER SIX: EVERYTHING CHANGED

TUESDAY, SEPTEMBER 11, 2001, was a warm and sunny morning, the perfect day to begin our new and ordinary phase of life. It started harmless enough. After arriving at the office early, I sat down to write some memos and answer some mail.

Those were the early days of the internet, so we still talked to people on the phone and wrote real letters. There were no cellphones, text messages, or social media, and people congregated around the coffee pot to say hello and catch up on things. We had a great office, full of talented people and interesting personalities.

There were about twelve of us in the Governor's Policy Office. Judy and Karen, the office assistants, ran the show. They knew everything that happened in our office and around Harrisburg. Friendly and professional, they always kept us out of trouble.

The rest of the office was mostly analysts. We would review state policies and make new proposals for the governor to consider. All my peers were very smart. Melia, Russ, Glenn, and Christine all had reputations as the best in their fields. Tammy, Sherry, and Brenda had expertise in international commerce and were always planning trade missions. Pete was the boss and had a strong grasp of just about any subject. Together, our group of policy wonks could tackle just about every topic you could imagine.

We were a tight-knit group. My office colleagues had thrown Susan and me a huge baby shower just before we had Will and kept in touch while we were in Texas. Whenever I had to leave for military training, everybody pitched in to cover my workload.

So it was in this collegial environment that we first realized something was wrong. It was before nine in the morning, and people were still milling around. As always, Judy and Karen heard the news first. There was a plane crash in New York City, they said, and it looked pretty bad. I nodded and continued to work.

Within a few minutes, people started to get up and congregate in the conference room, where the television news was on. I heard somebody mention the World Trade Center, heard the nervousness in their voices. I got up to see for myself what was going on.

A passenger jet had crashed into the North Tower. The news broadcasters had no idea what was going on. Was it an accident? Was it terrorism? The experts on TV were just getting their bearings, and we in the office were still on our first cups of coffee. Then we all watched as the second plane hit the South Tower.

At that moment, there could be no doubt. This was not an accident. We didn't need television experts to interpret the facts. America was under attack. Our lives had changed. There would be no ordinary life for Susan or me anytime soon.

I remember the office clamor as background noise. Nobody was panicking, but everybody understood that we were in some kind of war. Some of my colleagues stayed glued to the television; some hurried about to get their things in case of a hasty exit. All made phone calls to loved ones to let them know they were okay. Within a few minutes, everybody in Harrisburg was aware of the situation, and the Capitol Complex was under lockdown. People were being dismissed to go home.

Meanwhile, Susan and Will were spending the day alone in their new home, setting up things and cleaning. I figured they were oblivious to all that was occurring just ninety miles away in New York City. Our phone still wasn't hooked up yet, and we didn't have cellphones back then, so I had no way to get through to them. My parents were both at work. So I called Grandma Phoebe.

Grandma Phoebe lived by herself about five miles from our new house. She was eighty-one years old, four and a half feet tall, and had fiery red hair.

You didn't mess with Grandma Phoebe. She was as independent, feisty, and tough as they came. Her father was a machine gunner in World War I, her husband was a fighter pilot in World War II, and her son, my dad, was a fighter pilot in Vietnam. She had spent her entire life supporting her men in uniform as they went off to war. She would know what to do. In fact, she was expecting my call.

"Grandma," I said, "are you watching the news?"

"Yes," said Phoebe. She knew what it meant.

I told her that I couldn't reach Susan and asked if she would drive over to our house and tell her in person that I was okay. I said I needed to go into the Air Force base and that I probably would be home late.

It was a short conversation long on meaning. I don't think I would have needed to say anything to Phoebe, and she would have delivered exactly the message I needed to convey. Phoebe knew her grandson probably was going to war, and she was springing into action. Susan was in good hands.

I hung up the phone and told Karen that I was going to the base. She wished me well and gave me a hug. I gathered my things, hopped in my truck, and made the half-hour drive from my downtown office to the Harrisburg airport. Since transferring to the Air Force, I had 588 days of practice. Now it was real.

I remember pulling up to the front gate at the 193rd Special Operations Wing. The base always has a strong security presence with physical barriers and gate guards. But the difference this time wasn't the weapons in the hands of the Security Forces or the fences at the entry control point. It was the look on the faces of the airmen protecting the base. They knew it was real too.

I was wearing a suit and a tie, making me the only guy around who was not in uniform. For a moment, I felt out of place. But then I felt proud. I was able to go from my civilian job to active duty in less than an hour. By ten-thirty in the morning, I was on orders for Operation NOBLE EAGLE, the military mission to protect the United States from further attacks. *That's what it means to be a "citizen-soldier,"* I thought.

Although the National Guard is a part-time reserve force, both the Army and Air components have a significant contingent of full-time people to keep things running when the part-time Guardsmen aren't around. The Army Guard is about 80 percent part-time soldiers with 20 percent full-time. In the Air Guard, the ratio is about 70:30 because the Air Guard needs more full-time people to keep airplanes flying. Full-time Guardsmen have a unique status in the military that can be very difficult to understand.

Some of the full-time Guardsmen are permanently assigned to their National Guard units while enjoying the same military status as their active-duty counterparts. These members are part of the "Active Guard and Reserve" (AGR). AGR Guardsmen get most of the benefits of full-time military service without the requirement to move from base-to-base every few years. Until very recently, AGR positions were coveted and rare.

On 9/11, most full-time Guardsmen were considered "dual-status technicians." These are full-time civilian employees of the Department of Defense who get paid like civil servants but wear military uniforms to work every day. Dual status technicians only are on official military status when they are on military orders, such as during weekend drills, training exercises, or on deployments.

If this all seems confusing, that's because it is. The concept of a civilian technician in a military uniform is so strange, nobody in the active-duty military appears to understand it either. In fact, except for the technicians themselves, sometimes I wonder if anybody understands it. I guess that is one of the main reasons why the military is transitioning most of the full-time Guardsmen from technician to AGR status. That process is well underway.

Of course, the overwhelming majority of the National Guard is made up of part-time, "traditional" Guardsmen. The Air Guard calls part-time airmen "DSGs" for "drill-status Guardsmen." The Army Guard calls them "M-Day" soldiers for "Mobility Day." Part-time Guardsmen can volunteer for additional training or special duties and get activated for state emergencies or wars. Otherwise, we are obligated to spend one weekend a month plus fifteen days a year in training. That's a minimum commitment of thirty-nine days in uniform each year, just like the recruiting commercials used to say.

I was about to realize that my new commitment would be much, much more.

The news showed the Pennsylvania State Capitol in Harrisburg, where Kevin worked, being evacuated. My immediate concerns were *Where is my husband?* and *Is he safe?*

I had no way of calling Kevin because there were no cell phones, and he had no way of calling me because our phones were not hooked up yet. He and I had only been in our brand-new, first house for one week, and the phone company had not made it a priority to hook up our phones.

I continued watching the TV as the destruction escalated, and I prayed for the safety of all the other air passengers that day. I worried about the well-being of the President on Air Force One. I tried to get up to do some work around the house, but I couldn't quite move from the TV set. I doted on Will, though, and took every opportunity to hold him.

By now, the towers had collapsed, and the destruction and devastation were mind-boggling. The loss of life was staggering. I thought, *How many more lives are going to be lost when we go to war?*

About noon, a knock on the door brought some answers to my questions. Kevin's grandma came to tell me that Kevin had called her. He was safely out of the Capitol and had gone directly to the Harrisburg Airport to the 193rd Air National Guard base. He knew I would be worried and had asked Grandma to fill me in on what was going on.

Grandma and I sat somberly in the living room. We didn't say the thing we were thinking most. She held the baby as long as he would let her, and then it was time for his nap. So Grandma went home. I put Will down for a nap and went back to the TV set. My mind was whirling.

Back at the base, I was greeted by Captain McKissick and Technical Sergeant Darren Zimmerman, each a full-time Guardsman whose collective job was to run the intelligence shop when the part-timers were at their civilian jobs.

Captain McKissick was the most respected intelligence professional on base. He was smart and insightful, with a knack for thinking outside the box.

Technical Sergeant Zimmerman was just as smart but in a different way. He had memorized the engagement zone of every surface to air missile (SAM), the speed of just about every combat aircraft in the world, and the maximum effective range of every piece of enemy anti-aircraft artillery (AAA) our aircrews might encounter. He was a walking encyclopedia of intelligence knowledge with the demeanor to match. People called him Buzz Lightyear.

Captain Sharon Hedges was the other full-time intelligence analyst, but she was away on Temporary Duty (TDY) that morning. Captain Hedges was an up-and-comer in the Wing. A concert pianist in her spare time, she could recognize matters of strategic importance through the clutter of massive amounts of information. She would go on to become the first intelligence officer with the rank of colonel in the history of the Pennsylvania Air National Guard and one of the highest-ranking female officers in the state.

It was an all-star team of intelligence professionals at the base. I imagined it was as good as any core group of analysts found on active duty. Although they had things under control, the full-timers were surprised and happy to see me that morning, even if they did rib me for my suit and tie. They were overwhelmed with requests to find out what was going on, and I was a badly needed extra body, especially with Captain Hedges away on TDY.

By the time I arrived on base, the unit's crisis action team was in full swing. Everybody had three things on their minds:

How many more attacks were still coming?

What could we do to help right now?

And how should we prepare for what happened next?

The first problem was urgent. In about the time it took to drive from my office to the base, two more airplanes had crashed, one into the Pentagon and another into a field in Somerset County. We had no idea if we were done after four attacks or if we should expect twenty more.

Technical Sergeant Zimmerman was on it. He got plugged into every classified network you could think of and was relaying information back and forth between our unit and every three-letter agency you could name—the Federal Bureau of Investigations (FBI), the National Security Agency (NSA), the Defense Intelligence Agency (DIA), the Central Intelligence Agency (CIA). If he couldn't find it online, he found somebody on the phone and gave them a call. I was so impressed by his network of people and systems. He kept us informed about every detail.

Although it didn't affect our unit directly, we were tracking the different civilian airplanes that remained in the air over the United States. By about 9:45 in the morning, all airspace had been shut down, and the military had scrambled fighters to intercept any airplanes that didn't land or prepare to land.

As the day progressed, we came to realize that four airplanes were all they had, and the attack was over. But in those anxious moments between ten o'clock and noon, multiple civilian airliners had had malfunctioning equipment, made mistakes, or simply didn't follow orders to land. People don't understand how close the US military was to shooting down civilian airliners during those critical few hours. Thank God for levelheaded fighter pilots who held their fire instead of jumping the gun.

Soon, the base focus shifted from gaining situational awareness to preparing to assist. The new wing commander played a high-profile role in the initial planning process. He was from California and had hair like a Ken doll—a little too poofy and a little too perfect. A lot of the local guys didn't like him. He was an outsider who had replaced some popular leaders, sipped wine instead of chugging beer, and sometimes came across as a know-it-all. But he would become a competent wartime commander, and on that day, like most days, he was calm amidst the chaos.

The 193rd Special Operations Wing flies the "Commando Solo" airframe, the only craft of its kind in the world. Basically, it is a flying radio and television station with all sorts of extra bells and whistles. You can always tell people who are unfamiliar with our airframe because they call it "Commander Solo," as if it were named after the guy from *Star Wars.*

Our wartime mission is called airborne psychological operations (PSYOP). During the Obama Administration, they changed the name to a more politically correct version: "Military Information Support Operations" (MISO). Recently, the military is once again using PSYOP. Whatever they call it, it's all the same thing—delivering airborne radio and television broadcasts to civilian and military populations to achieve desired behavioral effects.

On 9/11, we thought the federal government might need to use Commando Solo to make radio broadcasts to Americans, not for PSYOP but for emergency communications. If networks in New York City were too damaged or saturated for people to get basic information, our airborne transmission platforms could provide temporary assistance. They also could have provided command and control capabilities during the heightened defense posture throughout the continental United States. And we were prepared to use our stripped-down C-130s (slicks) for miscellaneous regional airlift if required.

Most of the afternoon, the base was responding to inquiries about what we could do or volunteering information about it. By the evening hours, it became apparent that Commando Solo was probably not going to be needed to fly missions in support of domestic operations. The airspace was secure, communications were degraded but sufficient, and the attacks were over. Starting on 9/12, we were preparing for combat operations.

Driving home that evening, I had a full ninety minutes to think about how my life had changed. Although we didn't even know for sure who was behind these attacks, we all knew enough somebody was going to pay for them. I didn't know when or where, but I was pretty sure I was going to war.

I thought about my dad. He was a Navy fighter pilot who did three tours in Vietnam. He always said that he went to war so his kids wouldn't have to. Would he somehow feel like a failure if I had to go to war?

I thought about my mom. She supported my dad for two years while he was away flying combat missions. I was born while my dad was overseas. Would it be different for her with a son deployed instead of a husband?

I thought about our children. Will was entering his toddler years. Would I miss a critical time in his development? The new baby was due in January. Would I be there for the birth? You can't get those moments back.

Mostly, I thought about Susan. She had Grandma Phoebe and my parents around for help, and they were old pros at supporting military spouses. But this was brand new for Susan, her parents were five hours away, and there was no military support structure at our new home in Kutztown. She was going to have to succeed mostly on her own, with God's help.

I pulled into the drive of our new home, still with no furniture, late in the evening. I was wearing the same suit I had put on at six o'clock that morning and needed a shower. I had so much to talk about with Susan, but it was late, and I was exhausted. Plus, I had to return to base in the morning to assume my role in the battle rhythm—this time in uniform. We hugged, recapped the day, and both went to bed.

Kevin got home sometime around ten o'clock at night. He told me it had been a crazy day and that he was exhausted. We went to bed and held each other. He got up early the next morning to report to the base for an active duty day. I still don't know exactly what he did because it is all classified, and I have learned it is easier not to ask. After a day at the base, Kevin assured me he had no orders to deploy, at least not right away.

Thursday, Kevin went to his civilian job. A rather uneventful day. I made it a priority to have the telephone hooked up. I also recall the deafening silence outside. There were no planes. Our house was under a frequently traveled airplane route, and it was eerie having none flying overhead.

That evening, we watched President George W. Bush give a speech about Tuesday's tragic events and what immediate measures were going to be taken. He announced the formation of the Office of Homeland Security with Kevin's boss, Tom Ridge, at the helm.

We stayed up rather late, discussing whether Kevin wanted to throw his hat into the ring for a job at Homeland Security. We had just bought a house in Pennsylvania, but he certainly had the background, the connections, and the security clearance. He would be an ideal candidate. We went to bed without a clear decision.

The next week was a whirlwind of activity. I split time between going to the base and going to my civilian job. Long workdays and three-hour commutes left little time for Susan and Will. Mostly, I saw them late at night and did my best to be good company.

Meanwhile, the US response to the attacks was materializing. National intelligence agencies confirmed that a little-known organization called "al-Qaida" was responsible for the attacks, led by a terrorist named Osama bin Laden. He operated in Afghanistan under the protection of the Taliban, a radical Islamic organization that ruled the country with an iron fist.

The Secretary of Defense, Donald Rumsfeld, had been traveling around Southwest Asia delivering a blunt message: *You are either with us or against us.* Most nations fell in line and allowed us to use their bases, airspace, and other resources to prepare for a pending invasion. This included Pakistan, which had been protecting the Taliban up to that point. It did a sudden about-face when given the ultimatum.

President George W. Bush had been preparing the country for imminent war. Not that he needed to whip anybody into a frenzy. People of all political persuasions were fighting mad. Everybody seemed anxious to go after those responsible.

At the 193rd, planning shifted from possible contingencies to actual missions. Within days, we knew where we would be based and where we would be flying. Soon, we received our deployment dates and gained clarity about the mission. The only thing we didn't know is how long we would be gone.

Unlike active duty, where members of the military are on orders all the time, National Guard soldiers and airmen are only on orders for specified periods of training or during emergencies. Either the state or the federal government can activate Guardsmen in a crisis. In this case, we were being called up by the President for the pending war in Afghanistan. This was a so-called "Title 10" activation, which refers to the federal law that authorizes the call-up of reserve forces. We were being ordered to war.

Putting reservists on Title 10 orders is a big deal. So when an emergency occurs, the military must strike a careful balance between minimizing the disruptions to civilian careers and generating enough human resources to support the mission. One way the Air National Guard does this is by setting rotation schedules.

Rotations are different for every activation, but generally, they follow a similar pattern. First, the unit receives orders to go somewhere in support of a contingency (such as war). Next, we figure out how many people from each different specialty are required to complete the mission, and for how long. Then, we break the deployment into manageable chunks and take volunteers for the duration. In the Air Guard, rotations can be as short as six weeks or as long as six months or more, depending on the mission requirements and available workforce.

So, for example, if we needed two intel bodies to support a six-month-long mission, we might set up three two-month rotations and cycle six people through the deployment. In practice, this meant that our base needed more qualified people to accomplish the mission, but those people stayed in the combat zone for shorter durations. This was a practical compromise for Guardsmen who still had responsibilities to their civilian employers.

A week after 9/11, Susan and I both were becoming impatient about whether and when I would deploy, although for different reasons. The whole intel shop had been spending time in the office to help with mission planning, and everybody was contributing in various ways. We all wondered who would get the call to go out the door first.

About ten days in, Captain McKissick pulled me aside. He knew that I was anxious to get in the fight, but he explained that I was also his least experienced intelligence officer, fresh from training with no operational experience. He told me that although I would likely have a chance to go on a future rotation, he wanted me to stay behind in Harrisburg for a while before heading overseas. I definitely would not be going out the door first. He simply needed a more veteran team.

I understood his logic, but I was a little upset. I was rightfully concerned about going to war and had no delusions about what I might face. But deploying to fight if our nation was attacked was the main reason I had joined the military in the first place. I didn't want to sit on the sidelines while the varsity team was on the field.

On the other hand, Susan was thrilled. When I went home that evening, I explained the whole thing and how disappointed I was to be left behind. She pretended to be upset for me, but I know she was relieved. A delay in the deployment meant that it might not happen at all, and she would rather have me commuting to the Harrisburg airport for a while instead of fighting in the combat zone.

The next day I put on my uniform and went back to the base. I was trying to hide my frustration as I resigned myself to an indefinite stateside role. In contrast, Susan was more relaxed then I had seen her in weeks as she sent me out the door.

Her reprieve didn't last long. As soon as I arrived at the base, Captain McKissick called me into his office.

"Plans have changed," he said. "The first rotation leaves tomorrow. You are on it."

I asked him why, but I didn't listen to his answer. I was leaving for the combat zone in twenty-four hours, and my mind was going 100 miles an hour.

I called Susan on our newly installed telephone line. The conversation went something like this:

"Susie, I know I assured you just last evening that I wouldn't have to leave for at least a few months, but I found out this morning that the schedule has changed. I am going on the first rotation, and we leave tomorrow." I tried to hide my excitement. "I can't really explain everything now, but I will be home around five o'clock this afternoon. I'll need to pack all my gear and get everything ready. Can you please buy new batteries for my flashlight? I'll be in the SCIF all day, so you won't be able to reach me. See you tonight. Love you."

The base had asked Kevin to come in for an active-duty day on Friday. It was an early morning. He had to make the long drive to Harrisburg. Will was his usual cheerful self that morning. I had coffee and started to read the newspaper.

About seven-fifteen in the morning, the telephone rang. It was Kevin. "Sus, I'm going, and I'm leaving tomorrow."

I was dead silent. What do you say? I finally let out a meager, "Okay."

Our decision about whether to go to Washington, D.C., with Tom Ridge was a moot point. We now had to face something that few people in this nation can understand—a military deployment.

I didn't know what to do next. I made a mental list of everything Kevin laid out on the bed when he went on his two weeks of training with the Army as an infantry soldier. I went back to the Kmart and bought everything I could from that list—deodorant, toothpaste, sunflower seeds. . . The whole morning seemed surreal.

I went through the motions, but I was in a fog, constantly distracted thinking about the change that was occurring in our lives. I brought all the items home and laid them neatly out on the bed so that he could pack easily.

Sometime that afternoon, I received another call from Kevin. His family was coming over that evening. Not just his mom and dad and sisters, but his cousins, his aunts, and uncles. I had nothing in the house for guests to eat and drink. So I was off to find a beer distributor and supermarket.

Kevin got home and hugged me for a long time

We ate some dinner, and the family came. There was blatant disbelief that another generation of Dellickers was going to war. Kevin's father had fought in Vietnam, his grandfather in World War II, his great-grandfather in World War I. The events of the week had been so confusing for everyone. Sending a family member off to war against an enemy about whom many of us knew little was simply scary.

I appreciated the support of the entire family but at some point, in the evening, I wanted them all to leave. I wanted to be alone with my husband; I wanted him all to myself. I had never imagined him going to war, and this was not exactly how I pictured my last evening with my husband before he went.

After everyone left, Kevin understandably wanted to put Will to bed. So I cleaned up the kitchen and then watched him pack. He couldn't believe all the things I had remembered from his Army days. Some of them were completely obsolete for an Air Force deployment, I'm sure. But he was gracious about the gesture and was able to use many of them.

He packed meticulously. He was so focused, and I was still in a state of profound shock with more questions than answers.

Kevin told me, "I can't tell you where I am going, I don't know how long I'll be gone, and we'll have no contact while I'm away."

Okay, then. How do you respond to that?

That evening was one of the strangest nights of my life. After getting my call, Susan contacted my parents and told them I was leaving in the morning. In turn, they called all my relatives within a two-hour drive. Soon after I pulled into the driveway, I saw aunts and uncles and cousins, all there to wish me well as I went out the door. I felt very blessed that my family cared enough to show up and felt better knowing they would be there to help Susan while I was gone.

But in all the turmoil, it seemed like I hardly got to talk to Susan. She had one simple wish: to spend a few moments together with her husband and son before I departed. Yet here she was entertaining people she barely knew and putting on a show of strength for my extended family. I was the center of attention, but she was left holding the bag.

That evening, after everybody left, it was very late, and I still had to pack. It was the first time we were able to talk.

"Susie," I said. "We are going on a classified mission to a classified location. I will call you from Europe as I head in-theater and I will call you again from Europe when I am returning home. Otherwise, we will have no way to communicate while I am gone."

To this day, she doesn't know where I went or everything I did. That night, I went to bed with anticipation. She went to bed with dread. We both were exhausted.

Despite everything, I slept well that night. We awoke to a bright and sunny Saturday morning. Kevin had to report by noon. So we didn't have to rush out at five-thirty in the morning. We had coffee. We played with Will. The time came to say goodbye. We went outside to the driveway, and I was in tears.

"Howdy, neighbor," says a stranger carrying a handful of fresh beets.

I was so annoyed. Usually, I would have been thrilled to meet a new neighbor but not right now.

Kevin told the guy, "Now is not a good time." He didn't get the idea right away, but eventually, he left.

There was no delaying the inevitable—Kevin was gone. I had to keep moving forward.

The red beet incident is one of those stories that seem too strange to be true but too weird to make up. The morning of my departure, after things finally slowed down, we all got up early and had breakfast, just Susan, Will, and me. I was in civilian clothes with my bags in the truck. There was no marching-band sendoff—I would drive myself to the base where we would change into our uniforms and fly from there. All that was left was to kiss my wife and son and goodbye.

For a moment, we were finally alone. After all the turmoil of the past few weeks, we were about to experience that moment you see in the movies, when the brave husband reassures the faithful wife that everything will be okay. Instead, we met Dave.

"Hey, do you like red beets?" he said.

Dave could have had two heads and six eyeballs with a foot growing out of his chest, and Susan and I probably wouldn't have noticed.

"I'm Dave from across the street," he said. "Welcome to the neighborhood. Do you like green peppers?"

Susan and I snapped out of our trance. That's when we realized we had been so busy during the last few weeks that we had forgotten to meet the neighbors.

Dave was an Army veteran and one of the nicest guys you could ever know. He usually worked the night shift, so he was around a lot during the day when the kids were home. To our boys, he would become the beloved "Uncle Dave." But on that morning, I wanted to see Dave as much as I wanted a root canal.

"Hi Dave, I'm Kevin, and this is Susan," I said. "This is my son Will. I appreciate your friendliness, but now is just not a good time to talk. I'm leaving to fight the war in Afghanistan."

Dave was still in small-talk mode for a second, and I thought he might offer up another vegetable. But then it sank in. "You mean right now?"

"Yes, right now. I'm getting in the truck as soon as I say goodbye."

Suddenly, Dave became apologetic and embarrassed. He offered his full support to Susan and quickly gave us space. I felt bad for Dave because he felt so awful about his awkward intrusion. But I felt even worse for Susan. Our fine farewell had been interrupted, and now I was late and had to rush. I couldn't even give Susan a proper goodbye. Still, if it bugged her, she didn't let it show. We shared kisses and hugs, and I went on my way.

On that long and solitary drive to Harrisburg, I don't remember thinking about how rapidly our lives had gone from normal to completely abnormal. I was focused on going to war. But I was leaving a huge burden on Susan.

The moving van with all our furniture still hadn't arrived, so she would have to unpack. We had chosen to plant grass ourselves to save a couple of bucks on the house price, so now she was going to need to plant the seed and water the lawn. All this with a toddler in tow and baby due in three months. And except for red-beet man, none of the neighbors even knew I was leaving.

As planned, I called Susan from an airport in Europe as I switched planes for the final leg of my journey. My job in Harrisburg as a policy analyst was an afterthought, and my role as a husband and father was on hold. Today, I was an Air Force intelligence officer.

CHAPTER SEVEN: OFF TO WAR

WILL KEPT ME BUSY. The moving van was coming Tuesday to deliver the majority of our belongings. There was a lot of work to do. My mom and dad told me to buy a new bed for the guestroom. They were going to come out the following weekend and help me unpack and give me a break from Will. Not exactly how I imagined my parents' first visit to my first home, but I guess they were now part of a military family too.

The moving van came, and I had them place boxes in the right sections of the house as best I could. I knew that I couldn't lift any of the heavy ones myself because of the baby. If I wasn't sure of their contents, they went into the dining room because we didn't have a dining room set anyway.

I was overwhelmed at first. It was difficult to watch Will and accomplish any serious unpacking. Kevin's grandma came to help. Between the two of us, we got the kitchen in order. That was the most important room in the house. Everything else could wait.

My parents showed up on Friday and slept in the guest room, which had exactly a bed in it, nothing else. It had been delivered Thursday. My mom went right to work on some of my boxes. Knickknacks and "pretties" were placed up high or not unpacked at all because Will had a habit of breaking everything he could get his hands on. Dad finished hooking up the phone lines to various rooms throughout the house. It was an exhausting weekend, but we got a lot accomplished.

After a long flight, we landed at a secret location in the heart of the Middle East. Our base was a series of tents adjacent to an airstrip that could handle C-130s. It was hot and sandy, just like you would expect the Middle East to be.

We were part of a new special operations expeditionary unit established to fight Operation ENDURING FREEDOM (OEF), the official name for the war in Afghanistan. Its original name had been Operation INFINITE JUSTICE, but that was deemed too inflammatory. Eventually, OEF became part of the overall fight called the Global War on Terrorism, which included campaigns against all kinds of terrorists all over the world.

I always thought that the Global War on Terrorism was a ridiculous name, akin to fighting a Global War against Warfare. Terrorism is a method of fighting, a strategy used by inferior forces against a superior foe. How do you target a method? In my opinion, military power is best used against a tangible enemy that can be named and defeated with bombs and bullets. But those big-picture concerns were not on my mind in October 2001. Instead, those images of burning buildings in New York and Washington, D.C., were fresh in my mind. On that day, I wanted to help kill terrorists.

But the 193rd Special Operations Wing doesn't actually kill terrorists. We don't drop bombs, shoot rockets, or rain bullets from the sky. Instead, we take terrorists out of action in more creative ways, through a type of information warfare that can be even more powerful than airstrikes alone. That was our mission in Afghanistan. Here's how it works.

During the first days of a military campaign, the US and its allies hit an array of priority targets with missiles and fighters. At the top of the list is the communications infrastructure of the enemy. We want to impair their leaders' ability to exert command and control over the military and to disseminate propaganda to the civilian population. So we send in jets to take out both military communications nodes and civilian media centers such as AM/FM radio and commercial TV stations.

After destroying the transmitters and receivers and rendering the antennas useless, we can employ Commando Solo to come up on the same frequencies and broadcast our own transmissions. We use carefully crafted messages to influence behavior in ways that don't necessarily require dropping bombs.

In Afghanistan, this was highly effective in winning the "hearts and minds" of civilians and an incredibly powerful force-multiplier against enemy soldiers. Instead of hearing military orders on their normal frequencies, the enemy soldiers heard Commando Solo in their native language, telling them how to surrender. Imagine how unnerving that must be for a guy in a bunker. And we didn't just broadcast idle threats. The PSYOP guys would coordinate with the bomb droppers for added emphasis.

First, we'd use their radio frequencies to tell the enemy soldiers that we would bomb certain locations at certain times and that there was nothing they could do about it. Then we'd send the fighters in to blow up the exact positions at the exact times we had described. Next, we would pause to give them enough time to check with their fellow soldiers and verify that we really did drop the bombs. Finally, we would come back on the same frequency, warn them of new attacks, and give them instructions for how to surrender. This technique was responsible for the surrender and capitulation of hundreds of enemy troops.

Commando Solo also was critical to lowering the rate of civilian casualties and keeping the general population away from the fighting. Afghanistan is not a tech-savvy country by any measure. But the Afghans still listened to the radio, even in some of the poorest and most remote parts of the country.

With Commando Solo, instead of hearing the bad guy's propaganda, the civilian population got to hear the truth in their own language. We would broadcast the American version of the news to combat Taliban lies about our country. And we provided instructions about how to receive humanitarian aid and stay out of the most dangerous areas. Quite simply, our broadcasts helped save lives.

We also delivered entertainment. Often, the broadcasts in Afghanistan included native music and dancing, which the Taliban had banned and the general population craved. Soldiers and civilians working in Fort Bragg, North Carolina, collaborated with native Afghan citizens to develop culturally relevant programming delivered by the 193rd Special Operations Wing. These broadcasts helped advance our cause and reassure the population that our country was opposed to the Taliban and al-Qaida, not Afghan civilians.

The Fort Bragg Army guys were from an outfit called the 4th Psychological Operations Group (4th POG). We called them "poggies." The first poggy I ever saw was sitting shirtless and cross-legged outside a tent at our base, playing mystical-sounding music with some kind of wooden flute. At first, I thought he might be a native snake charmer who hadn't gotten the message that Americans were in town or a misplaced foreign worker who had lost the rest of his group. No, it was an American soldier from the 4th POG, and he was a weird one.

Later, I'd get to know that guy and other members of his unit. He wasn't nearly as strange as my first impression led me to believe. He was, however, along with almost everyone I met from that unit, extremely in-tune with the human and cultural factors of our battlespace. In a sense, the flute playing made him a better soldier. By immersing himself in the culture, he was able to understand our adversaries and local allies better and ultimately produce a better PSYOP production for our airplanes to disseminate.

As an intelligence officer, I also had to understand the enemy, but not quite in the same way. Our unit's job was to deliver the PSYOP content, not produce it, so I was far more interested in the enemy's defenses and weapons capabilities than their musical preferences. My primary role in OEF was to help the aviators plan the best routes for our airplanes that would maximize broadcast effectiveness and minimize the threat to our aircraft and the aircrew.

While most of the enemy air defenses had been taken out in the first few days of combat, the Taliban still had capable weapons dispersed or hidden throughout the country. Enemy SAMs and AAA were always a danger to US aircraft, but especially to slow-moving and less maneuverable airplanes like our EC-130s.

Each day, I would study the reports about enemy activity and capabilities from the various intelligence agencies monitoring the battlefield. This included imagery intelligence (IMINT), or overhead pictures of the landscape; signals intelligence (SIGINT), intercepted communications and electronic transmissions; and human intelligence (HUMINT), reports from people on the ground. We also scoured dozens of daily reports from soldiers and Marines on the ground and aircrew in the skies about what they observed as they carried out their missions. These theater-wide intelligence summaries (INTREPS) and mission reports (MISREPS) added to the information gleaned from national and international intelligence sources to paint a complete threat picture for coalition aircraft. During the time I was deployed, the US lost no aircraft to enemy fire.

The days after my parents left went by relatively quickly. I had Will to take care of, often I enjoyed a nap when he napped, and I kept organizing and unpacking.

My most vivid memory of the end of September was planting grass. We lived on an acre lot that was all dirt, so every time the wind blew, it blew dirt through the screens right into the house. I decided I could plant grass.

We had a new spreader and the seed, and I had the time. I spread seed over the entire front and side yard. Every evening I went out after dinner and would water the seed with the sprinklers. Will would always be right behind me and soon discovered that the water made all that dirt into mud. He loved playing in the puddles and would be covered head-to-toe with mud. After I was done moving the sprinklers for the last time, off we would go to the bathtub for a good scrubbing. It was our evening ritual, and it kept me sane.

I did wonder what the neighbors thought. We had moved in, and within a week, my husband had disappeared. I was obviously pregnant, with a baby constantly in tow, and must have looked rather ridiculous working on the yard with my belly protruding out in front of me. And a baby getting muddy behind me.

It was simultaneously thrilling and alarming to be plugged into our national network of intelligence during this time in our history. While we were flying missions against enemies in Afghanistan, our intelligence agencies were still trying to figure out the extent of al-Qaida's reach and what they might do next.

Congressmen were getting letters filled with apparent anthrax powder. Schools were receiving threats of shootings. Airlines were under constant warnings of new and different kinds of attacks. Osama bin Laden was becoming a kind of boogeyman responsible for all sorts of things. A bump in the night? It must be al-Qaida.

I remember thinking this way during these early days of the war. Even though I was older (I turned thirty-one in the combat zone), it still was my first deployment. Inside the perimeter of the base, we lived and worked with military men and third-country nationals from some of the same places that formed the core of al-Qaida. We were surrounded by people openly cheering the success of Osama bin Laden.

Yes, we had our own weapons and security forces on base, but mostly we were dependent on host-country security forces. I wasn't sure I trusted them either. I remember wishing we were better armed.

Eventually, I got used to the uncertainty and learned to relax. I realized that al-Qaida had limited resources and posed no real threat to our base. Plus, we were near a bunch of snake-eater special operations types, the kind that wear beards and brown t-shirts with their blood type in magic marker scrawled on their chests. I felt pretty safe with those guys around.

I also felt safe with Lieutenant Colonel W. in charge. He was the commander of our detachment from the 193rd, and he was no rookie. An electronic communications systems (ECS) officer in the Gulf War, Bosnia, and Kosovo, Lieutenant Colonel W. looked and acted the part of a grizzled veteran. He reminded me of those Army Air Corps flyers in World War II movies with the wispy hair, suntanned faces, and cigarettes dangling from their lips.

Every time I got spun up about a threat, Lieutenant Colonel W. calmed me down. He did that for everybody. Lieutenant Colonel W. just didn't get excited. He always seemed to have everything under control. Eventually, he would become a major general.

I was deployed with three other intelligence professionals from my shop. Captain McKissick and Technical Sergeant Zimmerman were there. The other was Airman Joe.

Airman Joe was a real character. He was fresh out of tech school when 9/11 hit. He must have been about nineteen years old and didn't exactly have a lot of life experiences to draw from.

Intel analysts work every day with pilots and aircrew. Sometimes, they need to be entertaining to get the flyers to pay better attention. It's not uncommon to work some humor into otherwise dry briefings to keep the aircrew engaged. Knowing when to be funny and when to be serious is an art, not a science.

Airman Joe was part of the briefing crew tasked to explain all the enemy threats to Commando Solo operations. For many of the pilots and aircrew, which consisted of officers and enlisted airmen that operated the radio broadcast systems and kept the C-130 in the air, this was their first combat deployment. To put it mildly, the pucker factor was pretty high.

On one occasion, at the beginning of the war, we went through this list of horrible things that could go wrong during our missions. Potshots from terrorists at the end of the runway. Small arms fire during takeoff and landing. AAA fired from boats. Small, man-portable anti-aircraft missiles (MANPADS) fired from mountain ridges. Mobile SAMs. Chemical warheads.

Everyone's heads were spinning with real-world enemy threats combined with the normal hazards of flying at night through bad weather and overcrowded airspace in unfamiliar territory. We finished the briefing by summarizing the litany of dangers to a serious and sober group of brave but anxious flyers.

After all this, Airman Joe put up a slide of a squirrel with massive testicles and made some comment about the need to have really big nuts to accomplish the mission. The whole room was quiet. One officer glared at him. It was the most awkward moment I had experienced since Dave tried to give me red beets.

Finally, one of the loadmasters let out a sight chuckle, and the whole room erupted in laughter. Crisis averted. We all got on with our business. Airman Joe ended up being one of the best and most mature NCOs our unit would see, eventually going on multiple deployments before becoming a Pennsylvania state trooper.

Captain McKissick let Airman Joe and me jump right into the operational mission. He didn't have a choice—there was no training program in the combat zone. There was a lot of work to do. Regardless, I immediately felt like a fully integrated player on the varsity team. I was always grateful to Captain McKissick for that.

One of the highlights of the deployment was getting to brief a colonel from our host nation's air force about our progress in the war. I was just a second lieutenant—a mere "butter bar"—and low-ranking officers typically didn't associate with high-ranking officers in the military culture of our host nation. Nonetheless, Captain McKissick gave me full rein to prepare and deliver the in-depth briefing, which was well-received by the colonel and our military allies despite my junior status.

In addition to briefing the aircrew about their mission and enemy threats, I had the pleasure of briefing the maintenance crews about war progress and their impact on the mission. This was another initiative of Captain McKissick's, who thought it imperative to keep all members of the support team engaged and involved with the big picture. So most days, after getting our airplanes launched safely, we prepared and delivered special briefings in the maintenance section.

These were always fun. We would intersperse updates on the war with football scores about Penn State, the Eagles, and the Steelers. The maintainers had no access to stateside news and appreciated the lighthearted information about what was going on at home. They always had tons of great questions about what was going on in the war and how things were progressing. They were in the hangars away from the action, so I think they sometimes felt a bit out of the loop. Our briefings helped keep them involved and helped them understand why their contribution was important. And it certainly was.

The maintenance men and women were incredible. We had fifty-year-old airplanes that might have been mothballed if our maintainers hadn't taken such good care of them over the years. Unlike active duty, where maintenance professionals move to a different base and a different airframe every few years, our maintainers could spend an entire career working on the same C-130 aircraft. They knew every nook and cranny of these airplanes and could keep them flying in the most demanding conditions.

One of the airplanes was tail number 7773. We all affectionally called it "Triple Cripple." It was commissioned for duty in 1953. Somehow, our maintenance guys kept that thing together with duct tape and glue for all those daily flights without missing a single mission during the entire deployment. It was an incredible feat I feel privileged to have witnessed.

There were so many other things I saw that made me proud. Our aircrew flew long and tedious missions day after day under threatening and stressful conditions. Our intelligence community was delivering products that gave us a comprehensive view of the battlespace. I got to interact with foreign military personnel supporting our wartime efforts and learn some of their military customs and courtesies.

One night, I was following military communications about a

US fighter that had become disabled over Afghanistan due to a fuel leak. A tanker flew up to meet him low and slow, coupled with the fighter, and became a flying gas tank. The two airplanes flew tethered together for hundreds of miles over enemy territory until they landed safely. Our military men and women were regularly performing incredible feats like this, and few people at home knew anything about them.

One of the most amazing operations was occurring in the north of Afghanistan, near the city of Mazar-e Sharif. Secretary of Defense Rumsfeld had insisted upon a small footprint of US ground troops in Afghanistan that relied on Special Operations Forces and indigenous fighters. That strategy was being put to the test in late 2001 as US Special Forces worked hand-in-hand with Afghan warlords against the Taliban.

In a campaign made famous by the movie *12 Strong,* an A-team of Green Berets known as the horse soldiers successfully liberated northeastern Afghanistan using local ground troops and American airpower. Acts of heroism like these made me honored to be a part of the US military. Even though I wasn't kicking down doors or dropping bombs, I was a small part of the overall effort and felt like I was making my own important contributions.

Then one day, just like that, my deployment ended.

While we were launching airplanes and planning missions, the rest of the unit back home had solidified the rotation schedule for the long haul. We would be doing six-week rotations for the duration of the fight. For the intel shop, this meant groups of two analysts for each rotation. After barely getting acclimated, it was time to go home.

I remember seeing my replacement, Captain Hedges, getting off the airplane for our swap out. I was standing in line with my bags packed to leave as she disembarked. We spoke for a few seconds, and then, along with a bunch of other airmen from the 193rd I got on the same airplane she had come in on. We left our makeshift base to head home.

Our first stop was at a classified location in an international airport somewhere in the Middle East. There we would wait in an airplane hangar for further military transportation home. One of our senior NCOs, Senior Master Sergeant Mike, got tired of sitting around and hatched a plan. He talked to the Embassy liaison and convinced them to give him a van so he could take a bunch of guys out to a nice dinner in the nearby city.

Senior Master Sergeant Mike was nicknamed "Milo" after the character from the book *Catch-22*. He was one of the most experienced airmen on the trip and had already been to the combat zone in the First Gulf War, Kosovo, and Bosnia. He was also one of the most resourceful. Milo always seemed to be plotting something.

Given the unpredictability of the terrorist threat and the lack of American support if something went wrong, I didn't think Milo's idea was a good one. I kept imagining how tragic and stupid it would be for me to have survived my first combat-zone rotation only to get blown up by terrorists at a fancy restaurant in the Middle East on the way home. Plus, my thoughts were still dominated by the unfinished business of Afghanistan, and I wasn't yet ready to relax with a luxurious meal. I declined to attend.

About a dozen guys went out into town with Milo, and I worried about them like a parent worries about his teenage driver out past curfew. Nothing happened, except that they all had a wonderful time. When they returned, they spoke of the amazing food they had eaten and the incredible cultural scene they had experienced.

Looking back, skipping that dinner may be the only thing in my entire military career that I truly regret. I didn't realize it at the time, but that simple meal built a bridge from wartime to normalcy for all those guys. Milo knew that, thanks to his years of experience. But I didn't understand. The guys who went to the restaurant spent the next few days talking about their awesome meal. I was still talking about Afghanistan.

Nonetheless, all of us were safe and on the way home.

The next day, we left the Middle East and stopped in Spain to refuel. I called Susan and told her I'd be home tomorrow. She was shocked and relieved my tour was over so fast, and I was thrilled to speak with her again.

But then I hung up the phone, and my thoughts immediately returned to the war.

Was Captain Hedges able to understand all my notes?

How was Technical Sergeant Zimmerman handling his unforeseen extension?

Did we finally take Mazar-e Sharif?

CHAPTER EIGHT: UNFINISHED BUSINESS

LUCKILY, THIS DEPLOYMENT WAS short. Kevin ended up being gone for only about a month and a half. The evening after he got home, we went to a Halloween party at his cousin's house. Everyone was so happy to see him. The whole time I kept wondering what a "culture shock" it must have been for him, going from a war zone to a family party. He seemed to handle the transition seamlessly.

He may have handled it better than I did. I had developed my own routine and system for doing things in our new house, and suddenly he wanted to do things differently or not at all. I felt like I had done all the work of setting things up and that my way was the only way. He did not see it that way, and of course, deep down, I knew I was wrong.

I came home to a hero's welcome. My family met me at the house with hugs and kisses. Dave introduced me to all the other neighbors, who all ribbed me about burning down the field. Will was happy to see me, and Susie looked beautiful eight months pregnant.

Susan and I went to a Halloween party the next night at my cousin Josh's place. I dressed up like a baby with a bib and a diaper. Susie went as a flapper from the 1920s. We had a blast, and everybody treated me like a conquering general.

A week later, my Aunt Sandy and Uncle Dan invited me to a play they were doing at the local high school. In the middle of the performance, they stopped everything and shined a spotlight on

Susan and me and announced to everyone that I was just home from the war. I got a standing ovation.

All this recognition was very nice and made me feel understandably gratified, but I was more than a little embarrassed by it. I was no war hero. My deployment had lasted less than six weeks, and I had been safe and sound on an Air Force base. Those Army Rangers that jumped into Mullah Omar's compound in Afghanistan were heroes. Those "little bird" pilots who flew up and down the streets of Kabul were heroes. My dad was a hero. He never got a reception like this.

I've never completely come to terms with this whole "support the troops" movement that has swept our country and remains in place today. On the one hand, I am profoundly humbled by the heartfelt expressions of thankfulness and the persistent outpourings of support. Indeed, eighteen years after 9/11, hardly a day goes by when somebody doesn't thank me for my service when they see me in uniform. I still get my 10 percent discount at Lowe's. I am very appreciative of my friends' and neighbors' sincere gratitude.

On the other hand, I wonder what my father and his fellow Vietnam veterans think about all of this. My dad got spit on when he walked through the airport after Vietnam. When he got off active duty, he kept his wartime service a secret for two years so he wouldn't get harassed in college.

Sometimes I wonder if any of the old guys who buy me a cup of coffee today were the same young protestors who spit on my dad fifty years ago. They didn't all just die off, so they either changed their tune or decided to keep their mouths shut. They deserve forgiveness too, but the wounds from that time in our history still aren't fully healed. Regardless, the current pro-veteran sentiment in our country could fall apart in a moment, and we cannot take it for granted. I wish my dad had experienced more strangers thanking him for his service while in uniform.

It's similar with Susan. As the man in uniform, I get all the glory, all the thank-yous, all the invitations to speak at the Veteran's Day events. Susan is mostly anonymous. Such is the role of the military spouse. They are always serving faithfully in the background. I suppose it has been like this since the first war in human history. Thank God for them.

In one critical way, the life of a National Guard spouse is even more difficult than an active-duty spouse. National Guard families lack full access to the military's family support infrastructure. As we experienced in San Angelo, active-duty military bases offer extensive resources to military families, from counseling and mental health services to fun activities for kids to babysitting and dog walking services. These resources are designed to make life a little more bearable for military families, especially during deployments. When soldiers and airmen go overseas, the entire base pitches in to help the families left behind.

That's just not the case in the National Guard. The reserve component only gets a tiny fraction of the resources allocated to the active duty for family support. While active-duty bases have buildings full of support personnel, Guard units are lucky if they have one full-time person dedicated to helping families.

Even more of a problem is distance. Guardsmen often travel very long distances to serve at their units, so even if services are available, they are not accessible. This is especially true for the Air National Guard, which typically only has a few bases in any given state. In Kevin's unit, it's very common for airmen to travel sixty miles or more just to attend monthly drills.

When he left for the Afghanistan War, the 193rd tried its best to help the families. They did have functions for spouses and children and invited me to attend those activities. But they all were held ninety miles away at the base in Harrisburg while we were home in Kutztown. It wasn't practical for us to spend three hours in the car for a one-hour family support meeting, even if it would have been nice to commiserate with other wives in the same situation.

My old Army National Guard unit in Kutztown might have been able to provide some assistance to Susan, but they didn't even know I was gone. That's because the Army National Guard and Air National Guard do not effectively communicate with each other about family support. Nor do the Reserves or the active duty. Susan did contact some of my old army buddies who were prepared to help in an emergency, but those plans were the result of my friendships, not any official ties. There simply is no institutional capacity in the Army National Guard to help a family in the Air National Guard, even if they live right down the road.

It's been almost two decades since the reserve component has been called upon to support the Global War on Terrorism, deploying time and again to fight overseas. Yet there remains no practical mechanism to deliver adequate support resources to families in the communities they live as opposed to where the soldiers and airmen train. It is long past overdue that the military create a fully funded, regionally-based family support infrastructure that can help the thousands of National Guard spouses in Susan's situation.

Kevin did have one issue that was really bothering him. He kept telling me he had left before his work was done. That is, he had set things up in his combat-zone office to run smoothly, but the job wasn't complete. He said this almost every day. At night he would get up and go on the computer to look up things that were happening in Afghanistan.

One night at about three in the morning, there was blaring Middle Eastern music—like a call to prayer. I sat up in bed, startled awake, and yelled, "what is that?" He apologized and turned it down.

I realized then that he was trying to live in two places simultaneously. His body and heart were here, but his mind was still very much in the war zone. I had only half of my husband home.

It took a while, but eventually, he came around and adjusted. It was hard because we couldn't talk about his experiences. They were classified, and I couldn't help him "work through" his emotions. There was always a distance between us. Of course, he couldn't know about the isolation that I felt being away from the base and knowing none of the neighbors. It was always an uncomfortable disconnect.

But he was home safely, and that was all that truly mattered. We slowly got into a new routine in our new home, met the neighbors, and grew together as a couple.

I was experiencing a pretty bad case of Guardsman whiplash. I had gotten back on a Thursday and was back at my civilian job the following Monday. I went from planning combat flight routes for the Commando Solo one week to working on a new tax reform proposal in Harrisburg the next. Even though I was glad to be home, it didn't feel right to be back. I was constantly thinking about what was going on in Afghanistan.

One night, soon after I got home, I couldn't sleep and was searching the internet for news about the war. I stumbled upon a website run by a ham radio operator who was recording Commando Solo's short-wave radio broadcasts in Afghanistan. I forgot to check the volume on the computer speakers before I clicked on a link, and suddenly some Pashto music started blasting.

I was familiar with this music because we had been broadcasting it along with news and information in native Afghanistan languages for the past month. Susan was not. She must have thought the Taliban were invading the house in the middle of the night: she came running out of the bedroom with a look of abject terror on her face. I think she thought I was losing my mind. Maybe I was.

I was struggling at work too. Nothing I did seemed nearly as important as the work I was doing to help topple the Taliban and defeat al-Qaida. I was constantly checking the news and calling the base. I was annoyed at people who didn't understand what was going on in the war. I had returned from the combat zone with a chip on my shoulder and a potty mouth.

My boss told me that I needed to ease up and stop being such a "bulldog." Susan told me I needed to stop swearing. All I wanted to do was get back in the fight. Instead, I went back to my civilian job, which had suddenly become very dull.

Governor Ridge had been replaced by his lieutenant governor, Mark Schweiker, who didn't have the same credentials as my former boss or the same style. I didn't know much about him except for a story I had heard from a friend in the Air National Guard a few years prior.

Lieutenant Governor Schweiker had been assigned by Governor Ridge to assist with state emergency operations, things like floods, tornados, and snowstorms. Since lieutenant governors don't have many official responsibilities besides waiting to replace the real governor, Schweiker took his assignment very seriously.

During one particularly nasty snowstorm, a young Army private was answering the phones at the Joint Emergency Operations Center (JEOC) when a certain lieutenant called and demanded to speak to the officer in charge. That happened to be a very busy Air Force lieutenant colonel, who informed the private that he had no time to talk with some junior officer he didn't know. After the private told the "junior officer" that the colonel would not take his call, they all got a tongue lashing from "Lieutenant Gaveener." It was Lieutenant Governor Schweiker himself on the line.

So it was in the Schweiker Administration. Under Ridge, opinions were respected, discussions were serious, and work seemed important. Under Schweiker, my work felt like drudgery. I think it was me that had changed more than the administration. Regardless, I didn't last very long. Within three months of returning from my deployment, I said goodbye to Lieutenant Gaveener and quit my government job.

Things were not all bad. Susan gave birth to our son Jacob in January 2002. He was a happy and healthy baby who grinned like a monkey and screamed like a pterodactyl. Jake seemed to smile all the time. Now we were blessed with two baby boys. Having Jake snapped me out of my funk. I was myself again, enjoying life with Susan and the family.

Everybody warned us that going from one to two kids was the hardest step in raising a family. I guess they were right. Will was only eighteen months old and still required our full attention. But Jake required our full attention too. We were extremely fortunate that Susan was home with the babies. She seemed genuinely happy with the two boys.

After quitting my job in the Capitol, I had the perfect chance to start a new career without such a long commute. After all, I was still driving ninety miles each way from Kutztown to Harrisburg. But I had no experience except for working in government, and I had little time to look for a new job. I found out about a new company called Affinity Group, launched by some former colleagues in the Ridge Administration, that needed some help. And although it was based in Harrisburg, they would let me do most of my work from home. It was an ideal arrangement. I started my new position in April.

Initially, the work at Affinity Group was similar to the work I did in the governor's policy office. It was part government relations and part public communications. Some of its employees conducted straight-up lobbying, which I had no interest in doing. Others were public relations professionals who helped to craft press releases and manage media events. I wasn't qualified for that either. Instead, my role was to create a new line of business, helping organizations use information technology to improve core operations.

This was right up my alley. I was especially interested in broadband telecommunications, which had become an area of niche expertise during my work in the Ridge Administration. I started working to help schools, colleges, and universities improve their broadband infrastructure.

Meanwhile, the war was progressing more rapidly than most

had expected. By the New Year, the US and its allies had overthrown the Taliban and liberated all major cities in Afghanistan. Rumsfeld's strategy of using American special operations forces and airpower combined with local ground forces was a resounding success.

Although major combat operations in Afghanistan were winding down, the military was ramping up its nation-building capabilities in the country. In addition, the US and its allies launched a protracted counter-terrorism operation aimed at destroying the remnants of al-Qaida. The 193rd contributed to both missions, so my peers at the unit and I expected engagement in Afghanistan for a long time to come.

Soon, it became apparent that Afghanistan would not be our only destination. By the summer of 2002, President Bush was intent on achieving another goal in the Global War on Terrorism, the toppling of Saddam Hussein.

I remember being on vacation with Susan, Jake, and Will at the New Jersey shore just after Labor Day. On the drive home, Susan and I listened to the President make his case to the United Nations for invading Iraq. I'm sure that was compelling radio for the two babies in the back.

Up to that point, President Bush had discussed many different reasons for getting rid of Saddam Hussein: his sponsorship of terrorism, his constant threats to the region, his past atrocities. But in this speech on September 12, 2002, President Bush made it all about weapons of mass destruction.

I remember saying to Susan, "I hope he knows where they are."

From that point on, my unit and my family started getting ready for war with Iraq. We all knew better what to expect. And we had certainly had more time to prepare. But first, I had to get caught up on some overdue training.

I attended a course to better familiarize myself with all the different units and capabilities of our special operations forces, of which the 193rd was a component. That was one of the many classes I would take over the years from the United States Air Force

(USAF) Special Operations School, a Florida-based military training institution. The school would either send experts to your location or bring you to them to deliver riveting training on relevant topics.

I also attended one of the most challenging and interesting courses I ever experienced: Combat Survival, also known as Survival, Evasion, Resistance, and Escape (SERE). Combat Survival is at Fairchild Air Force Base in Washington State among some of the most beautiful mountains in the Pacific Northwest. It's a three-week course that starts with some basic knowledge about how to live off the land. Then you practice navigating through the mountains and avoid being captured. Finally, you experience simulated captivity in a camp as a prisoner of war. Much of the course is classified SECRET, so I cannot go into details, but I can reveal some unclassified anecdotes about my experiences at Fairchild.

First, the instructors were complete professionals. It was like having a bunch of Bear Grylls teaching you survival skills one-on-one and in small groups instead of on television. We learned how to graze on native plants while strolling through the woods, set snares and traps for small animals and craft makeshift weapons and tools. We also learned which bugs to eat, which would come back to haunt me when I taught the same skills to my wife and kids. More on that later.

One of the things we learned was how to purify water. Back in 2002, we didn't have fancy filter pumps or chlorine pills. Instead, we used old-fashioned iodine tablets. The first day, our instructors led us to a beautiful mountain stream and told us to fill up our water pouches, big, clear bags made from durable plastic. The water was so pure and clean, none of us wanted to spoil the pristine taste with the stinky yellow tablets. Nonetheless, we complied and drank the yellow water.

The next day, we went to a slightly less appetizing water hole. Still, it was a mountain lake, and we could better understand the usefulness of the iodine. We drank up the water and didn't quite mind the aftertaste this time.

On the third day, the instructors took us to the nastiest, stinkiest swamp on the mountain. We had to move the pond scum aside to reach the water below and fill up our pouches. Tiny worms and other unknown creatures were wiggling around suspended in the bag, and this time we couldn't notice any color change at all from the yellow tablets. The water was already a greenish brown.

We all choked down that water to the very last drop—the instructors made sure of it. And despite some sour looks and smelly burps, not one of us got sick. And that was the point. The instructors were training us to trust the process and depend on our equipment in a real survival situation. It worked. From that point on, if those guys told me to stand on my head and beat a drum to make it rain, I would have put on my poncho and waited for the downpour.

Evasion was the best part of the training. They dropped you off by yourself in the middle of the mountains with a compass and an MRE. An MRE is a "Meal Ready to Eat," a complete military dinner in a freeze-dried pouch. It's also known as a "Meal Refusing Exit" if you eat too much of the cheese. Once you have your food and your compass, they gave you a few days to get from one part of the forest to the other without getting caught by one of the roaming enemy instructors looking for you day and night.

Mostly, this was three days of sleeping all day in the woods and walking all night so that the enemy couldn't find you. When I was at Fairchild in October, the days were still warm, the nights were not too cold, and the leaves were a beautiful autumn color. I think I could have stayed out there for months.

One day toward the end of my camping trip, in the middle of a deep mid-morning sleep, I awoke to the sound of footsteps nearby.

Dang, I thought. *I'm about to get captured.*

I did my best to remain as quiet as possible. Although I had camouflaged my position before I took the nap, I wasn't completely sure that all my equipment was hidden and in reach. Plus, I was still in that hypersensitive state that occurs right after you wake up suddenly. The footsteps got closer. I held my breath. Then I saw the enemy.

It was a moose.

If you never startled a moose that walks up on you in the mountains, I suggest you never try. I have seen moose on other occasions, including from a flat-bottom boat on the Snake River in Wyoming. When you are standing on a boat, and a moose is facing you from a riverbank 100 yards away, you see a big brown animal. When you are laying down on your back, and a moose is standing about two feet away from your head, you see a big brown wall, because that's about all you can make out as he blocks the sun with his massive body just inches away from your face.

Later, I would have welcomed a moose in my face, because soon I would experience a Mongo in my face. Mongo was my prison guard in the simulated prisoner-of-war (POW) part of the training. Mongo wasn't his real name. He just looked like a guy named Mongo, so that's what we all called him. He was one of the SERE instructors role-playing as a POW camp administrator, about six feet tall and 220 pounds. He had ripped the sleeves off his red uniform shirt to show off his arms, which were bigger than a moose leg. And I should know. I got very familiar with both.

For the next few days, Mongo tossed me around like a rag doll, doing his best to simulate the severe conditions we might expect if we ever got captured by the Iraqis or some other nasty enemy. He was always in my face and on my case. I had nightmares about that guy after I left.

This US Air Force SERE school has received a lot of criticism over the years for allegedly "torturing" people in training. What I saw was nothing of the sort. Yes, the instructors were harsh and physical. And I learned things I hope my kids never have to learn. But the purpose was to save my life in case I ever got captured. On that point, the instructors did an outstanding job. I felt supremely confident in my ability to honor the Code of Conduct in case of capture, and to help the aircrew I would be serving to do the same. All the instructors were consummate professionals.

Even Mongo.

Back home, I was trying to strike the proper balance between my military commitments, my civilian work, and my family.

My new job was going well, but it was hard to get in a rhythm when I kept leaving for training that lasted weeks at a time. More important, it's nearly impossible to stay focused on work projects when you know you will be taking off for war in a few months.

The family was great. Will was now in full toddler mode and was like a little man. From a very early age, he had a gift for gab and a great vocabulary. When the pediatrician asked Susan if Will had ever used full sentences, she laughed and said he was already speaking in paragraphs.

Jake also was doing well. He was a small child, just like his dad, and very athletic.

Susan's whole family always said Jake is built just like her grandfather, Dale Clarke, one of the best athletes of his era in Western Pennsylvania. Dale was about five foot four inches tall and played four sports at Thiel College in Greenville, Pennsylvania. He was an all-star halfback on the football team, the best point guard on the basketball team, and ran sprints for the track and field team.

His best sport was baseball, and he got drafted by the Cleveland Indians on a minor league contract. But that was during the Great Depression, and he got a higher-paying offer to work at the post office in Beaver County. Dale never made it to the big leagues, but he just might have if he had tried.

Jake got Dale's athletic genes. When he was an infant, Jake would be up in his crib drinking his baby bottle, and when he was done, he would whip it across the room. He did this all the time. Susan and I would be downstairs watching TV, and suddenly, about twenty minutes after we put Jake to bed, we would hear a crash against the wall where his baby bottle would hit. Sometimes he threw it so hard he would make dents. Thirteen years later, when we moved out of that house, we found an old baby bottle from Jake's infant pitching days that had somehow gotten stuck behind a hidden grate in the far corner of his bedroom. Gross.

Susan was also doing well. She was making friends and volunteering at the local church. It was sometimes strange for her because we lived in my hometown, so I had all sorts of relationships with people that she didn't know about. I'm not talking about anything romantic or sinister, just random previous encounters. Sometimes, this made things funny for the both of us.

Once, Susan came home after taking the boys to swimming lessons and told me about this interesting but unusual woman she met at the pool. Susan said she was super talkative and really funny. She had sons named after her favorite characters in cheesy action/romance movies like *Top Gun* and *Gladiator*. I got a chuckle out of Susan's story and told her she should stop hanging out with such crazy women.

The next week, Susan came home with an update from the pool. It turned out the crazy mom of the movie boys had been my date to the junior prom. Crazy indeed.

And so was our life. Somehow, Susan and I were getting used to the back and forth of daily transitions among military, civilian, and family obligations. One day I was on active duty getting beaten up by Mongo. The next day, I was cleaning up poop from Will and bottles from Jake. The day after, I was speaking to a chamber of commerce about how to improve the town's broadband infrastructure.

If you've ever seen that scene in *Happy Gilmore* where all the spectators' heads go back and forth as they watch the golf ball bounce around the obstacles, that is what our life was like in those days. We were head bouncers.

Susan and I justified this crazy lifestyle by trying to stay focused on the big picture. We believed in three priorities: God, Family, and Country. We figured our entire lives were going to be a constant struggle to achieve balance among those three. Susan seemed to get this right all the time. I struggled with it.

God would always have to be first, and I figured I could stay focused on Him while I did anything else. That would take prayers and discipline, and I knew I would fail at times. But the Bible commands it, and I knew it was right, so I would accept this idea and move along.

The other priorities were harder. I had a strong devotion to my country and felt compelled to defend our way of life, especially after 9/11. I was determined to stay in the fight. But I also knew plenty of soldiers and airmen who had put their military service above their families and lost a big chunk of what they were fighting for. I was not going to let that happen.

Fortunately, I have an amazing wife. Together, Susan and I struck a balance that allowed me to serve my country and have a family. When the military really needed me, Susan always let me go. But when my family really needed me, I had to tell the military no.

That wasn't as hard as it might sound. I respect the military, but it is never satisfied. The minute you step off the airplane at home, somebody asks you to get on the next one to someplace else. If you don't have the confidence and courage to say no when you must, you will never be home consistently, and your family will always play second fiddle.

Some Guardsmen never figure this out. They always go without question when the military calls and one day come home to an empty house. It is tragic, but it happens all the time. Eventually, I learned to say no to Uncle Sam, and it saved my marriage and family.

Part of this derives from humility. At some point early in my career, I discovered that I was not indispensable to the military. The United States was not going to lose the Global War on Terrorism if I wasn't constantly deployed. And the military was not going to kick me out if I didn't volunteer for every exercise and operation. I also came to peace with the realization that I probably would never reach the highest ranks if I didn't jump when they called, but who wants to risk sacrificing a family for rank? Not me.

I am not talking about shirking responsibilities or disobeying orders. I am talking about pacing yourself and being judicious about accepting additional obligations beyond what is required. This is critical in the post-9/11 military, especially for the reserve components.

There is no real reserve component anymore. It used to be that the Guard and Reserves were true "strategic reserve" forces, called upon to support the active component for major wars or specialized missions. But then the wars became permanent, and all the missions became specialized. The Guard and Reserve together are now just another part of the operational force, rotating in and out of the combat zone along with the active duty on a regular basis.

Perhaps I shouldn't have been so anxious for more real-world opportunities when I was a part-time infantry grunt bouncing around in old M-113s. We were still getting good training, and I'm pretty sure our enemies still counted us as part of the overall deterrent force that discouraged them from messing with the United States. Maybe training with hand-me-down equipment in case you are really needed is what the National Guard is supposed to be: a true strategic reserve.

George Washington said, "When we assumed the Soldier, we did not lay aside the Citizen."

That ideal is in peril.

Today, even if you are a part-time soldier or airman, the military wants you full-time. The longstanding concept of the "strategic reserve" has been replaced with the new doctrine of "operational reserve." I don't know what that is, but I know what it means. Members of the National Guard and Reserves must constantly resist the encroachment of the military into their civilian lives. Soldiers must learn to say "no" or plan to get out. Otherwise, they can't also be citizens.

I was determined to be both. But in late 2002, I was mostly a soldier again. That meant the citizen, and the family, would have to wait. We were going back to war.

CHAPTER NINE: BECOMING A VETERAN

IN THE FALL OF 2001, I was a rookie second lieutenant fresh out of intelligence school. By early 2003, I had already been to the combat zone once and was preparing for my second deployment for more than a year. I was becoming a veteran.

Susan was, too. She established herself independently in her adopted community and could survive and thrive on her own. She understood what to expect when I went overseas and had adapted to my time away and short-notice obligations. She knew who to call when she had a problem and could rely on the neighbors for help and support. This next deployment would certainly be longer than the last time around, and Susan now had two boys to care for instead of one. However, Susan and I felt both better equipped to make the transition back to full military mode, and somehow, we both thought the second time would be less disruptive, even easier.

The military effort was a different story. We had a much harder task to complete in Iraq compared to Afghanistan, and we were bracing for a long and difficult fight. In Afghanistan, a small but focused military effort had toppled the Taliban in a matter of months. Enemy air defenses were mostly old and poorly maintained, and the primary threats to air operations were large-caliber AAA and MANPADS. A fixed-wing aircraft like Commando Solo could avoid those by flying high and avoiding populated areas, so the biggest concerns were random potshots on takeoffs and landings, when the airplane had to fly low.

In Iraq, the US military was preparing a major air and land offensive. We had amassed armored divisions in Kuwait and fighter wings throughout the region. The Iraqi military was large, well-trained, and armed with an array of weapons that could inflict real damage on American soldiers and airmen. Plus, there was the potential danger of chemical or biological weapons. We were expecting a long and difficult fight.

The next war started with the search for weapons of mass destruction (WMDs). President Bush received intelligence that Saddam Hussein had them and was poised to use them. He felt he needed to act.

To the military wife, none of the politics really matter. They should, but somehow all you can fixate on is the deployment. The safety of your loved one becomes almost all-consuming. But I am getting ahead of myself.

It was 2003, and I was still a stay-at-home mom raising our two boys, Will age three and Jake age one.

Even though we figured he would have to go to the Iraq War, one afternoon, Kevin just came and simply said, "I am being activated."

I looked at him and asked, "When do you leave?"

The answer surprised me. "Tomorrow," he said.

We didn't have time to call the entire family this time. But his grandma, parents, and sister came to say goodbye. He had to pack, this time without the aid of my meager contributions from the Kmart.

We made love.

And in the morning, we had a tearful goodbye in the driveway. Kevin was on his way to war again.

But late that afternoon, I got a phone call from the base. The transport airplane had slipped a day. Kevin was coming back home. And they would leave the next day.

What an unexpected joy to have him home again for one more

night. After putting the boys to bed, we spent some time together planning for his absence, and then we made love.

The following morning was difficult, another tearful goodbye. The boys weren't sure what to make of any of it. But late that afternoon, a phone call came again. The transport had slipped a day. He was coming back home. And they would leave the next day.

Yes, you read that correctly. It happened again!

I asked to speak with Kevin's commanding officer. And I asked, "Is this for real, or is this some ploy Kevin has going to get sex?"

He laughed and assured me that the transport didn't work out and that they would be leaving as soon as they could. I still had my suspicions.

Kevin finally left for real the following day. Destination: unknown. Duration of trip: unknown. All I could do now was pray.

The 193rd was being sent to multiple locations throughout the Middle East in its largest-ever deployment. One group would head south, another would go north, and the third was assigned to a special task force without regional constraints. To send three sets of aircraft to three different places required all our resources. Virtually the whole wing was activated. No volunteers were required; we were all ordered to go.

I was to go north as part of the "advanced echelon" (ADVON) team to head overseas early and prepare for the rest of the force. I thought it was a real honor to have this responsibility as a first lieutenant, and I was excited to go. In reality, the unit was stretched so thin that I was one of the only officers left to handle the duty.

I was part of a team of eight professionals, each with different duties. Captain Esteban Diaz from the aircraft maintenance group was the senior officer and group leader. Captain Mike Hackman, whom we called "Hacker," was an electronics communications systems officer and the mission expert. Senior Master Sergeant Jim was the logistics officer responsible for getting us in and out of theater. And Technical Sergeant Rick Shirk was a late addition to handle billeting, food, and living arrangements.

We also had two junior noncommissioned officers with our ADVON team. Technical Sergeant Shaun was an avionics expert on his first deployment. And Technical Sergeant Jason was a radio communications specialist who also served as our team bouncer; you didn't want to get in the way of his 220-pound frame. Finally, we had Staff Sergeant Dennis, an Army psychological warfare expert. He would be the 193rd's liaison to the 4th Psychological Operations Group at Fort Bragg, which provided all the broadcast material that Commando Solo would transmit over Iraq.

Our orders were to fly to an Air Force base in Turkey and set up shop as part of Joint Special Operations Air Detachment North, which would have control over our deployed group of 193rd airmen. From there, Commando Solo aircraft would be able to broadcast across northern Iraq and reach military and civilian populations from Mosul to Baghdad.

Unlike Afghanistan, which happened quickly without prior planning, the Iraqi invasion was preplanned well in advance. Although I didn't know exact dates, I knew that unless we reached a diplomatic solution, the war would start sometime in late winter/ early spring of 2003. So I had plenty of time to get ready.

During January and February, I had transitioned my civilian work to other people in the company and made sure they could take over my projects. My bosses, colleagues, and clients were extremely supportive.

I prepared a new will and power of attorney for Susan and did my best to explain what was going on to the boys. They were still too young to really know what was happening. This time around, there was no need for a last-minute farewell party; my friends and family had stopped by over the past couple of months to wish me well. My cold-weather gear and green uniforms were packed, my training was complete, and all I needed to do was receive my military orders. They came on March 1, 2003.

The suspense of this deployment had been building up so long that it was a relief when the orders arrived. This time around, Susan and I had the experience to understand better what was coming and plenty of time to rehearse our goodbyes. That morning, we all shared hugs and kisses, I threw my bags in the truck, and Dave with his red beets was nowhere to be seen. It was finally like that scene on the Hallmark Channel. I gave my heroine a final kiss and drove off to go to war.

Only I didn't.

When I got to the base, they told me to go back home. Something about our Turkey arrangements was delayed, and we would leave tomorrow. Since everything was all packed and ready to go, I guess they figured we might as well spend time with our families instead of killing time out at the base. We didn't have cellphones back then, so there was no calling or texting. I just left.

Imagine Susan's surprise when I showed up in the driveway a few hours later. She had just finished a good cry and gotten herself together when I came walking back through the door. She kind of looked at me the way she does when the boys run in the room with mud on their shoes to give her a hug right after she cleaned the floor. Susan was happy to see me, but I had made a mess.

So we replayed the scene from the day before. I kissed Susan and the boys goodbye, got in the truck and drove to the base. And the same thing happened again.

The first time back was disruptive but pleasant. We considered it a blessing to have another day together. The second time was just plain weird.

Dave and the neighbors didn't know what to think. My dad, the retired colonel, couldn't believe they were just letting me drive back and forth. Susan was perplexed, and even jokingly accused me of faking the whole thing to get her amorous attention. "That's a really good idea," I told her, but I wasn't that clever. This really was me expecting to get on a plane and then coming back home because something wasn't ready.

If she didn't believe me at first, she believed me soon after. Later that evening, I got a call from the unit. I was definitely departing the next day, but the circumstances had changed. My destination was different, but they wouldn't tell me where I was going. I needed to pack hot-weather gear and cold-weather gear, green uniforms, and brown uniforms, plus a whole bunch of extra equipment. Our leisurely evening turned into a frantic rush to find everything, clean it, and repack all my bags. Susan was still doing laundry at eleven o'clock in the evening. So much for the Hallmark Channel goodbye.

When I got to the base, I found out why they couldn't tell me my final destination. They didn't know where it was.

Negotiations between Turkey and the Bush Administration had hit a snag, and the US still didn't have permission to use Turkish bases. Although the State Department expected to resolve the problem soon, we were kind of in a hurry. The war was supposed to start in two weeks.

So instead of heading directly to Turkey, our new orders were to head in that general direction and wait for further instructions. That way, we could move quickly to prepare the way for the main body in time for the start of the war.

We were headed to Romania.

Prior to that morning, I didn't even know we had a base in Romania. The only things I really knew about the country were that it used to be part of the Warsaw Pact and that it was the home of Dracula. But they gave us an address to a former Soviet airbase near the Black Sea and told us the secret knock. We only had two more things to do before heading out the door.

First, we all got smallpox shots. The US thought Saddam Hussein had stockpiles of biological weapons waiting for us, so we got immunized against all kinds of diseases from anthrax to measles.

The smallpox shots were especially dangerous because they used a live smallpox virus. If you touch your arm and then rub your eye, you can get smallpox on your eyeball. That's pretty bad.

It's also pretty bad if your toddler touches your arm and sticks his fingers in his mouth and gets smallpox too. That's why they give you the shots when you've already left your family. The good news is your family doesn't get smallpox. The bad news is that you get to sit on a plane for two days with a big swollen knot under your arm and a nasty scab full of oozing pus that really freaking hurts.

Last, we had to eat, but that effort would prove to be unsuccessful. The bus to take us to the Baltimore airport was late, and we were all getting hungry. So I ordered a sub from the local sandwich shop and sent one of our intel guys, Technical Sergeant Sean, to go and get it. Of course, as soon as he left, the bus arrived, and we all had to hurry up and leave. I got stuck with no food, and Technical Sergeant Sean got stuck with the $5.95 bill.

We flew commercial from Baltimore to Bucharest. They told us to keep a low profile. Right. All eight of us on the ADVON team had short haircuts with sand-colored backpacks and olive drab duffel bags that said "US" in bold black letters. Just call us the inconspicuous eight.

The flight was long but uneventful, and we arrived in Bucharest mid-afternoon Romanian time. All we had was a bunch of bags and an address. After a brief conference with Captain Diaz, Hacker, and Senior Master Sergeant Jim, we decided to do what most people do when they get off the plane in Bucharest—rent a couple of cars.

I walked over to the first rental car place I saw and pulled out my government credit card. I think it was an Enterprise, but I'm not sure. The guy behind the counter said, "Oh, Lieutenant Dellicker, we've been waiting for you. Your cars and driver are out back."

That was weird. There must have been a dozen rental car places, and I had just picked the first recognizable American brand on the strip. I wasn't in uniform, didn't pull out my military identification card, and had no reservations. This was James Bond stuff.

The rest of the guys were equally befuddled, and we dragged our bags outside to witness this deal. There before us were three vehicles and a guy out front waiting for our arrival. He was big and round with enormous hands, a shiny bald head, and big pointy ears. It had to be Dracula.

"Velcome to Romania!" he bellowed. "I am Vlad, your driver."

I was still pretty sure he was Dracula.

"Who sent you?" said Hacker.

"The American Embassy," said Vlad.

"Do you have identification?" asked Sergeant Jim.

"No," he said.

"Then how do we know you are not a terrorist?" I asked half-seriously.

"You vill just have to have to take my vord for it," said Vlad.

This back-and-forth went on for a while. Somehow, with no instructions or prior knowledge of any such liaison, we had randomly picked a rental car company from a dozen possibilities that had three cars reserved in our names and a driver who knew everything about us, ready to take us to a secret base in Romania. We were either experiencing an amazing feat of friendly statecraft or were about to be led to our deaths.

Senior Master Sergeant Jim was the most experienced and seasoned veteran among us. We asked him what he thought we should do.

"Get in the cars," he said.

So we did.

The next three hours in those cars may have been more dangerous than the next three months in the combat zone. Two guys went with Vlad in the first car, and the rest of us spread out in the other two. I was in the last car as a passenger with Technical Sergeant Rick Shirk as the driver.

Rick was a country boy who knew how to drive fast. But Vlad took off like a bat out of hell, driving seventy miles per hour through the streets of Bucharest. None of us had any cell phones, we didn't know where we were going, and we couldn't let each other get separated. After all, we still weren't sure that Vlad wasn't Osama bin Laden's Romanian uncle.

We drove into the night without stopping. We went from city streets to country roads to winding dirt paths through tiny little towns. We dodged tiny old ladies with straw brooms sweeping gravel sidewalks, little old men with donkey carts hauling metal parts, motorcycles, tractors, mules, and potholes. Most of the roads didn't have streetlights, and traffic laws were more like traffic suggestions.

Our entire mission from our number three car was to stay on the bumper of that number two car. To succeed, Rick borrowed tactics learned not from his military training but from *Cannonball Run, The Dukes of Hazzard,* and *The Fast and the Furious.* Somehow, he stayed locked on that number two, which stayed locked on number one, which Vlad was driving. By two in the morning, we were running out of gas.

Then suddenly, Vlad pulled off the highway. We followed him slowly to a combination gas station/roadhouse restaurant where we got out of the cars. Even though it was the middle of the night, the place looked crowded. I think we were somewhere in Transylvania. Vlad looked hungry.

Relieved to be together and in one piece, the "Romanian Eight" followed Vlad into the building. It was packed with about 100 people, all eating and drinking like it was seven in the evening, not two in the morning. The place got silent, and everybody stopped and stared. I figured this was when they all turned into werewolves and ate us or something.

Then an amazing thing happened. We got a standing ovation. The entire place stood up and started clapping, crying, and giving us hugs like we had just liberated their country.

"We love America!" an old lady cried.

"What took you so long?" said a young man.

In twenty-four years of military service, I have never seen such an outpouring of gratitude from anyone to a group of American servicemen and -women. And it came from a group of farmers in rural Romania in the middle of the night.

The rest of the evening was a blur. They had a feast prepared for us with soup and chicken and all sorts of beer. Vlad was having a blast. We heard stories, sang songs, and felt genuinely welcomed. After a couple of hours, we said thank you, exchanged handshakes and hugs, and went on our way.

Around four-thirty in the morning, we arrived at a Romanian army checkpoint and got out of the cars. They searched all our vehicles, inspected our paperwork, and spoke in Romanian to Vlad. Then, just like that, we were inside the base and ushered in to meet our American counterparts, safe and sound.

To this day, I don't know how any of this happened. We never figured out who Vlad was or who had sent him to meet our group. We never understood how our random choice of rental car companies already had everything arranged. And we never knew who organized or paid for our late-night feast with all those friendly people.

We had just experienced the adventure of a lifetime, and the war hadn't even begun. We had full bellies, no fears, and no vampire bites. The Romanian Eight slept well that morning as we rested for the next phase in our quest.

As we got settled in Romania, the rest of our unit remained in flux. C-130s are tactical aircraft with propellers designed primarily for intra-theater airlift. That means they fly slowly and need to make a lot of stops. To make it to the war on time, the mission aircraft had to depart Harrisburg for the war zone early, before they knew where they would be going, just like us. It would be the job of the Romanian Eight to figure out where that would be.

Captain Hackman was the guy for this job. He knew everything about the aircraft's capabilities and how it should be optimally employed. The rest of us were mostly waiting around for Hacker to work his magic. But it didn't happen as fast as we expected. Mostly, it was out of his control.

While we were waiting, they put us up in a resort hotel that had been taken over by the US military. Every day, we put on our uniforms and went to the base to participate in meetings and discussions about where our airplanes would be based and how we would get there. There would be lots of waiting around, and then suddenly, we had to be available for a face-to-face discussion or conference call immediately. Some of these were high-level matters. One of the calls with Captain Hackman included the Secretary of State, Condoleezza Rice herself.

But when we weren't in meetings, we were mostly killing time. We went to the gym a lot. We talked to a bunch of people from all kinds of units. In the evenings, we spent hours in the hotel restaurant getting waited on by beautiful Romanian waitresses who normally just served tourists in the resort. Since it was March, we were there before the tourist season kicked off, so the hotel staff was happy to have us there.

The Romanian people remained exceptionally friendly. To this day, I have never experienced another country that treated me with so much respect and hospitality. I will be forever grateful for the treatment I received there.

Meanwhile, the 193rd mission aircraft and aircrews were getting bounced around Europe as they waited for the Romanian Eight to figure out their final destination. Hundreds of airplanes were flying from West to East and back again, ferrying soldiers, transporting equipment, and generally getting ready for the impending war. There was no room for airplanes to take up space at key logistics hubs in Europe, and there weren't enough hotel rooms to accommodate all the transient servicemen and -women.

Generally, this was no big deal, but it did have a significant impact on one of my colleagues, Lieutenant Colonel James McGovern. "Guvvy," as everyone affectionately called him, was a traditional

Guardsman and my boss in the intelligence section. In his civilian career, he was a teacher and golf coach at a local Catholic high school. In his military career, Lieutenant Colonel Guvvy was the most experienced guy in our shop, known for his strong grasp of complex issues, his cool head under pressure, and his ability to see through clutter and focus on the big picture. He also really liked to drink beer.

Officially, Guvvy volunteered to fly on the mission airplane instead of taking a direct flight to our wartime base because he was one of our unit's primary classified couriers. That is, he needed to transport a classified laptop and a big envelope marked "SECRET" from our base in Harrisburg to our deployed location in the Middle East. Unofficially, Guvvy volunteered because he expected to have at least one night in Frankfurt where he could go out and have his fill of good German pilsner.

The problem was, the unit kept having to move from place to place on short notice, and every time the airplane landed at a different base, Guvvy had to babysit his classified material. The laptop was no problem because he could lock it in the safe on the plane with the other classified electronics, but the big manila envelope marked SECRET wouldn't fit. So every time he landed at a new base, instead of running out to go drink beer with the rest of the guys, he had to find the Air Force Security Forces, fill out a bunch of paperwork, and make sure that somebody would protect his stash of classified information. If the security forces were too busy or there was no room in the base safe, Guvvy had to sit in his hotel room and babysit the envelope himself. Poor Guvvy.

Back in Romania, we were still stuck and running out of time. At first, the routine of getting up at the resort, going to the base, and going back to the resort was a nice break. But after doing that day after day, we all were feeling very bored and very useless. Plus, the war was supposed to kick off in a couple of days, and they weren't going to wait for us. We were failing at our primary job—preparing for the main body.

Finally, after two weeks of good Romanian hospitality, Hacker had a breakthrough. Turkey was a definite no-go, but we found another base much closer to our target area that would allow us to accomplish our mission. The location of this base was classified SECRET, and I am still not permitted to reveal where it was. Regardless, now it was up to Senior Master Sergeant Jim, our logistics NCO, to get us there before the war began. That was no easy task.

The biggest problem was there were no direct flights from Romania to where we were headed. So we hopped on an airplane and took a trip back to the main logistics hub in Germany, figuring that this high-traffic area would be the best place to hitch a ride. After two days, we were starting to worry because everything was so jammed full, but we caught a C-130 to a small base at a classified location in the heart of the Middle East, where we were supposed to have a liaison with a Navy Chinook that would take us to our destination.

We arrived at our interim location in the middle of a blast of cold weather and slept in tents near the airport runway waiting for our helicopter. It was freezing. We didn't know exactly when it was supposed to arrive, but it was supposed to be a touch and go, so we had to be prepared. We sat with our bags adjacent to the runway, just waiting for this thing to arrive. One hour late. Two hours late. Finally, after seemingly waiting there all day, we got word that the Chinook wasn't coming. We were out of options and stranded in the desert.

Hacker wouldn't buy it. Frustrated by the bureaucracy of the logistics process and worried we would miss the start of the war, he did the most foolish yet most awesome thing I've seen at an airport since retrieving Bob Dole's podium. While we were still hanging around the apron, a British C-130 landed and taxied down the runway. Hacker ran up to the airplane while it was moving. He's lucky he didn't get shot by Air Force Security Forces.

Somehow, Hacker got the attention of the pilot and explained who we were, how we got there, and where we needed to go. Amazingly, the British C-130 guys agreed to give us a lift. Right then and there, we threw our gear on the airplane and climbed aboard. We departed immediately.

On American C-130s, everything is by the book. All the equipment is tied down, all the gear is in perfect order, and everybody is strapped in with earplugs and helmets, as required. You don't pass gas without the loadmaster giving you permission.

On this British version, we just climbed on top of a bunch of stuff and spread out willy-nilly. Only after we sat there awhile did we realize we were sprawled out on a bunch of crates of Stinger missiles. Now that would make some interesting lawn furniture! We thanked the British guys and went on our way.

We arrived at our destination just a few hours before our mission aircraft and all the rest of the 193rd crew. We had less than a day to get everything ready before the war was supposed to start. We found our tents, located our workspace, and learned our way around the base. Amazingly, we had made it in time.

The ADVON team was in our new makeshift office when our 193rd teammates arrived. The guys from the mission airplanes came in first, and Guvvy greeted me with a hiss.

"This better be important!" he growled as he slammed the manila envelope on my desk with the "SECRET" markings on the outside. "I had to babysit this damn package for five days while the rest of the crew got to go out and drink beer."

I looked at the envelope. Immediately, I noticed something was wrong. Sure, it said, "SECRET" on the package in the same color scheme as an official classified coversheet, but it didn't contain any of the standard disclaimers and official handling instructions. Instead, it contained gibberish about James Bond, secret agents, and a whole pile of made-up crap.

"Guvvy, did you actually read this label?" I asked.

Before he could respond, I got my answer. As we opened the envelope, the whole office was overcome with an unbearable stench.

Inside the package was the two-week-old sandwich I had ordered while waiting for the plane in Harrisburg.

Technical Sergeant Sean had gotten his revenge for the $5.95 I owed him, but I would have paid $100 to see the look on Guvvy's face when that stinky sandwich fell out of the envelope. It was a mix of terror, anger, and humiliation, and I thought he might either have a heart attack or kill me. Fortunately, Guvvy was also known for his sense of humor. We would laugh about that moment for years to come. He never lived it down.

Guvvy ended up going on ten different combat-zone deployments before he retired. He is a true American hero.

I had another surprise that same day. Up to that point, intelligence analysts were responsible for handling all aspects of SERE preparation for aircrew in the warzone. That's why we got sent to survival school and had to go through all that training. But upon arriving in theater for Operation IRAQI FREEDOM, we were informed that trained SERE professionals were being deployed for the first time to support the mission directly. We would have two guys attached to our unit to help us handle all the survival and personnel recovery issues.

I was ecstatic to have the extra help and all that expert knowledge. So I found out where they were and went to introduce myself. Then I had my own Guvvy moment. Standing right there before me was Mongo himself. Yes, the same guy that had tossed me around like a ragdoll at SERE school and found his way into my nightmares like Freddy Kruger was now going to be my colleague for the duration of the war. He remembered me too.

The next day, just to mess with me, Mongo left a neatly folded red shirt with the sleeves cut off on my desk. It was exactly like the one he had worn in the fake POW camp when he had terrorized me. We spent a lot of time together and ended up working together very well. But I always secretly wanted to punch him in the head.

Kevin and Susan today.

Kevin and Susan in Harrisburg around 2000.

This page and next page: Summertime training at Fort
Stewart, Georgia and Fort Pickett, Virginia in 1996 and 1997
with Charlie Company, 1-111th Infantry.

Will and Kevin, September 2001.

Captain Diaz, Hacker, and Kevin
waiting around in Romania.

Kevin in the desert for Operation IRAQI FREEDOM.

Kevin in the sandstorm at the start of the war.

Kevin and Lieutenant Colonel James McGovern (Guvvy) together
again after the safe delivery of the SECRET sandwich
to the Commando Solo base.

The crew from Commando Solo at CJSOTF-West.

Easter Sunday in the desert, not too far from where Jesus rose
from the dead. What an amazing experience.

Homecoming 2003.

Halloween 2003 with Will and Jake.

Disney World with Jake, Eli, and Will, 2005.

Curt and Susie with the boys, right after Kevin's deployment
was cancelled January 2006.

Will, Jake and Eli hanging out.

Susie, Curt and Sally at Conneaut Lake Park in 2006.

Camping at the Delaware Water Gap in 2007.

Just back from Operation IRAQI FREEDOM II, 2007.

Susie and Eli in between deployments, summer 2008.

A bunker in Afghanistan, 2009.

A divot from a dud rocket outside a hut in Afghanistan.

Nighttime in Afghanistan.

Coming home from Afghanistan, May 2009.

Kevin and Susan, back at home, spring 2009.

Wrestling with the Dellicker boys, Jake and Eli.

Promotion ceremony in State College, Pennsylvania, Summer of 2015.

Bill and Trudie and the boys at a Phillies game, 2016.

All grown up. Will, Eli and Jake in late August, 2018.

Kevin and Susan relaxing.

CHAPTER TEN: WAR STORIES

AFTER JUST A WEEK by myself with two toddlers who weren't even in preschool yet, I couldn't take it anymore. I would spend the entire day with the boys, sit down for dinner, and jokingly ask, "What did you do today?" Of course, I always knew the answer because I was with them all day.

Worse, I would put them to bed at seven in the evening, turn on the news, and get into my head all the things that could go wrong. I thought about all the ways Kevin could be injured or even killed.

I called my parents and asked if I could stay with them for a while. I talked with my in-laws about keeping an eye on the house, I forwarded the mail, and off to Beaver I went.

The official launch of Operation IRAQI FREEDOM was March 19, 2003, when President George W. Bush addressed the nation. Although we had to hustle, our airplanes were in position, the crews were ready to go, and our work and living spaces were all set up and prepared for the start of major air operations.

As is customary for the US military, the war started with a big bang. The opening salvo of the air war was dubbed "Shock and Awe" by Pentagon planners to convey the message we sought to deliver to the Saddam Hussein regime. The phrase stuck and was used ad nauseam to describe our air operations in the early days of Iraqi Freedom. It also was similar to the name of Toby Keith's album that got him in a fight with the Dixie Chicks, but that's a different story.

As expected, our enemy in Iraq was much more formidable than that of Afghanistan, and the entire strategy was different. In Afghanistan, the plan was to use overwhelming air power and a few special operations forces to help rebel fighters topple the Taliban and create a new government. In Iraq, we still planned to use overwhelming air power, but there was no organized rebel force in the southern half of Iraq to support. We needed a full-out ground invasion.

The initial plan for Iraq was to have US Army divisions simultaneously invade from the north and the south to converge on Baghdad from both directions. With Turkey not cooperating, the northern part of the plan fell apart. Instead, the US relied heavily on Kurdish fighters in Northern Iraq to attack key northern cities and keep the two-front strategy intact. The Kurds had support from US airpower, special operations forces, and about a thousand paratroopers from the 173rd Airborne Brigade. As always, the Kurds were stalwart allies of the US and fought bravely and effectively alongside US troops.

The main American effort came from the south. The US Army's 3rd Infantry Division rolled in from Kuwait along with the 1st Marine Expeditionary Unit. As US and coalition aircraft pounded preselected targets, soldiers and Marines made rapid progress toward the heart of Iraqi territory.

During those early days of the war, I remember experiencing an incredible sandstorm. The sky turned blood red from the swirling dust, and the winds seemed to be hurricane force. We had to jam rags into every crack and crevice to block the blowing sand, and going outside was nearly impossible. When we did emerge from indoors, we had to wear airtight goggles and wrap our heads and faces in big cotton rags. The suspended sand was so thick it obscured the sun during broad daylight, and you really couldn't see anything outside.

This sandstorm affected the entire region, and I remember the press coverage when it occurred. Western reporters, who seemed uniformly opposed to the war, created a narrative that US ground forces were "bogged down" just a few days into the conflict due to the storm and the tough Iraqi resistance.

In reality, as tanks and trucks from both sides paused to wait out the storm, American airplanes flew above the clouds and plinked the enemy vehicles one-by-one like ducks on a pond. By the time the sandstorm ended, US fighters and bombers had destroyed much of the Iraqi armored force and paved a clear pathway for American soldiers and Marines to roll right into Baghdad.

This left an impression on me. The negative reporting about the apparent slowdown, parroted by nearly every Western news source, was entirely wrong. From that point on, we would look for stupid news stories and include them in our daily intelligence briefing for comic relief. I guess that was "fake news" before President Donald Trump started using the term.

My detachment supported the Combined Joint Special Operations Taskforce West (CJSOTF-W). The name said it all. The "combined" part meant it included military units from other countries, specifically the United Kingdom and Australia. The "joint" part meant it included forces from various US military components, including the Air Force, the Navy, and the Army. We had so many different uniforms on that base it looked like the cantina scene from *Star Wars*.

The "special operations" part also is self-explanatory. Our 193rd contingent would be working with Army Special Forces (Green Berets), Navy SEALs, British special operators, and Australian commandos. On the air side, we would fly with all kinds of Air Force Special Operations Command (AFSOC) assets like the AC-130 Spooky gunships and the MC-130 Combat Talons.

The CJSOTF-W commander was Colonel John Mulholland, whose work we knew well from our previous deployment in Operation ENDURING FREEDOM. Colonel Mulholland had been the leader of those Green Berets featured in the movie *12 Strong*. He led Task Force Dagger, which sent a dozen Green Berets on the mission to fight on horseback alongside the Northern Alliance to defeat a force of 50,000 terrorists. He was and remains a true legend in the special operations community.

For those of us in the 193rd, the environment was a bit surreal. Yes, I was an intelligence officer, but that still was my part-time job. Mostly, I was a technology consultant. My counterparts from Harrisburg were in the same situation. Guvvy was a teacher. Hacker was an environmental engineer. Our detachment commander, Lieutenant Colonel Jerry, was an airline pilot. Our operations officer, Lieutenant Colonel Kevin, wrote software for the textile industry. Our first sergeant, Drew Horn, was a manager in a state agency.

This is what makes the Guard so unique. Two weeks earlier, each of us was doing something completely different, wearing civilian clothes and leading a normal life in eastern Pennsylvania. Today, we were wearing Air Force uniforms conducting combat operations alongside the highest-speed group of experienced and professional special operators in the world.

I think that may be the part about Guard service that most people just don't comprehend, neither civilian nor military. People simply cannot relate.

My civilian friends have no idea what I do when I'm in uniform. Some of this is because of secrecy. Much of what we do is classified, so we can't just blab about our adventures. But I think the real reason they don't understand is that it seems too implausible. Some guy down the street, whom you only ever see in jeans at a youth baseball game, disappears for a few months at a time to wear the air combat uniform at a secret base in the Middle East? And he's working for the *12 Strong* commander? It sounds like a corny Hollywood script. But for hundreds of Guardsmen, it is the truth.

I remember returning from one of my deployments and going to visit a family friend. He's a great guy who I've known for many years. When I told him that I got deployed with the Air National Guard, he asked me if they sent me to pull security duty at a regional airport.

"They don't actually send you guys overseas, do they?" he asked.

"Yeah," I said. "We got uniforms and everything," I added, quoting one of my favorite lines from *Major League.*

Recently, I was interviewed by a radio talk show host about my service in the military. Over a staticky connection, I described some of my experiences with the Air National Guard. He sounded puzzled, then I realized why. He thought I was a proud member of the "International Guard." I guess he thought I worked for the United Nations or something.

While most civilians don't know much about the Guard, neither do most people on active duty. Just as civilians generally don't comprehend that we put on a uniform and get right to work, our military counterparts who have never experienced the Guard firsthand can't fathom the concept either.

One reason is you can't tell us apart from the active duty. We all wear the same uniform. No insignia says "Guard" or "Reserve" on the sleeve. A clever observer may figure out that we are in the Guard by our airframe (only the Guard flies the Commando Solo), or by our age (we tend to be older), but otherwise, you can't tell the difference at all. I'd bet that 95 percent of the soldiers and airmen we encountered at CJSOTF-W never knew we were in the Guard.

Now don't get me wrong. Our part-time airmen at the 193rd don't claim to be door-kicking, snake-eating tough guys. We don't fly through Mogadishu on little bird helicopters, and we don't ride horseback through Afghanistan.

But despite our part-time status, we are expected to deliver real-world combat power as part of the total force. And as bona fide members of the special operations community, we Guardsmen get to wear a unique patch on our sleeve just like every other member of AFSOC, identifying us as "Air Commandos" too.

It was early spring, and my mom was working long hours because of her job as a tax collector. My dad was newly retired from teaching, so we all got to spend a lot of quality time with him.

One of the biggest extras about that spring was they were working on the street outside my parents' front door. There were bulldozers, steamrollers, and trucks of every variety. The two boys would eat breakfast and then watch the men working for as long as I'd let them.

Sometimes my dad would take them outside to sit on the neighbors' steps to get closer to the action. It was little boy heaven. We would go to the park and play. Usually, we would walk and visit along the way. My dad was happy to show off his grandsons.

I was able to do the grocery shopping, cleaning, and cooking, so my mom was not as busy as she usually was during the tax season and she could enjoy the boys during the evening. Most importantly, though, my mom had made some phone calls, and she was able to get me a spot in the local Community Bible Study chapter. It was the same organization that had helped me so much in San Angelo during our year in Texas, and I had a wonderful experience with them. I was able to go to Bible study once a week and focus my mind on Scripture throughout the week. It kept me grounded and focused on the bigger picture of what is truly important.

I also rekindled friendships with some women from high school. In particular, I had one friend whose husband was also deployed. We took the kids to a museum in Pittsburgh and attended a Blue Star Mothers' rally in Beaver Park. Mainly, we talked about our fears and our hopes for when our husbands would return home.

At CJSOTF-W, the 193rd was part of an interesting and important mission. The entire western half of Iraq is a vast, arid desert. It is the perfect place for Baath Party officials, insurgents, terrorists, and assorted bad guys to hide. It is also a great location from which to launch SCUD missiles and conceal potential weapons of mass destruction. Plus, it is a transit route to other nasty regimes in the Middle East like Bashar Assad's Syria. Much of CJSOTF-W's work was to keep this vast desert under control while the rest of the coalition fighting force marched to Baghdad and toppled the government. We simply didn't have the troops to cover that much land, so the job went to special operations.

The British guys were great. They had special tactics guys spread out all over western Iraq and would provide daily reports about their situation. One day, a British officer gave his daily briefing to Colonel Mulholland and the rest of the headquarters staff about a situation his troops had encountered the day before. They had rolled up on a group of Iraqis, identified them as Fedayeen insurgents, and captured the whole gang of twenty bad guys without firing a shot.

The Americans were impressed, and one Green Beret asked the Brit, "How were you so effective in identifying the Fedayeen when we have such a hard time telling apart the bad guys from the normal civilians?"

The Brit deadpanned that one of his translators heard one of the Iraqis whisper to the other in Arabic, "Tell them whatever you want, but don't tell them we are Fedayeen."

The Australian commandos were the coolest cats in the desert. They wore these polka dot camouflage uniforms, including cargo shorts. That's right; they were authorized to wear shorts. The Americans were bound by General Order One, which prohibited drinking any alcohol, possessing any war trophies, having any contraband, and a whole bunch of other activities. The Australians, well, not so much. They knew how to work hard and play hard no matter where they were. I don't know how they got away with half the stuff they did.

Of course, most of our interactions were with American special operations forces. The Green Berets had plenty of soldiers in western Iraq, and I made daily trips to visit their liaison officers for updates on their positions and situations. The real-time information from special forces on the ground was extremely valuable to our unit as we planned missions targeting their locations with various information warfare platforms.

We also had daily discussions with the poggies from the 4th Psychological Operations Group. Besides developing the broadcast programming, they also had soldiers setting up temporary radio stations, broadcasting from loudspeakers, and dropping leaflets from C-130s. They handled the overall PSYOP strategy.

Staff Sergeant Dennis was a poggy assigned to the 193rd as our liaison. We had already gotten to know him well because he had been part of the Romanian Eight who traveled across Eastern Europe on the way to the Middle East. In this position, he lived and worked with us instead of his fellow Army soldiers.

For him, that was a good thing. Anybody who has ever been in the military knows the Air Force takes a ribbing for being soft compared to the other service components, especially the Army and the Marines. Mostly, it is totally deserved. The Air Force is coddled compared to the other divisions. I know. I started out in the infantry.

Staff Sergeant Dennis ribbed us hard about the Air Force, but deep down, I think he wished the Army treated its people as well. One area of difference that we observed firsthand related to malaria medicine.

In addition to all the other vaccines we got, everybody going to the Iraqi theater had to take pills to prevent malaria. The rumor was that the Air Force distributed the new, better medicine to its airmen, but the Army gave out old, crappy stuff with all kinds of side effects. I don't know if that is true, but one night we saw the results of the Air-versus-Army dichotomy with respect to these particular prophylactics.

Staff Sergeant Dennis had been taking these Army malaria pills and was worried about the side effects. He'd heard about the scary stories involving vivid dreams and crazy nightmares. Maybe it was psychosomatic, but one day, he freaked out.

After a long shift at work, we returned to the tent to get some sleep. The tent slept about twenty people in two rows. Since it was only used for sleeping, it was usually dark. Staff Sergeant Dennis was already there and had been sleeping for some time. The lights were off, and we were all drained.

Suddenly, we heard this horrible scream from the far end of the bay. Everybody immediately jumped out of bed to see if we were getting attacked or something. It was Staff Sergeant Dennis. He was sitting up in his bed, yelling at the top of his lungs. Even though his eyes were wide open, he was fast asleep and the middle of a nightmare.

A crowd gathered around. I tried to talk to Staff Sergeant Dennis to wake him up, thinking he would snap out of it. Instead, as I got closer, he grabbed me by the neck and started screaming even louder.

Now, Staff Sergeant Dennis wasn't a big guy, but he was super strong. I seriously thought he was going to snap my neck. Fortunately, the rest of the group subdued him and pulled him off me. We were all standing there in our underwear, wondering what the heck happened. Eventually, Staff Sergeant Dennis came to his senses. He had no idea what had happened either.

Later that day, he went and got the Air Force malaria pills instead. Thank goodness.

One night, Kevin called from overseas. I was thrilled! But I could immediately tell something was not right. He was irritated.

Kevin started asking who had been over to the house and how I had been spending my time. He asked in a very accusatory way. I didn't know what I had done and was very confused and upset. He ended the call by hanging up abruptly. I had no idea what I had done or said.

A few days went by, and I was still clueless as to the reason for Kevin's mood and implied accusations. Then he called, and much to my relief, he told me he had watched the movie *Unfaithful* about a cheating wife. Apparently, he had transferred all his emotions from watching the film to me.

I was so relieved. I laughed out loud. He still wasn't over his feelings of hurt and betrayal, but when he realized what he had done, he apologized. I ask him what kind of idiots thought it would be a good idea to show a movie like that to a bunch of deployed airmen.

The 193rd had its own workstation near several other special operations airframes. That allowed us to interact regularly with pilots and aircrew from other AFSOC units flying similar airframes like the AC-130 gunships. We were able to develop good relationships that were extremely helpful in doing our jobs. Since the special operations community is so small, my colleagues and I would run into these people at different places around the world for years to come.

Soon after the war began, we all settled into a battle rhythm. Each day, the 193rd would receive its next mission from the PSYOP guys, which would include the target area, the type of broadcast required, and the platform. Then the mission planners, which included Lieutenant Colonel Jerry, Lieutenant Colonel Kevin, and the intel shop, would map out the next day's mission. Once they'd fully planned it, we would work with the mission aircrew to finalize the details and launch the airplane. Inevitably, things would change. But mostly, we had a routine.

Each day, about six hours before the aircrew arrived, I would get to work. The first order of business was to review all the intelligence reports that came in while I was sleeping. Some of these were waiting in my email when I arrived. Others were posted on various classified websites that I visited in sequence every day. Then at the same time every day, I would walk over to the CSOTF-W SCIF.

The SCIF was the heart of the task force's intelligence work. There were representatives from all the different components and services. They had specialists who knew how to collect and disseminate the latest SIGINT, IMINT, and ELINT. Everybody got a chance to brief intel from their own point of view and share information about their various missions. It was a great give-and-take that consisted of some really smart people.

My favorite part was getting to know the different individuals who represented the various units. Just talking to them could yield a treasure trove of information invaluable to mission planning. Despite all the electronics equipment, information systems, and technical expertise, it was always the people and the relationships that provide the best usable intelligence.

For example, our Commando Solo aircraft was tasked to fly into an area with a lot of anti-aircraft capabilities. Most of the weapons were mobile, so it was tough to pinpoint where the enemy might be able to take a potshot at a loitering C-130. I had built a relationship with an Australian liaison officer who was exchanging intelligence back-and-forth with Australian commandos on the ground in western Iraq.

On my request, he could ask Australian soldiers in Iraq questions about when and where it was safest to fly, based on where the Australians were operating. The 193rd then used their intelligence to plan our flight routes. It was pretty cool that commandos from Australia were helping Guardsmen from Pennsylvania accomplish the mission.

We also worked closely with the SERE guys. Mongo was around, but mostly I worked with a different NCO, whom we called Batman. Soon after arriving at our secret base, Batman and I had to deliver an in-depth briefing to the aircrew about what to do if their airplane got shot down. There were lots of nasty rumors about what the Iraqi forces had done to Kuwaiti POWs during the first Gulf War. Everybody was taking this training very seriously.

There was an old auditorium on the base, big enough for a large briefing, but it looked like it had been locked up and unused for many years. There were dust and cobwebs everywhere, and all kinds of creepy creatures to watch out for, like big camel spiders and little desert mice. Later, I would witness a camel spider fight one of those mice. But on that day, the creature of interest was a bat. Just as we stood up on stage to deliver the briefing, it started flying all around our heads.

Somehow, in a split second, this SERE guy pulled out a knife and stabbed the bat against the wall. Then he stood there in front of the entire squadron and presented the impaled creature, announcing, "Hah, another for my collection."

We weren't quite sure if he actually had a bat collection, but none of us would have been surprised if he did. After this feat of manliness, the aircrew was very confident in Batman's advice and did everything he said.

For me, the highlight of each day was mission planning. Guvvy and I had a great professional relationship with Lieutenant Colonel Jerry and Lieutenant Colonel Kevin, our two primary bosses and mission planners. Both were aviators, and anybody familiar with unit intelligence knows that a good relationship between intel and aircrew is not guaranteed.

Sometimes, the intel guys act like they are a bit too smart for their own good and come across as either too technical or just too nerdy. Sometimes, the aircrew can get a little too full of themselves and act with arrogance or dismissiveness toward the non-flying team. One of our intel guys used the phrase "zipper-suited sun gods" to describe pilots who think their crap doesn't stink. Fortunately for ourselves and our mission, our team of intelligence professionals and aviators was working together exceptionally well.

We developed a grid system that would allow planners and aircrew to establish routes to fly in and out of the target area in the safest and quickest manner possible. It was a simple color-coded scheme: green was the lowest risk, yellow was medium risk, and red was high risk. It was presented in a giant map on the wall for everybody to see. If somebody asked why we changed a grid square from yellow to green overnight, we could tell them that the Australian commandos on the ground had cleared the sector and that it was safe to fly. When the aircrew got that kind of answer, they knew we were doing our homework. It inspired confidence and helped to develop a great rapport.

I also really enjoyed preparing and delivering briefings. I would brief anybody who would listen on any subject they wanted to know. If I didn't know the material, I would research it. If I did, I would try to offer my own unique perspective and not just parrot somebody else's work. I always hated delivering somebody else's briefing. Preparing the briefing myself was the best way for me to learn the material and communicate it effectively.

A briefing is nothing more than short presentations on a particular subject. Usually, we used PowerPoint slides. Often, we used maps and charts. Sometimes, we just talked with no props at all. Regardless of the form or format, briefings were designed to provide relevant information to decisionmakers clearly and quickly.

At various times in my military career, I have delivered some memorable briefings. I briefed a group of Army Rangers about the Taliban just before they parachuted into Afghanistan. I briefed an Air Force colonel and his staff from a Middle Eastern ally about US actions to minimize civilian casualties. I briefed a general about the potential nuclear fallout of a hypothetical attack on an American city. I briefed a Congressman about the situation in North Korea. I briefed an audience of several hundred Guardsmen about the religious beliefs of al-Qaida and the Islamic State.

Preparing and delivering Air Force intelligence briefings taught me how to think and how to communicate my ideas—be short and to the point. It also taught me you should never make up stuff you don't know. Delivering briefings is one area where my military training and practice has spilled over into my civilian career with great benefit. It has instilled in me a love of public speaking.

Besides the pre-mission briefings to the aircrew, there were two regularly scheduled briefings I enjoyed the most. One was the current intel brief to the maintenance guys. We continued this tradition, which I learned from Captain McKissick in the Afghanistan War, into Operation IRAQI FREEDOM. The maintenance crews continued to appreciate the information and were as engaged and interested as before.

The second briefing I looked forward to was our daily standup at the SCIF. This was when intel professionals from all different backgrounds had the opportunity to present in front of their peers to provide relevant information, ask questions, and generally share good intelligence.

We didn't always speak at this meeting because there wasn't always something important to say. But it was fascinating getting to hear all the updates about the special operations on the ground and in the air. And it was humbling to contribute to such a prestigious and professional group.

Sometimes, these discussions were really funny. A lot of the guys had a great sense of humor, and some of them had us in stitches. We tried to do our part. Guvvy and I once briefed that a Baath Party official and his family were stopped at the border trying to sneak into Syria in a water truck. When the border guards caught him, they detained the official and his wife but let the infant son continue.

"Why?" somebody asked.

"Because they didn't want to throw the baby out with the Baath water."

Okay, so that's bad, but the Brits thought it was funny.

We witnessed some heroic deeds by our soldiers and airmen. I brought home an autographed copy of the *Time* Magazine cover detailing the rescue operation of Private Jessica Lynch and her fellow prisoners of war. It was signed by the aircrew of the gunship who flew in support of rescue forces on the ground.

There was a leader of a small city in Western Iraq who had a stranglehold on the population and was sympathetic to Saddam Hussein. Since we didn't have enough firepower on the ground to take the city by force, we had to find another way. An enterprising Army sergeant found out that the leader was deathly afraid of US fighter jets. So on a day when he was supposed to deliver an inspiring speech to his citizens, urging them to resist the Americans, the NCO called in for any available aircraft to buzz this guy's podium.

It sounds silly, but it worked. The Air Force sent a volley of fighter airplanes, I think it was at least two F-16s, for a low-level flyby right on time, and the guy turned into a blubbering idiot on stage. He ran away in terror, setting the stage for an A-team of US Green Berets to walk in and take the town unopposed.

Our mission was to send radio and television broadcasts to Iraqi citizens, assuring them of our good intentions and giving them instructions about how to stay safe. We also broadcast information to enemy soldiers about how to surrender, why their fight was a lost cause, and why our war was just. Our unit was credited with saving thousands of civilian lives and initiating hundreds of military capitulations. In a sense, our slow-moving C-130 could be a more powerful weapon than a supersonic fighter full of 500-pound bombs.

The Air Force delivered plenty of those bombs too, and soon there wasn't much left of the Iraqi defenses. US Marines and Army units spread out across the country, and within a few months, the American military had destroyed the Iraqi forces and toppled the regime. We watched the Marines tear down the big statue of Saddam Hussein on televisions in the base cafeteria, and we knew we would be going home soon.

Easter came, and our Bible study paralleled Holy Week. It was a special time. The Easter Bunny managed to find the boys at my parents' house, and we went to my aunt's for Easter dinner. It was a warm day, and we ate outside.

Kevin's buddy Chad was there. He had been the best man at our wedding and was dating my cousin. They had met at our wedding three years earlier. Chad was sweet enough to help the boys put together the new balsa wood airplanes they'd found in their Easter baskets.

May 1, 2003, was the day of President Bush's infamous "Mission Accomplished" speech on board the aircraft carrier USS *Abraham Lincoln*. In that address, Bush wore a Navy flight suit to declare that major combat operations were over and the nation's wartime objectives had been fulfilled. Little did we know that this announcement would portend the start of a guerrilla war that would cost hundreds more American lives and lay the foundation for the rise of the Islamic State.

Nevertheless, for the time being, our job was done. We stopped flying combat missions by early May, and then it was just a matter of waiting around to go home. The airplanes had already flown back to Harrisburg with most of our gear, and all the other American units at our secret base were long gone. With thousands of soldiers, airmen, and Marines waiting to get home, the Pennsylvania National Guard did not seem to be a top priority. We were literally just waiting around trying to get picked up, and we might still be stuck there if not for the resourcefulness of my former AMS partner, Lieutenant Dawn.

When we had been in officer school together, Dawn had demonstrated a penchant for straight talk with no nonsense. She could get the job done, whatever that might be. Since going through official channels was taking forever, Dawn decided to try other methods. She started making phone calls.

Soon, she found a flight home that could fit all our people. The problem was the flight was departing the next day, and we were hundreds of miles from the pickup point. Undeterred, Dawn somehow was able to get a bus and a driver to take our entire unit from our secret base across the country to our departure point.

It was a crazy plan. We had no weapons and were not exactly driving through friendly territory. Instead, we drew curtains over the windows and tried to look as inconspicuous as possible. I peeked out through the curtains as we drove through little villages and big towns. There were camels in the fields and Bedouins herding sheep. It was like an RV trip across the states, except we were in a dilapidated bus in the heart of the Middle East while a war was still going on. Then, of course, halfway there, the bus got a flat tire, and we almost missed our flight. We should have just gotten more rental cars from Vlad the Romanian.

Maybe that crazy bus caravan across the desert was the transition I needed in place of the meal I skipped on the way back from OEF. Because by the time we arrived at the airport, all I could think about was going home. We arrived at our departure point just in time for our flight and jumped on an airplane out of the country. On the way home, we stopped in Rome and Ireland, where I bought Susan a necklace at the airport. We learned the unit was planning a big homecoming welcome for us at the airport, and I was so excited to see Susan again.

Eventually, I returned to Kutztown. I had been gone for almost two months, and it was time to go home. One evening at about eight o'clock, I got a call from the base family support office. Kevin would be back the next day at eight in the morning. I was thrilled!

I called Kevin's parents, Bill and Trudie, to see if they could babysit the boys the next morning at six in the morning so I could drive to the base. Of course, they said they would. I was so excited I couldn't sleep.

I was tired the next morning when my in-laws arrived, but I jumped in my Jeep and off to Harrisburg I went. I got about ten minutes away from the base when I suddenly lost control of the car. It was raining and slippery, and I suppose I just wasn't paying enough attention. I hit the guard rail to the right, bounced across the median strip into oncoming traffic, and spun around at least once. It was a blur, really, and I thought I was going to die. Then suddenly, I stopped in the median grass strip.

I got myself together and tried to start the car again; it was dead.

All I kept thinking was that I was going to miss Kevin's arrival ceremony. I jumped out of the Jeep, and a car pulled over to see if I was okay. I couldn't believe my luck. It was an airman!

I asked the airman if he was going to the 193rd, and he said yes, but first, he wanted to know if I was okay. I had already forgotten about the Jeep and just wanted to see Kevin. He asked me again if I was okay, and then he gave me a ride.

By the time I got to the base, I had already missed the arrival ceremony. So I went directly to Kevin's office. He opened the door, and I threw my arms around him. Then I stepped back, looked him in the eye, and told him I had wrecked the Jeep. I explained how some wonderful Good Samaritan had given me a ride to the base. I was so sorry I was late. We needed to rent a car.

It was a lot for him to take in. We got a ride to the rental agency and got a car. I called the police, and we waited for them to come. We kissed and kissed and kissed the entire time we waited.

On May 19, after two days of travel, we touched down at Harrisburg International Airport. I could see the crowd of families waiting at the flight line for their airmen to arrive. When it was time, I got off the airplane, grabbed my bags from the pallet, and made my way to the crowd of families and friends.

But Susan wasn't there. I thought maybe she was in the intelligence section with people she knew, so I made my way through the crowd, saying goodbye to my fellow airmen and chatting with their families. This took a while, and I still didn't see Susan.

Susan isn't exactly known for being on time for everything, but I couldn't imagine she would be late for my homecoming. When I walked back to the intel shop and she wasn't there, I started to get a little worried. She was more than half an hour late, and the other families were already beginning to leave.

Then, just like that, she knocked on the door, and I instantly forgot about her lateness. She stood there looking as beautiful as ever with a huge smile on her face. We exchanged hugs and kisses and chatted with some of the families still around, including those in the intel shop. Then after a few minutes, it was time to go. I wanted to get out of there as fast as possible. But Susie seemed to be lingering, which was unusual.

Eventually, I got more insistent. "Susan, let's go home." That's when I learned why she was late.

"Uh, we can't," she explained. "I think I totaled the Jeep."

On the drive to the base, she had been so distracted about my homecoming she'd almost missed her exit and swerved to make it. She had spun out on the wet road and ended up hitting the guardrail. Fortunately, she wasn't hurt, and a uniformed Guardsman had stopped and given her a ride to the base. The Jeep was still parked on the median strip of the highway about five miles away.

She was embarrassed and started to cry, and I did my best to reassure her that I didn't care about the Jeep. We laughed and spent the next couple hours calling a tow truck and renting a car, and eventually made it back home.

It was great to see the boys. Susan and the kids had spent most of the time visiting her parents in Beaver while I was gone, so they hadn't been home much in Kutztown either. Will was almost four years old, and Jake was seventeen months. Although Jake was kind of distant at first, it didn't take long for him to open up. It was time to get back to normal again, even if "normal" meant something very different than most people imagine.

But first, I had to get off active duty, and that was a challenge of its own. Unlike my previous deployment, this time I had been involuntarily mobilized. That meant the Big Blue Air Force had something to say about me getting back to my civilian life, and they weren't in any hurry.

Even though I got home on May 19, the Air Force kept me on orders throughout June. It was a real pain. I had to report to the unit along with everybody else to a crowded office with very little to do. Driving ninety miles twice a day to wait around and bump into other impatient people got old very fast.

They offered me a hotel room in Harrisburg, but after being away in the Middle East for three months, I certainly didn't want to stay overnight away from my family in Harrisburg. We should have been celebrating my homecoming, but instead, we were stuck in redeployment limbo, wasting time and money. So I commuted and complained.

Soon, I realized that complaining did nothing to get me released earlier; it just made me grumpy and made Susan upset. So I just commuted and stopped complaining.

Finally, I got my release. In early July, on our fourth anniversary, I got off active duty. For the past three years, Susan and I had faithfully done our duty to our country. Now it was time to prioritize our family.

CHAPTER ELEVEN:
ACCEPTING THE NEW NORMAL

WHEN KEVIN CAME HOME from Operation IRAQI FREEDOM, I had already decided I wanted to try for a third baby. Luckily, he had independently decided the same thing. It was just a couple of months after he got home that I found out I was pregnant again.

However, I was nervous thinking about caring for three babies at the same time. I couldn't imagine how I would ever get out of the house with three little children.

It was time to give the kids and Susan the attention they deserved. I jumped right into being a dad and a husband, and those were good times in the Dellicker house. Susan seemed happy, the boys were doing great, and we were going to have another baby. It was nice to see Susan smiling again. She really seemed to enjoy being a full-time stay-at-home mom, and the boys truly benefited from that decision.

In Harrisburg, my civilian colleagues at Affinity Group seemed happy to have me back. Chris was co-founder of the business and owner of its parent company, Bravo Group. John was a senior team member and former Ridge Administration coworker. Everybody was supportive of my military service, and they all let me leave with no questions asked whenever I had to put on the uniform.

When I got home from the war, Chris and John threw Susan and me a big welcome-home party. Since they had good relationships with the media, they invited a television news crew to cover the affair. The nation was riding a wave of patriotism after our quick dispatching of Saddam Hussein's forces, and everybody was anxious to be a part of the story.

It was obvious they were using my homecoming to generate free publicity for the firm, but I didn't mind. I figured it portrayed the Air National Guard in a positive light. Plus, Susan thought it was a sweet gesture.

Chris was my boss. He gave me broad flexibility to develop my own book of business. As long as I kept generating enough money to pay my salary and make a little extra profit, he allowed me to pursue the work I wanted. Essentially, I was an entrepreneur without the risk of owning my own company. I decided to revisit a subject of interest from my time in the Ridge Administration, improving broadband access for education.

Several years prior, the governor's people had asked me to develop a policy proposal to help solve the so-called "digital divide" among Pennsylvania schools. A few school districts across the Commonwealth had fast and affordable Internet access, but the rest had slow and expensive service. I had researched all kinds of solutions, but when 9/11 hit, all that work went on the back burner. Now that the world seemed to be getting back to normal, some of those issues were coming back to the forefront, and I thought I could make an impact.

With some Affinity Group colleagues and a local engineering firm, we came up with an idea for combining the purchasing power of a bunch of schools to get a better price on internet access. It was like the Wal-Mart approach to buying broadband services. The idea sounded great in theory; we just had to see if it would work in practice.

The first organization to try our experiment was the Capital Area Intermediate Unit, an educational service agency that represented twenty-four school districts in south-central Pennsylvania. The Intermediate Unit had a smart and savvy technology director named Kathy, who had attempted a similar project the year prior.

Her member schools had bailed on it before she could see it through. With help from our team at Affinity Group, she succeeded the second time around, and a bunch of her schools saved a lot of money.

Other schools took notice, and shortly after the first endeavor, we started another project, this time in eastern Pennsylvania. It was a lot easier the second time around, as we avoided several pitfalls from the first effort and had a much smoother time of it. I was convinced that we had a viable model that could be replicated time and again, maybe even in other states or in different industries.

But first, we had to solve the problem of scalability. We needed big projects to get big results, and it was going to be very labor-intensive to round up enough schools to make our new idea work. Most districts had other priorities besides better broadband access, few had extra money lying around for technology projects, and hardly any were interested in financing "new ideas." If we were going to transform our good idea into a viable business, we had to get lots of schools to pay attention and somehow solve the problem of rural telecom economics. Then we stumbled onto "Chapter 30."

Chapter 30 of 1996 was an obscure law. Almost nobody in the general public knew anything about it. It was Pennsylvania's telecommunications statute, and we learned it was up for reauthorization in 2003. Chapter 30 governed the state's entire wholesale pricing and regulatory structure for the telecom industry. Hundreds of pages of arcane text, the statute was about as interesting reading as the phone book. But it was important. With the internet emerging as the dominant innovation of a generation, most of the new law was going to be about broadband access. And it was a battle of the telecom titans: AT&T versus Verizon.

We figured a winning outcome for either side was worth billions of dollars, so we crafted a crazy plan. Bravo Group would organize a coalition of broadband consumers and plant it right in the middle of the debate. If we could generate enough political clout, one of the two sides might cut a deal for the support of our coalition and give the schools what they needed. We were seeking policy changes to incentivize rural broadband investment and more money to help schools build better networks.

I was responsible for developing the policy, and my colleague Athan was responsible for the politics. Athan was very young, only about 25 years old, but also very smart. Perhaps more important, he was too naïve to know when to be afraid. Together, we created this new coalition called "Project e-Quality" and set out to solve Pennsylvania's digital divide.

We recruited a diverse group of about a dozen different organizations to influence the debate. In one of our very first meetings, Athan explained our strategy to a friendly state legislator. He asked how much money we thought AT&T or Verizon might agree to finance as part of a grand compromise. Athan said $100 million. The representative burst out laughing. From then on, he called Athan the "$100 million man." Eventually, we would get the last laugh.

But at first, we were both in way over our heads. Verizon took out an op-ed in the *Pittsburgh Post-Gazette* attacking me by name. That was unnerving. Legislators called my company and told them I ought to be fired. I think Athan was getting flak from his bosses for going along with my scheme. We needed a better plan.

That's when John got the idea to create the big red maps. At some point, I had shown him a list of how much it cost to buy a standard commercial broadband connection in every county courthouse across Pennsylvania. Since it was easier to serve big cities and harder to serve rural communities, the price disparities were stark. The same service that cost $500 in Philadelphia might cost $2,500 in rural Bradford County.

John ordered the creation of about 500 table-sized maps that plotted the cost of broadband on a red-yellow-green color scale by legislative district. Green was good. Red was bad. Except for a couple of specks of green and yellow, almost the whole map of Pennsylvania was bright red.

That was what we needed to turn it around. Legislators from rural areas might not even know the difference between broadband and a rubber band, but they didn't want their district to be red on the map. Suddenly, the debate turned into a rural versus urban contest that pitted the wealthy Philadelphia suburbs against the rest of the state.

Sensing the change in politics, Verizon tried to muscle through its own version of the legislation around Thanksgiving of 2003, before the situation got worse. But it didn't have the votes. Our ragtag coalition of schools, business groups, and healthcare organizations armed with big red maps stopped the legislation in its tracks.

A few months later, Verizon agreed to legislative changes. The new law would provide incentives for telecom companies to build infrastructure in rural areas, offer discounts on commercial broadband services to underserved consumers, and create a multi-million fund for better broadband in schools. In return, Verizon would receive regulatory relief worth well over a billion dollars.

With our coalition endorsing the Verizon compromise, the bill passed with bipartisan support. It was a great policy win that ultimately united legislators who were both urban and rural, liberal and conservative, pro-business, and pro-consumer. Essentially, it was a market-driven solution, also championed by advocates of students and underserved customers.

Schools across Pennsylvania now had the necessary resources to solve the digital divide, and Bravo Group had the pieces in place to scale our broadband business. In the end, the total value of discounts and new funding for broadband in schools was just about $100 million, exactly as Athan had predicted when that guy had laughed at him.

Thankfully, my pregnancy with Elijah was uneventful. The baby was to come around Memorial Day 2004, but my water broke several weeks before my due date. I had a regular appointment scheduled that morning, and after I saw the doctor, they sent me to the hospital. I endured a long day of sitting in the hospital and waiting for the Pitocin to work.

I suppose my induction was typical of most women's experiences: uncomfortable, prolonged, and painful. But after my epidural, the situation improved. Thank goodness for anesthesiologists.

Eli came quickly after that. And he was beautiful. His eyes were so smiley and bright for a newborn baby. He slept well and ate well. Simply put, he was a pleasant and easygoing baby. Boy, was he going to need that mentality to survive our house.

Jake and Will came to meet Eli the following day. Both were thrilled to have a baby brother. But then we came home, and they were a little disappointed. They wanted to play with Eli right away, but all he did was lay on his back and grab at the toys hanging above him on his play mat.

On the other hand, the older boys soon learned that when it was time to feed Eli, I would read them all a book together, which they really liked. I guess they figured Eli was good for something.

Susan and I knew Eli was going to be different from the outset. Will and Jake were light-skinned redheads. Eli came out of the womb looking like he had a summer-long tan with a tousle of thick, dark hair on his head. And he acted as cool as he looked. Susan's dad Curt nicknamed him "Silent E" because he just kind of smiled at you and pointed until you gave him what he wanted.

With a third baby in the house and Susan firmly established as a stay-at-home mom, we started to experience stability in our family life for the first time in a while. I was commuting less to Harrisburg, and our financial situation had improved. And a year after I'd come home from Operation IRAQI FREEDOM, even my military obligations had calmed down to a manageable level.

After our great success with Chapter 30, I was anxious to see how far we could advance our broadband ideas across Pennsylvania.

With my visions of grandeur, I suppose I just expected Chris to invest a bunch of money in marketing and hire a team of people to support my emerging practice. Instead, he made it clear that although he approved of my work, his focus remained on public affairs. Broadband would be ancillary to his core business.

In hindsight, I realize Chris made a perfectly rational business decision. But at the time, I thought he was making a big mistake. I started to wonder if I should start my own business aimed at promoting broadband in schools. For the first time in my life, I thought about becoming an entrepreneur.

Many entrepreneurs get the bug early on. They have parents who owned businesses, or they idolize some captain of industry. Some just want to try to get rich. Not me. I don't think I considered starting my own business until that period in the fall of 2004.

The timing was not ideal for our family. Susan had finally gotten comfortable in her role as full-time mom, and it was clear she was not going back to her teaching job any time soon. Paying the bills would be my exclusive domain, and with three growing boys, that was only getting harder. Plus, I was trying to devote more time to being a dad and husband. Adding to my workload was not in the plan.

Fortunately, my military commitments had eased up quite a bit. The nation was still immersed in both Iraq and Afghanistan, and we all expected to be sent overseas again. But since returning from Operation IRAQI FREEDOM, my farthest trip was to Fairchild Air Force Base near Spokane, Washington. There, I received additional survival instruction to supplement the three weeks of training I had already completed in 2002 with Mongo and his counterparts. This training, which we affectionately called "Advanced Beatings," was another course in our ongoing SERE sequence designed to make us ready in case of capture.

Our unit also got tasked by the State Department to conduct a long-term, classified mission that involved weekly broadcasts with Commando Solo for several years. It was a massive commitment, and every mission required at least one intelligence professional. We would end up having to support these so-called "weekend trips" for several years.

Fortunately, the trips were to a pleasant, tropical location, a stark difference from the nasty, isolated places we normally went. But like everything else the 193rd did for the Global War on Terrorism, they added even more time away from home. Ultimately, I went on six of those trips over three years until we completed the mission.

Around September 2004, just after I returned from one of the weekend trips, Susan and I started to take the business idea more seriously. We could do it together. I would do the customer work, and she would be the office manager. The concept of being able to work from home part-time was appealing to Susan, although the question of how to do that with three preschool children seemed to be an insurmountable barrier.

Through the holidays, conversations turned into plans. We considered starting the new business while I remained employed at Affinity Group but rejected that idea. It would be too much work, and most entrepreneurs advised against such an approach. Besides, Chris probably would have said no to that. My part-time drill pay would help, but not much. Guard drill pay was just about enough for a car payment. If we were going to do this, we had to jump in with both feet.

I met with my minister and longtime friend Pastor Bob to ask his advice. I told him what we were considering and then explained all the reasons starting a business was a bad idea. Neither Susan nor I had any meaningful experience. We had no extra income, no money in savings, and three babies at home. Plus, I could get called back to active duty at any time.

"If I mess this up," I said, "we could lose our house."

To my shock and horror, Pastor Bob said, "So what?"

"What do you mean, so what?" I responded. "Didn't you hear what I said?"

Pastor Bob doubled down. "If you lose the house, you'll find a different place to live. You have a good education, and so does Susan. If you fail in your new business venture, you'll eventually find new jobs. Mostly, you need to have some faith and trust in God."

He was right.

I put together a new plan for Susan to consider. We would take out a home equity loan, the maximum we were qualified to receive. We would use that loan to start the business and pay for living expenses until one of two things happened. Either we would earn enough money from the venture to pay it off, or we would exhaust the loan and run out of money. At that point, I would get another job and close the business, but we wouldn't risk another dime.

At most, we would lose the money from the loan. That was a huge sum, but it wouldn't ruin our lives if we lost it. Susan and I decided to take the chance.

First, I needed a place to work. The basement would become my new permanent office. I had learned how to build things from my dad and summer jobs with local building contractors, so I decided to build a home office myself with the help of friends and relatives. The funniest part was sitting on the shoulders of my 350-pound brother-in-law while he carried me around to fasten the drywall to the ceiling. Working nights and weekends, it only took a few months to build a comfortable space in the basement from which to work. But it also exhausted about 20 percent of our available funds before we even got started.

Next, I needed to file the paperwork. Fortunately, I had access to PA Open for Business, the award-winning one-stop shop for entrepreneurs I had created for Governor Tom Ridge. Sitting in my basement with a cup of coffee, I proudly logged in, ready to join the ranks of entrepreneurs who already had benefited from my good work. The first screen popped up and prompted me to start the process, asking me a series of questions. They might have been the exact questions I wrote myself two years ago. Here I went, question number one. . .

Except I couldn't answer it. The question asked something about the type of business structure I wanted to create, and I didn't understand the differences among them. Undeterred, I skipped that question and went to the next one. But I couldn't answer that one either.

Click after click, I realized that despite all my work on this project and all the awards it earned, the website was virtually useless to an entrepreneur without prior experience. It was unwieldy and complicated. It had replaced incomprehensible paper forms with incomprehensible online questions. It seemed to have been written by a bureaucrat who had no idea about what it really took to start a business.

Wait a minute. *I* was that bureaucrat.

I closed my screen, went to a local law office, and paid an attorney $900 to incorporate my business. I never went on that website again.

It's hard to overstate the impact this episode had on my life. Since my first job in New York, I had pondered my good fortune to be a young man with such little experience yet tremendous responsibility in government, first in Albany and then in Harrisburg. From time to time, this caused me to pause and question my qualifications, but I would quickly put those thoughts aside as I observed so many others around me who were both younger and less experienced. I realized that being young and uninformed was perfectly normal among government decisionmakers.

It took me ten years and a lousy website to realize that this was very wrong.

I'm not trying to disparage young people who have government jobs or paint everybody under forty years old with a broad brush. The problem derives from a lack of experience, not from being young. But in state legislatures and capitol buildings across the country, the rookies are running the show. And from what I know about Congress, they are running the show in Washington too.

I'm convinced this is one reason our government is so messed up. Instead of learning a skill or a trade first and then applying that practical life experience to government, bright, young people are jumping into electoral politics right away, either as staffers or elected officials themselves. And they often do very well for themselves, thriving in a system that values education, charisma, and intelligence, which they all have.

But that system also rewards less desirable traits like elitism, superficiality, and craftiness, and is very different from the day-to-day reality of life outside the halls of government. And when these bright young people never leave that political system, they end up in powerful positions making important decisions from a narrow and perverted worldview. They are doomed to fail.

When I was in my late twenties working on PA Open for Business, I didn't think there was anything unusual at all about a person who never started a business building a website for people that wanted to start a business. In government, we did that kind of stuff all the time. To compensate for our lack of experience, we called in "experts" from different business organizations to provide advice and feedback.

In hindsight, I realize that most of those "experts" were employees of trade associations who represented the business owners but were not business owners themselves. In other words, they were young and inexperienced, just like us. The real business owners were too busy running their businesses.

Through this episode, I learned something that all my college degrees never taught me. You cannot replace experience. It is nearly impossible to know what a business owner goes through without being a business owner. Just like it is nearly impossible to know what a teacher goes through without being a teacher, or a doctor without being a doctor, or a soldier without being a soldier, or even a parent without being a parent.

That doesn't mean young people can't be effective business owners, or teachers, or doctors, or soldiers, or parents. But it does mean young people probably ought to avoid making too much government policy affecting those people unless and until they have some experience doing those things themselves.

And regarding all the older people who have spent their entire lives making rules about things they know little about, well, maybe they all should take a break and get some experience too. Then they can return to public life and become better public servants.

CHAPTER TWELVE:
A WELCOME REPRIEVE

PREPARED OR NOT, I was about to gain some valuable life experience. On March 1, 2005, Susan and I launched Dellicker Strategies, LLC. We were going to make a run at school broadband projects and see how far we could go. Within a month, we had a half-dozen clients and more work than we could handle. I even went back to Affinity Group and hired my former colleagues as subcontractors to help me with the workload. By the end of summer, we had already paid off the loan.

Our family settled into a comfortable routine. I got out of the house *almost* every day. There was that occasional day when Kevin would come home from work and I'd still be in my pajamas. I'd look at him and say, "It just wasn't in the cards for me to take a shower."

One such morning the state police even came because Eli had called 911 while he was playing with the phone. I was so embarrassed because our three boys were running around half-dressed in a disaster of a kitchen and I was still in my pajamas. I would love to see that trooper's report.

Honestly, I *was* working. Soon after Eli was born, we started our business. I was helping with office work like invoicing and paying the bills. I suppose I tried to blame my poor mothering on my work.

The most amazing time of day came about two in the afternoon when all three boys would take a nap. It would be so quiet, and I often collapsed into bed too. I remember the doctor saying, "When the baby sleeps, you sleep." I took his words to heart.

Having three children less than four years old is an incredible blessing. It was a challenge when they were little, but it was worth every difficult day.

There's more to that story about the police.

About a year earlier, we got a visit to our house in Kutztown from the newest state trooper at the Fogelsville Barracks, Airman Joe. My old friend from the 193rd had finished his enlistment in the Air National Guard and just graduated from the State Police Academy.

Soon after starting his new assignment, Trooper Joe stopped by our neighborhood one afternoon to say hello. Hearing the kids playing in the backyard, he walked around back and was greeted by three happy boys. They were all buck naked, splashing in a plastic swimming pool, and very enthusiastic to see a real-life police officer.

The next visit by Joe was a couple of months later, this time in the evening. Susan was giving the boys a bath. When they saw Trooper Joe pull in the driveway, they excitedly jumped from the tub, ran out the front door and greeted him a second time, again in their birthday suits.

When another policeman stopped by the house just a few weeks later, the officer came to the front door and rang the bell. The boys jumped up and down, excited that Trooper Joe must be visiting again.

Susan yelled a greeting through the window.

"Hi, Joe, we're coming," she said. "But we're fully clothed. Just give us a minute while we all get naked first."

Trooper Joe would have thought that was pretty funny. But it wasn't Trooper Joe. Eli had been playing with the phone and somehow mistakenly dialed 911. The responding officer wasn't amused. I would have loved to hear the ribbing that the real Trooper Joe got from his fellow state troopers after that encounter.

The focus on our new civilian business venture was made possible by a reprieve from our military duties. In 2005, for the first time since I transferred to the Air National Guard, I had a "normal" training cycle—one weekend a month and two weeks a year. Susan and I both wondered how long the break would last.

The US military had toppled the enemy regimes in Afghanistan and Iraq much faster than expected, and most of our soldiers had come home victorious. The passage of time was healing our nation; the acute memories of 9/11 were receding from the forefront of the national psyche. It's not that people had forgotten those terrible events. They were just ready to move on and get back to normal.

Indeed, most of the country was already back to normal. There had been no new terrorist attacks against the US homeland, and the economy was booming again. Military operations had shifted from outright war to nation-building, which did not generate the same dramatic headlines in domestic newspapers. Visitors to the US during the mid-2000s would scarcely have known that the nation was still at war because there were virtually no domestic indicators of a conflict going on overseas.

As the war gradually receded from the public view, the national mood began to change accordingly. The presidential election of 2004 was highly contentious, and President George W. Bush became a deeply polarizing figure. Lots of pundits were saying the Iraq War had been a big mistake, and people were becoming more outspoken in their criticism. Personal attacks increasingly characterized the national discourse, a trend that has continued ever since. And although support for the troops remained sky-high, servicemen and -women were getting caught in the political crossfire.

I remember my first experience with this new attitude. In the summer of 2005, I had to go for a week of military training at Hurlburt Field, Florida. It was the Dynamics of International Terrorism course, where intelligence professionals and security forces personnel get training in how to protect airmen and military facilities from terrorist attacks. It was pretty important training for my career and would impact the safety of 1,800 unit members in my wing.

The course was only a week long, so managing my business while I was gone was no big deal. I couldn't do any substantive work during the day, but I could return important phone calls on breaks and respond to emails in the evenings. Otherwise, my subcontractors or Susan handled things while I was gone.

Well, something happened with one of my projects, and the client wanted to reach me right away. It turned out to be a trivial matter, but she was angry that I was unreachable for her "urgent" problem. She was sick of her people carrying the load while I was away "playing Army," she barked.

As soon as she said that, I think she realized she had overreacted because she immediately backtracked and changed the subject. But those flip comments were typical of the gradual coarsening of civil discourse that defined the 2004 election cycle and has only gotten worse. She would never have described my service in such disparaging terms a few years earlier, but politics was creeping into everything.

Meanwhile, Susan and I took advantage of the lull in the military action to focus on building the business. By September, we had a dozen clients. By October, we had organized them into buying groups and completed all their needs assessments. By November, we issued seven bid specification documents to help them all buy faster broadband service.

In early December, we started receiving proposals from dozens of telecommunications providers. Our team was knee-deep in the evaluation process. We were on track to help about 200 districts drive a massive broadband upgrade in their schools. And if we were successful, it virtually guaranteed follow-on work with hundreds more. Dellicker Strategies was well on its way to establishing itself as the market leader in this niche opportunity and becoming a viable small business.

Then we got the call Susan and I had been dreading.

I was getting deployed.

Some small mission in Iraq was becoming a larger mission, and the 193rd needed more bodies. I was part of a short-notice deployment that would last for at least two months. I had about six weeks to prepare.

The timing was terrible.

Susan and I had both expected this at some point, but not during the first year in the middle of seven huge projects. If I failed during this first go-around, I might never recover. So I did all I could. I asked Affinity Group and the engineering firm to take over my contracts and do the best that they could while I was gone.

On December 19, 2005, I sent a letter to all my clients. Some of them didn't even know I was in the military. It read like this:

"As you may know," I wrote, "I serve part-time as a captain in the Pennsylvania Air National Guard. Recently, I have been given notice that I am needed for a mission in support of the new Iraqi government. I will be deploying to the Middle East on or around January 25, 2006, and returning in late March 2006..."

I told them that they could either continue working with my subcontractors, put the projects on hold, or cancel them outright. While I waited for their answers, I focused on having the best Christmas possible with my family as I got ready to leave again. The boys would be five, four, and almost two years old this time around, so this deployment would be much harder on them. Plus, Susan now had the added stress of keeping the business afloat while I was gone. What a mess.

Then just like that, the deployment got canceled.

The unit called me right before the New Year's holiday to say that the mission had been postponed indefinitely. They didn't say why, but I didn't care. Susan and I felt like we had received a stay of execution from the governor.

On Monday, January 2, 2006, I sent another letter to all my clients, alerting them to the false alarm.

"The situation in Iraq has improved to the point that my unit has been sent home early from our mission there. Members of my unit who already were in the Middle East arrived home safely on New Year's Eve. I will not have to deploy after all..."

Mostly, everyone was gracious and gave me the benefit of the doubt. The "playing Army" lady was especially nice. Nothing much happened over the holidays anyway, so I was able to pick up where I left off. But we had dodged a bullet. From that point on, we had to be much more careful about managing the risks of deployment and planning for military contingencies that might wreck our new business.

Throughout 2006, Susan and I worked hard to grow the broadband business and establish our new company. We enjoyed being home together, tackling challenges as a team, and seeing a different side of each other. Susan was the company chief financial officer, responsible for paying all the bills, invoicing all the clients, and managing the budget. She was a consummate professional. She put on a suit when required but mostly worked from home with the kids all around, sometimes in her bathrobe. Watching her switch back and forth from business-mode to mother-mode was impressive. She was really good at both jobs.

Our unique living and working arrangements provided ample time for family activities. We were both disciplined about not working too much on the weekends or in the evenings, spending as much time as possible together with the kids. Susan and I both wanted to make sure that in pursuing our military and business commitments, we didn't neglect our family.

At some point, Susan bought a small picture of an old barn with the three words inscribed on the bottom:

God. Family. Country.

That picture hangs in our kitchen to remind us of what is most important. We were fortunate to learn these values from our parents, and our hope is that we pass them along to our boys.

Susan's mom and dad met at a church camp near Pittsburgh and became lay leaders in their congregation. Curt devoted much of his free time to the study of Martin Luther. He became an amateur scholar on his subject, learning German and traveling to Europe to study original sources. Sally immersed herself as a church volunteer, becoming a national leader in the women's group and organizing conferences across the country.

From an early age, Susan witnessed how Curt and Sally placed God at the center of their lives. At home, prayer and worship were ubiquitous and meaningful. At work, Curt led the local Fellowship of Christian Athletes and helped students have a safe place to practice their faith. Together, they laid a foundation for Susan that would help her develop a deep personal relationship with Jesus and develop her commitment to being part of a vibrant church community.

My parents did the same. I, too, was raised in a Christian household and attended church regularly. At one point, my mom Trudie was the church secretary, and I remember sitting on the living room floor with my sisters, helping her fold bulletins. My dad was on the church council and would attend meetings in the evenings when I was a boy. From the time I can remember, my parents were reading the Bible to me and teaching me about Jesus. Like in Susan's childhood home, God was a regular part of our lives.

So was the military. In the Frank household, Susan's exposure to the armed services was limited to stories about her grandfather. She grew up in a home that respected military service but never experienced it. In the Dellicker household, the military was a big part of everyday life.

My grandfather, Willard C. Dellicker, was a fighter pilot in World War II flying P-38s in Italy. He remained in the Air Force Reserves for decades after he got off active duty, and I remember visiting his old unit as a young boy.

My father, Bill, retired as a colonel in the Air National Guard. He is a bona fide war hero, completing three tours of duty on aircraft carriers in Vietnam. At one point, he was the youngest combat pilot in the Navy. He is a member of the Pennsylvania Air National Guard Hall of Fame, a rare honor that serves as a fitting capstone to an outstanding military career.

My mom, Trudie, learned firsthand the trials of a military wife, moving around the country and giving birth to me while Bill was away at war. She could write a book on her feelings about people she loves serving in the combat zone. Was it harder for her when her husband was flying over Vietnam or when her son was on the ground in Afghanistan? Only she knows.

From the A-4 tailhook mounted over our fireplace to the pictures of my parents and their military friends on the wall, military service and patriotism were prominent features in our household and strong influences in my life.

Susan and I wanted our children to understand their heritage and learn these values, but we didn't want to leave it up to chance. They weren't learning all they needed about Jesus from weekends at church, and they weren't learning about God in the public schools. Although our boys had firsthand experience with the military, they didn't understand what it was all about. We made a concerted effort to do more and make sure they were learning what we thought was most important.

Susan and I decided to create an informal program of learning for our children that would reflect the priorities we sought to convey. The "curriculum" would supplement the boys' Sunday school lessons and regular school district learning to reflect our values. In a play on our last name, we called it the Dill Creek School for Boys.

We came up with age-appropriate "lessons" in our three priority subjects: God, Family, and Country. Each year, from first to twelfth grade, our three boys would learn something substantive in each category, and we would keep a record of their progress that we would give to them when they graduated high school. Essentially, it would be a scrapbook of memories that would reflect years of lessons and learning.

On the subject of God, we would start slow and get more rigorous as they got older. In the early lessons, our boys had to learn stories of Biblical heroes and memorize the Ten Commandments. Later, they would read books like *The Screwtape Letters* by C.S. Lewis and listen to lectures from intellectuals like Ravi Zacharias and Alistair Begg. We made it a point to help our children feel comfortable talking about their faith.

For the "Family" component, we made the kids pick a family member and write about their family tree. Then they had to come up with ten questions and record an interview with them on video. These videos are archived for the boys and hopefully will be treasured memories for them as they grow up and start their own lives.

The "Country" part consisted of two components—lessons about American history and corresponding instruction about different places around the world. Sometimes, these were rigorous assignments. For example, we made the kids identify all fifty states on a map in first grade and all the countries in Europe in second grade. We had them read and report on the Declaration of Independence, the US Constitution, and numerous biographies about the founding fathers while they were still in grade school.

Often, they complained. But by the time they reached high school, those extra efforts paid dividends. Dill Creek taught each of our boys about the Bible, introduced them to their extended family, and helped them understand what it means to be an American. Susan and I hope that it fosters a lifelong commitment to these priorities in our boys and that they will someday pass along the values of God, Family, and Country to their own children.

Meanwhile, my military obligations remained manageable. Compared to the early years of the Global War on Terrorism, serving in 193rd in the mid-2000s seemed like a piece of cake. I suppose that's how being in the reserves is supposed to be. When there is a big war, you get called up. Otherwise, you live a relatively normal life.

That's what I had experienced in the Army, and now it was happening in the Air Force.

With no new rotations to the Middle East, most of my service was related to my new additional duty: intelligence support to force protection. I was responsible for coordinating with the base security forces and wing leadership to prepare anti-terrorism plans for the base. I had already completed the Dynamics of International Terrorism class, which was the introductory level of training. Now I had to attend the so-called Responsible Officer's Course at Hurlburt Field, a more advanced course for military force protection.

It was pretty intense. We had to pretend we were in a foreign country and hunted by terrorists. The instructors would break into our hotel rooms and mess with our stuff, so you could never let down your guard. They would attach pretend magnet bombs to our rental cars in fast-food parking lots and take videos of our trips to buy groceries. Then they would show the videos to the class so you could see what a lousy job you did pulling security.

For most of that class, I was sure that somebody was going to call the cops on us for staking out public buildings and surveilling transportation hubs. But we got through the week without incident. Then I went home to do more broadband projects and play with the kids.

The unit family support group organized a C-130 airplane ride for spouses. I couldn't wait. I was going to fly on a military cargo plane to Niagara Falls.

We all got on board the airplane and took off. The flight was much shorter than I expected. When we arrived, we all took turns looking out the windows and peering out the cockpit.

The falls were breathtaking. I had seen them before, but this perspective was amazing. You could see the entire falls at the same time, from the river flowing down from the top to the mist rising up from the bottom. We flew home over Lake Ontario, passing so low at times it felt like we were waterskiing.

It was exhilarating. But the real value was understanding how Kevin and his fellow airmen traveled. There were no stewardesses, few windows, and mesh seats. And it was loud—so loud. The bathroom was a toilet open to full view. You could close the curtain, but I imagine many of the men probably didn't use it. It was just a little reality check for me, reminding me that his deployments were no vacation.

By early 2007, we were entering the third year of Dellicker Strategies, and the business was growing. But the workload was getting too much for Susan and me to handle alone, and I still didn't have a good plan in place in case I got deployed again. It was time to hire my first employee.

I put out feelers to friends and professional colleagues for an assistant. I figured I could hire somebody who could interface with the clients in a way Susan could not do as a stay-at-home mom and also handle some of the analysis and number crunching. Before I could get organized and formally advertise the job opening, I got a call from Christine.

Christine had learned about the position from a telecommunications executive whom she knew from a previous job. She was a marketing major working for a web design firm in Harrisburg as their chief operations officer with fifteen years of experience in the software industry. She didn't know anything about broadband, wasn't qualified to crunch numbers, and except for her work with the soccer booster club, had no experience working with schools. Plus, she wanted more than double the salary I was prepared to offer.

Right. I wasn't interested.

Undeterred, Christine found out where I was delivering a speech on broadband infrastructure and nosed her way into the audience.

Afterward, she asked to meet with me about the job. She had done her homework. In a half-hour discussion, she laid out the case that I didn't need an assistant. I needed an executive, somebody who could develop new business, interact with senior leaders, and manage subcontractors and future employees. Most important, she argued that I needed somebody to run the business when I got deployed.

Christine had guts. I didn't want to spend the cash to pay her what she wanted, but she made an intriguing case about what the business needed. I invited her to a follow-up interview with Susan at a diner halfway between Kutztown and Harrisburg, where she lived. Susan liked her, and we made her an offer on the spot. Dellicker Strategies had its first employee. Now I just had to figure out how to pay her.

Christine was a wonderful addition to the team. Smart, funny, and engaging, she connected with my clients and subcontractors. In the field of telecom and educational technology, almost everybody is a man. She added a fresh perspective to our work and new people skills to our team. When I ruffled feathers, she would smooth things over. She was always a fierce defender of the company, and more importantly, she had my back.

CHAPTER THIRTEEN: FINISHING THE JOB

IT DIDN'T TAKE LONG to test Christine's mettle. A few weeks after she started her new position with Dellicker Strategies, I got another call from the 193rd. The situation in Iraq had deteriorated, and the country was on the brink of full-blown civil war. President Bush, on the recommendation of his newly appointed commander General David Petraeus, had ordered a so-called "troop surge" to stop and reverse the violence. I would be a part of the surge.

I had just gotten about six new contracts, and the ink was barely dry on the agreements before I told them I had to leave. I was still using my old friends at Affinity Group to help with the technical work, so I wasn't leaving Christine in the lurch completely. But the projects were so new that I didn't have much time to get them started. They would succeed or fail based on her ability to manage them, and she had no experience in the field. I left for my second rotation to Operation IRAQI FREEDOM on the tenth of July. I would have no communication with her or my clients for the duration of the deployment.

Nor would I have any communication with my family. Susan was preparing to hold down the fort again. Will had just turned seven, Jake was five, and Eli was three. In the fall, all of them would be in school of some kind—Will in first grade, Jake in half-day kindergarten, and Eli in a part-time preschool program. But for the duration of the summer, they would all be home with Mom. She did her best to make it like a vacation, albeit a vacation without Dad.

Friends and family were a blessing. After our ignominious beginnings, we had become great friends with our neighbors in Kutztown. Next door lived Eric and Rebecca, who our boys called Eric the Dad and Mama Becca. They had two kids who were a few years older than our boys, Christopher and Elizabeth. Almost every day, Eric the Dad would be working in his garage, which faced our house, and the kids would be playing together in the driveway.

Across the street was Mrs. Anette and Uncle Dave, the former red beet man. If our kids weren't hanging out with Eric the Dad and Mama Becca, they were probably over at Dave's house. Most summer evenings, Dave would crack a Coors Lite and sit out in his driveway, joking around and teasing the kids. He had a refrigerator in his garage stocked with beer for himself and the neighbors and juice boxes for the boys. They would just go over and help themselves. Dave would tell them stories about fishing, push the kids on the swing, or even fight them with *Star Wars* lightsabers.

On the other side of the house lived Steve and Kathy. Kathy was a successful businesswoman who worked for a Fortune 500 company, and Steve was a mailman. They spoiled our kids with candy and stuffed animals. One time, Will was climbing on their fence and broke one of the rails. Kevin made him go over to take responsibility and apologize. Instead, Will came home with a handful of Kit Kat bars.

It was a wonderful neighborhood and a safe place for kids. We always had friends looking out for us and the boys, even when they did things that would make other parents cringe.

For example, Will heard us talking about the business one day and asked me if he could start his own. I told him the best businesses were those that provided something other people needed. Later that day, our neighbor Becky, who lived down the street, found Will with a red wagon full of toilet paper, selling rolls from our bathroom door-to-door for a buck apiece.

Not to be outdone, Jake used the same wagon two weeks later to sell cans of beer around the neighborhood for a dollar a can. By the time we found out, the wagon was empty, Jake had twenty dollars in his pocket, and the dads in the neighborhood were feeling no pain.

To break up the time when I was gone, my parents took Susan and the boys to the Jersey shore with the extended family. Aunt Sheri and Uncle Todd were there along with cousins Nolan and Reagan. Uncle Greg and Aunt Jodi kept the kids entertained. Greg especially made the boys laugh with his goofy stories and tall tales. Back at home, Susan could drop off the boys to go swimming at Grandma and Grandpa's when she needed a break.

Susan also spent a couple of weeks at her parents' house in Conneaut Lake. Since my last deployment, they completed their retirement move from Beaver in the Pittsburgh suburbs to northwestern Pennsylvania, where they had a bungalow near the lake. They decided to knock it down and build a new house that could accommodate our whole family coming to visit.

At the lake, Curt and Sally had a boat and a dock to go swimming and fishing. Visiting them was like being on vacation. Usually, Uncle Jimmy and Aunt Tina drove in from Pittsburgh to make it even more fun. The boys had a ball and probably never even missed me.

Or maybe they did.

It had been four years since I had gone away for more than two weeks at a time. None of the boys even remembered my previous deployments. This time though, they noticed my absence, and at least the older boys were beginning to understand what it meant to be fighting a war and that Dad was in it.

Will told his teacher that he feared terrorists hiding under his bed. Jake worried that "Salami Balata," his way of pronouncing "Osama bin Laden," was going after his dad. Although my kids looked normal as they played through the summer, they were dealing with secret boogeymen that other kids didn't have to face. Perhaps I will never know how this affected them. And Susan, instead of just having to manage her own feelings, now had to take care of the boys' feelings too.

Meanwhile, I was at a classified location in the Middle East, launching airplanes with the 193rd. It was hotter than anything I had experienced before, with temperatures routinely reaching 120 degrees. They would place pallets of bottled water at various places around the base, so you could just grab a bottle as you walked by. But if you drank it without cooling it down first, it was like guzzling hot tea.

They also had these cool-looking desert foxes roaming around the flight line. Mostly, they came out after dark, but you could hear them yipping and barking at all hours. They had beady eyes and huge ears, and despite orders to leave them alone, some of the guys treated them like pets. That was a bad idea.

One night, after a long flight over Iraq, one of those foxes slipped into a C-130 in search of leftover food. Whoever was the last person off the plane didn't notice, and that poor creature got locked in the airplane.

The next day, when the maintenance crew opened the hatch to prepare for the next mission, they got a surprise. I don't know who was more scared: the dehydrated, shell-shocked fox or the unsuspecting airman who got a face full of flying fur when he opened the door. The Iraqi terrorists couldn't stop our aircraft, but that little fox did. We missed a mission cleaning up fox feces and urine all over the plane.

Since we flew mostly at night, I slept during the day. I would wake up around three in the afternoon, put on my uniform, and go right to work. I would assist the mission planners with the flight route, prepare the pre-mission briefings, and then stick around to launch the airplane. Then I would go work out at the gym, take care of any errands, and go back to the mission control center to recover the plane and debrief the crew. By that time, it was dawn and time for my dinner.

Since the rest of the base was on a normal schedule, my dinnertime was always breakfast in the chow hall. So every day for the entire summer, my dinner was scrambled eggs with sausage gravy, bacon, and hash browns with a whole bunch of Tabasco sauce on top. Not exactly the healthiest routine, but I didn't snack, I didn't drink alcohol, and I exercised every day. As long as I didn't take a cholesterol test, I was fine.

At these Air Force bases, you could get fat if you weren't careful. All kinds of companies donated food for the troops, and you could grab an Otis Spunkmeyer muffin whenever you wanted to indulge. I learned to drink Starbucks coffee overseas since their employees donated truckloads of their product to military bases all over the place. I have loved Starbucks ever since.

Army guys coming through Air Force bases couldn't believe how good our food was. They were eating MREs day after day at these forward operating bases (FOBs) across Iraq, and we were getting hot meals of pork chops, chicken, and even occasional steak. We had salad bars and ice cream machines and all kinds of juices. And you could usually get a second helping if you wanted. I always looked forward to the Air Force food, but maybe that was colored by my past relationship with Army food, which wasn't quite as gourmet.

Others in the intel shop didn't share my sentiment. Once, during a family day event at the 193rd, I overheard Airman Joe saying to another guy in our shop, "Susan must be a really bad cook, because Kevin keeps saying how much he loves Air Force food."

Our deployment during Operation IRAQI FREEDOM II was to support the troop surge. Although we still were tasked with broadcasting radio messages to Iraqi civilians, our main mission was different this time. We were going to conduct an electronic attack in support of the soldiers and Marines on the ground.

An electronic attack involves many things, and the details of our mission remain classified SECRET. The basic idea is to transmit electrons over some frequency the receiving end can pick up. For radio broadcasts, this is simple. You play live or recorded content, like news or music, over a frequency that can be received by a radio receiver. But the same concept works if you blast white noise (static) over an enemy combatant's hand-held radios. If you know the frequencies and can transmit with high enough power, you can effectively render their battlefield communications useless. This is called jamming, and it's just one kind of electronic attack.

We had a whole electronic attack operations center at the base, which included our unit and other assets performing similar missions. One of the young officers from a different unit was a ring-knocking patch-wearer. Ring-knockers are condescending Air Force Academy graduates who want you to know they are special by the oversized class rings on their fingers. Patch-wearers are obnoxious graduates of various Air Force weapon schools who display prominent insignia on their uniforms and speak a specialized jargon designed to make you feel stupid.

Not all graduates of the Academy are ring-knockers, and not all graduates of weapon school are patch-wearers, but the stereotypes exist for a reason. Put a ring-knocker together with a patch-wearer, and you sometimes end up with a real jerk.

That guy tested my mettle as a captain. I don't remember his name. Let's just call him Lieutenant Patch. Clearly, he knew far more about electronic attacks than anybody else in the room. He probably had forgotten more about the mission than I would ever learn. But he treated people like dirt, especially young NCOs and airmen in the National Guard.

I first observed Lieutenant Patch belittling an airman from his own unit. The airman had made a minor mistake, and Lieutenant Patch was letting him have it. Not wanting to get involved in another unit's dispensation of discipline, I kept my mouth shut.

But it didn't stop there. Lieutenant Patch continued to ride this kid and others in the shop for all kinds of trivial things. He would bark instructions in his jargon nobody else understood, and people were too afraid to ask for clarification. Soon, this guy's tyranny was affecting the entire office. Even my bosses, who were lieutenant colonels, were intimidated by him. When he unfairly berated one of the airmen from my unit, I had to intervene.

Even though he acted like a general, Lieutenant Patch was still just a lieutenant, and I outranked him. I ordered him out of the operations center into a different room and lit into him like a drill sergeant at basic training. For about five minutes, I gave him the best dressing down I could muster. It was mostly an act, but I yelled so loudly I went hoarse. The entire building could hear me screaming at him. When it was over, I walked back into the operations center, sat down, and acted like nothing had happened.

I was sure I had just created a massive problem for myself, but I never heard a thing from my bosses or the other unit. I think everybody knew the guy was acting like a jerk and they probably appreciated my intervention, especially those young airmen. I'm pretty sure I didn't suddenly reform him into a more patient and empathetic officer, but Lieutenant Patch never gave me or anyone else in the office a hard time after that. Maybe he did listen to what I had to say. Sometimes a spanking is effective.

Besides that one guy, everybody else was a pleasure to work with. There were a lot of young people in the operations center, including twentysomethings from all different backgrounds. The commander of the operations center let them watch music videos in the background, and they found an Arabic television station that constantly played pop music from all over the world. I learned a bunch of songs from artists I would never have otherwise heard. My favorites were "Umbrella" from Rihanna, "Wake Up Call" by Maroon Five, and "Las da la Intuicion" from Shakira.

When we weren't singing along to Shakira's purple-hair video, our unit flew missions throughout the summer, supporting the US troops on the ground. As US forces brought new firepower against the terrorists and insurgents, we defeated the enemy strongholds one by one. Gradually, most foreign al-Qaida fighters either got killed or went home, and most of the native insurgents laid down their arms. President Bush's resolve had been strong, and General Petraeus' new strategy had been critical. But ultimately, it was the blood and sweat of American servicemen and -women who eventually finished the job and created the conditions for us to come home. The troop surge had worked.

The 193rd came home in September of 2007, knowing we had again been part of something important. Time and again, our electronic attack transmissions had helped American soldiers and Marines gain battlefield advantage by jamming the communications of enemy combatants. We had demonstrated the resiliency of our platform with a broader mission set and established the relevancy of our aircraft in combat missions outside of special operations. Our small group of part-time airmen had proven its value once again.

CHAPTER FOURTEEN:
DOMESTIC OPERATIONS

I RETURNED HOME TO Susan and three independent-minded boys. In previous deployments, the boys had been babies; they hadn't contributed any productive work to the household and had required no special handling. If they could speak at all, they mostly did what they were told.

But the boys were older now, and they were active participants in the Dellicker economy, both contributing and consuming resources. While I was gone, the boys had been given more responsibilities, and Susan had created a new routine to maintain order in the household.

When I got home, I messed all that up.

It was innocent enough. I didn't set out to be a monkey wrench in Susan's system. But I was. And my homecoming was not so pleasant this time.

The first day was bliss. Instead of having her meet me in Harrisburg, I told Susan to stay with the kids and that I would just drive home myself. I found out from my friend Joe that they were all going to be at his house for a family picnic, so I drove straight there from the base. I didn't even change out of my uniform. I surprised Susan and the boys and got to see a bunch of my friends in another storybook homecoming. I brought a bunch of Army hats for all the neighbor kids.

The following Tuesday was the first day of school. Susan had already purchased all the back-to-school clothes and student supplies, and the boys' schedules were all set. She had also signed them up for fall sports like T-ball and youth soccer, which were already underway. I was like an eager beaver, trying to assist her with all these tasks and priorities but mostly just getting in her way.

From my point of view, I just wanted to help. From her perspective, I was micromanaging her process and questioning her judgment. It was a textbook case of redeployment angst that has probably affected every military family since the beginning of time.

At some point, we lost it. Instead of providing a happy morning for our oldest boys, who were experiencing the school bus together for the very first time, Susan and I got engaged in a screaming match. I don't remember what set us off, but we were ridiculous. We barely got it together before we got the kids on the bus, and their back-to-school photos showed the angst on their faces. We blew it.

I'd like to say we just kissed and made up after that awful morning, but we continued to struggle for some time. She had managed the household just fine while I was gone, and now I was back home, disrupting her routine. There was no formula to fix the problem. We just gradually got back to normal, except for me singing songs by Shakira in Spanish.

On the business side of our lives, normal meant jumping right back into Dellicker Strategies. I had gotten home on Friday night, spent Labor Day weekend getting reacquainted with my family, and went back to work on Tuesday. I was less than one week removed from planning combat missions over Iraq and one hour removed from my screamfest with Susan, and now I had to figure out what happened with school broadband projects while I was gone.

Christine was happy to hear from me and filled me in on all the details. Some problems needed fixing, and some people were difficult, but overall, everything was on track toward success. She had performed very well in my absence and had earned my trust. I spent the rest of 2007 working with familiar people doing familiar things, helping even more schools get better broadband.

By the end of the next year, Dellicker Strategies would connect almost 350 public school districts to high-speed networks, more than two-thirds of all school districts in Pennsylvania. And we were driving big improvements in technology capacity, increasing average bandwidth by 850 percent. Our little company was accomplishing big things for schools, and we were starting to branch out into other areas.

With the business growing and successful projects piling up, Susan and I were increasingly confident in the sustainability of Dellicker Strategies. But after a demanding third deployment and unexpectedly difficult homecoming, we weren't quite as confident about the ongoing viability of my military career.

I had seen it happen to plenty of other guys in the unit. Some would get divorced. Some would get ultimatums. I remember one of our best young officers getting promoted to major. He had already demonstrated outstanding skills as a combat aviator and was poised to become a squadron commander. His wife was there to pin on his rank with a brood of young children, but her anxious eyes betrayed her contrived smile. A few months later, we heard his wife had given him a choice: *me or the military*. We never saw him again.

Susan wouldn't do that to me, although I really wouldn't have blamed her if she did. But she did express her opinions. She let it be known that the constant threat of getting sent overseas was taking its toll on her and the family. The regular deployments were incompatible with a normal suburban lifestyle, and something had to give. She was right.

One thing most people don't realize is that for many National Guardsmen, deployments are a financial burden. Ours were. Every time I got deployed, it cost us money.

The first time we experienced a reduction in pay due to prolonged military duty was when we went to intelligence school in Texas. My military salary as a second lieutenant was significantly less than what I earned in the governor's office, and Susan gave up a good-paying job to stay at home with Will. We took a pay cut again in 2001 for

Operation ENDURING FREEDOM and again in 2003 for Operation IRAQI FREEDOM.

With the business, I wasn't just forgoing a higher salary for lower military pay. Now I had to hire replacement workers to handle my contracts while I was gone. During the summer of 2007, those extra workers cost a lot of money. We lost several thousand dollars that year when I deployed.

I don't write about this to evoke anybody's sympathy, and I'm not complaining. The military pays quite well. But most active-duty servicemen and -women get bonuses when they go to the combat zone. Taking a pay cut to go to war is another aspect of part-time military service unique to the Guard and Reserves and affects thousands of soldiers and airmen.

Retirement benefits were a factor in our conversations about whether to stay in the Guard. I had already been in the service for twelve years and needed twenty before I could earn a military retirement. But National Guard retirement is very different from active-duty retirement, and I wasn't sure it was worth it.

On active duty, after you complete twenty years of service, you can retire and immediately start to draw a pension worth 2.5 percent of your average final three years of salary times every year of service. That means if you enlist at age eighteen, you can retire at thirty-eight and start drawing half your active-duty salary for the rest of your life.

Not so in the Guard. You still have to stay in twenty years to get any retirement benefit at all, but once you retire, your part-time service accrues a part-time benefit. Plus, you generally can't receive any retirement at all until you reach the age of sixty. New laws have improved this system for new recruits, but we were still in the old system.

So while we discussed financial issues, they weren't the deciding factor in our discussions about whether to stay in the Guard or get out. Mostly, we were worried about our lifestyle. Specifically, we were increasingly concerned about our ability to juggle all these priorities as our kids got older and demanded more of our attention.

The high operations tempo at the 193rd had not eased up like we thought it might, and our recent success in more mission sets virtually ensured that we would continue to go on the road. The unit was already asking me about returning to the combat zone in 2008. I knew that if I were to stay in the 193rd, I would need to plan for regular overseas deployments, at least every other year. Susan and I just weren't prepared to do that anymore.

So we came up with a compromise. I would stay in the military, but with a different unit with a less intense deployment schedule. After all, the 193rd was the most deployed unit in the Air National Guard, so anything would be less than what we were currently experiencing. It seemed like a great plan, but there was an important problem. I didn't know whether a job like that existed.

One promising area seemed to be in domestic operations (DOMOPS). Although overseas combat deployments dominated my own National Guard career, the rest of the National Guard retained its core mission to help US citizens respond to snowstorms, hurricanes, floods, and assorted natural disasters. Its importance was growing fast since the Guard was the first line of defense against domestic terrorism.

The attacks in New York and Washington had demonstrated the need for better coordination between the military and civilian authorities. So the federal government, in collaboration with state and local jurisdictions, created a new system to manage all this. It was called the National Incident Management System (NIMS) and the related Incident Command System (ICS). These new agreements laid out all the rules for how military and civilian leaders would work together in response to domestic emergencies.

Every state had a role, and the Pennsylvania National Guard was one of the first headquarters in the nation to establish a joint military command structure for domestic operations, known as the Pennsylvania Joint Force Headquarters (JFHQ). Leaders from the Air and Army National Guard developed an ad hoc organization to test these new capabilities and create a joint emergency operations center (JEOC) that could integrate a civilian and military response to anything from a flu pandemic to a 9/11 style attack.

My new boss at the 193rd, the newly promoted Major Hedges, knew I was looking for a change. She found me the perfect opportunity. She arranged for me to get the job of the first air intelligence officer to JFHQ. My new base would be Fort Indiantown Gap, half an hour closer to Kutztown than the Harrisburg Airport, and I would be on the ground floor of an entirely new organization. Plus, I would not have to deploy overseas.

I thanked Major Hedges and took the job. It was a bittersweet transition. I loved the overseas mission of the 193rd and was going to miss my friends there. But I owed it to Susan and my family to make a change. This seemed like the perfect opportunity. In the fall of 2007, I said goodbye to the 193rd and became a member of JFHQ. I was going to make the best of it.

I knew Fort Indiantown Gap well. I had spent many weekends there doing training with the Army and could find my way around the ranges and the garrisons. Since I would be working with soldiers in this new position, I figured my infantry background and familiarity with the base would provide instant rapport with my new Army counterparts.

I also knew about the Gap because of the 201st REDHORSE Squadron, which was also there. REDHORSE stands for "Rapid Engineers Deployable Heavy Operational Repair Squadron Engineer." That mouthful means "construction" in Air Force lingo, and they know how to build things. REDHORSE was the unit that my father used to command, and I had visited the squadron many times as a child.

When my dad got out of the Navy, he went to college at Penn State Harrisburg on the GI Bill and joined the Air National Guard. After getting his degree in mechanical engineering technology, he went to work at the 201st REDHORSE Squadron, the Air Force version of the Navy Seabees and the Army Corps of Engineers.

My father loved being in REDHORSE. As he described it, it had two separate flights—one that built things upward and one that built things outward. The "upward" flight made buildings and structures. The "outward" flight made roads and airfields. Together, REDHORSE could build just about anything.

A unit like REDHORSE is especially suited for part-time service because its members are often experts in their military trades as civilians, so there is no dropoff in skill levels when they put on the uniform. They contribute something to the fight that the active duty cannot even approach.

In the late 1970s and 1980s, when my father was in the unit, the US was still fighting the Cold War. REDHORSE had to do a lot of goodwill projects around the world. They built baseball fields in Germany, roads in Honduras, and buildings in England. These projects would ensure proficiency in their core competencies while making practical and useful things for our allies.

REDHORSE epitomized the motto, "Work Hard, Play Hard." Introduced by the first commander of the 201st, this idea guided subsequent commanders, including my dad, and would come to define the REDHORSE culture. The squadron earned a well-deserved reputation for outstanding craftsmanship and an equally deserved reputation for having a good time.

When I arrived at the Gap, I ran into some people from REDHORSE who knew my dad when he was commander. They told me stories about him and how he interacted with his airmen. Some of the stories were serious. A lot were funny. All of them ended with people working together to achieve amazing things. The airmen in REDHORSE loved my father, and he loved them right back. It was a real pleasure to hear them speak about my dad in this way.

Since JFHQ was brand new, there was no job description. I would need to make it up for myself. My new boss, Colonel Frank, gave me a list of names of people I would be working with, mostly Army officers and NCOs. He told me to introduce myself and ask about their expectations for my role. Then at the end of the weekend, we could regroup and get organized. That seemed reasonable to me. So I started to knock on doors and say hello.

One of the first people I met was Brigadier General John Gronski, the former commander of the 2nd Brigade Combat Team of the 28th Infantry Division (2/28 BCT), which had recently completed a tour of Iraq. He was pleasant and engaged and welcomed me to JFHQ. I didn't know much about him, but I knew he and his soldiers had experienced some of the heaviest combat in western Iraq and had fought with valor. He was an experienced veteran, and I was honored to be working with him.

The Army National Guard of 2007 was very different from the Army National Guard of 1998, when I was a sergeant in Charlie Company. Soon after 9/11, the Guard had gotten rid of its tin can M-113s and received state-of-the-art Strykers, the Army's newest armored fighting vehicles. My old unit in Kutztown had already deployed for a year to Kosovo for peacekeeping duties. Now they were preparing for a difficult combat deployment to Taji, Iraq.

Some of the most intense fighting of Operation IRAQI FREEDOM was borne by 2,100 Pennsylvania Army National Guard soldiers assigned to the 2/28 BCT.[1] Nicknamed the "Iron Brigade," this fighting force was a mix of Guard units from around the country organized in early 2005 to provide extra combat power to the active duty. There were infantry grunts from Pennsylvania, armored troops from Vermont, field artillery soldiers from Utah, and intelligence analysts from Kentucky. Nebraska sent a contingent of cavalry troops, Indiana offered a signal company, and Tennessee provided a maintenance unit.[2]

Most active-duty units train together for years before entering combat as a cohesive fighting force. But the Pennsylvania National Guard was already being used for other combat deployments and had to borrow troops from other states to accomplish the mission. By the time the 2/28 BCT made it to Iraq, they had Guardsmen and Reservists from thirty-five states and Puerto Rico, plus some additional Marines, Air National Guardsmen, Sailors, and Iraqi Army troops to round out the force.[3]

The Iron Brigade went into the heart of al-Anbar Province, the stronghold of the Iraqi insurgency and the most dangerous place in the country. Their enemies were as diverse as they were formidable. There were the al-Qaida extremists who fought for religious reasons, the nationalists who wanted Americans to leave, the former Baath Party officials who were holding onto power, and the criminals who just wanted to fight everybody to make money. Individually, each of these groups could wreak havoc on the local population and US military presence. Together, they created a cesspool of violence and strife. It was the mission of the Iron Brigade to get the situation under control.[4]

For almost a year, Pennsylvania National Guardsmen led near-daily combat missions against the enemy, killing and capturing more than 2,400 insurgents. The 2/28 BCT oversaw stable elections in December of 2005 and the establishment of a new police force in Ramadi. Their progress through mid-2006 set the conditions for the eventual defeat of the insurgency in western Iraq in 2007 after the so-called "troop surge."[5] But they paid a steep price. Eighty-two members of the Iron Brigade did not make it home.[6]

My former platoon leader at Charlie Company in Kutztown, Rich Howett, deployed with the 2/28 BCT as an infantry officer and served as battle captain and company commander of the BCT Headquarters Company. I knew Major Howett as a competent and disciplined officer who cared very much for his men, but also a hard and intense leader who didn't tolerate stupid mistakes.

He returned a different man. I saw him about a year after he returned from Iraq. He was not just a combat veteran, but an officer who had lost soldiers under his command. He still had that same tough demeanor and the wry grin, but there was a softer edge. He had learned, in his own words, "the price of sacrifice and a deep humility."

Rich, now retired, will retain to the end of his life the memory of those soldiers in his command who paid that ultimate sacrifice. And like many of those who served with the 2/28 BCT, he will retain the memory of violent scenes. Perhaps paradoxically for many who have served, Rich said that it was then, and is now, extremely difficult to relate those experiences to others who had not been present.

He opened up to me about his time in al-Anbar, and I listened attentively to everything he said. But even a fellow service member who spent time in the infantry and completed several overseas deployments himself cannot fully understand what Rich experienced in the hell of direct combat.

Rich does keep in touch with many of his former soldiers, but unlike many of our active-duty counterparts, keeping in touch is rarely personal. More often, it is via email, Facebook, and other social media. Outside of those rare times Rich does attend reunions, there is, to his knowledge, only one other person living locally to him who served in either Iraq or Afghanistan. Rich often goes about his daily life knowing full well the indelible mark his service in the Pennsylvania National Guard left on his life but also knowing he must shoulder that burden secretly and alone.

As I walked around State Headquarters that weekend, I realized that most other senior Army National Guard officers at the time didn't have the same experiences as Brigadier General Gronski or Major Howett. It seemed that if a soldier had the rank of major or below, he or she probably saw combat in the Global War on Terrorism. But with few exceptions, most soldiers above the level of lieutenant colonel generally had missed out on the recent deployments. That caused an interesting dynamic among the Army officers at headquarters, where the young officers had more combat experience than the older officers, some of whom never deployed anywhere.

I went through my list from Colonel Frank and had a good weekend talking to all my new colleagues. Everyone seemed eager to work with me and was forthcoming about the pros and cons of headquarters duties. I learned a lot about the unit's mission, the training requirements, and unit culture, at least so I thought.

The last guy I had to meet was an Army colonel. Let's just call him Colonel X—no need to disclose his real name. He was my direct Army boss and a senior intelligence advisor to the Joint Staff. I hadn't deliberately chosen to meet with him last; he just hadn't been around when I stopped in before. I knocked on his door, walked in, and smiled as I held out my hand to shake hello.

"Shut the door," he said to me. He didn't accept my handshake.

I shut the door, and for the next fifteen minutes or so, I endured a tongue-lashing the likes of which I hadn't experienced since my introductory weekend at Army OCS.

"How dare you talk to my people without my permission!" he barked. "You will never again speak to a brigadier general in this building unless he addresses you first, Captain!" he said. And so on, and so on.

I suppose I could have quibbled with him and protested that his boss Colonel Frank had told me to meet with all those people, but it didn't matter. He was offended, and I didn't know why. I decided just to stand there respectfully until he was through.

Finally, he scowled, "Do you understand?"

"Yes, sir!" I said and left his presence. Thank goodness.

Shell-shocked, I went back up to Colonel Frank to explain what happened and try to understand what possibly had gone wrong. Perhaps Colonel X was defensive about his authority or had some kind of inferiority complex? Maybe he was intimidated that a young Air Force intelligence officer with lots of experience had arrived on the scene?

Regardless, I was discouraged and disgusted. I had just completed my third combat zone tour and was a competent intelligence professional eager to serve in a new capacity. But my new boss had a chip on his shoulder and was angry at me for no apparent reason. It was one weekend into my new job, and I was already second-guessing my decision.

Colonel Frank told me to stick with the plan and lighten up. He would talk to Colonel X. Things would get better. Besides, Colonel X was retiring soon, and I would get a new boss within a year or two anyway. I decided to take his advice, put my head down, and plow ahead.

The next month, I tackled a simple task: preparing and delivering SECRET briefings for the Joint Staff. The leaders of the Pennsylvania National Guard rarely received classified intelligence briefings, and I was well qualified to fill this gap. I laid out a schedule for regular classified briefings on the places where Pennsylvania soldiers and airmen were deployed, the local terrorist threats, and other developments about military affairs and international relations for situational awareness.

That backfired. Colonel X saw this as another example of me trying to do his job. He worked to keep the briefings off the schedule, and I ended up delivering them for Air staff only. The Army would have to do without.

Undaunted, I thought that maybe we were just having a communications problem. I floated the idea to Colonel Frank of a state intelligence conference, where senior officers and NCOs from the Air and Army Guard intelligence units could get together, meet each other and share a little bit about what they do. Not only did this seem harmless, but it was also very useful. If we were going to work together on domestic operations missions, we'd better start understanding the various capabilities and limitations of units around the state.

That effort also crashed and burned. All the Air units immediately responded and agreed to participate, but the Army units were forbidden to attend. It seemed like a silly and petty response to a perfectly legitimate endeavor.

I had learned my lesson. Sticking my neck out to have it chopped off was a bad idea. So I became a turtle. I'd only stick my head out when it was safe. Otherwise, I'd stay inside my shell. That was not my style, but at least I could be productive. Plus, I refused to let others ruin my precious days in uniform.

I decided to use my time at headquarters to get more training. I got certified in NIMS and ICS. I attended conferences in Washington, D.C., and Fort Huachuca about domestic operations, the homeland response force (HRF), and various intelligence systems. I got smart in joint planning, aviation support to domestic operations, and incident awareness and assurance, which was essentially the application of intelligence-related tools and skills in a homeland security environment.

I stayed out of trouble. But it was boring. I kept telling myself that this was good for my family and that it wouldn't last forever, but for the first time in my military career, I hated going to drill. So I focused on other things.

The business was one. I was diversifying my broadband practice by focusing on other industries besides schools. After succeeding in the K-12 marketplace, I needed a larger set of potential customers. The schools were happy with the work I did for them, but after I set up multi-year contracts, they didn't need me again for a while.

I started work in the fields of higher education, healthcare, and economic development. By 2008, my clients included a local chapter of the Red Cross, several manufacturing companies, and even a coal mine. I did a bunch of projects with an old friend, Kelly, who worked for a prominent technology nonprofit. We were bringing the model that worked so well for schools to all kinds of other businesses, and I was enjoying the work.

My family also received more of my attention, a welcome and important development. I took advantage of my time at JFHQ to invest in Susan and the boys. That meant more time with her and launching myself into my kid's lives. One way I did this was through youth athletics.

I'm convinced that youth athletics delivers amazing benefits to kids and families, when consumed in bite-sized portions. I coached my kid's teams for fifteen years and loved every minute of it.

Unfortunately, everything today seems supersized, and that's not always good for the kids or their families. Crazy parents, coaches who think they are Vince Lombardi, and overbearing athletic associations are ruining youth sports. And the consequences are worse than just taking the fun out of friendly games. I think youth athletics as they exist today are harming the very fabric of American life.

Kids are practicing football, field hockey, and soccer all summer long instead of getting summer jobs. They are specializing in one sport while they are still young, getting injured and missing out on other opportunities. They are too caught up with travel teams that cost lots of money, waste tons of time, and diminish traditional neighborhood athletic programs. And they don't go to church anymore because they always have competitions on Sunday mornings. Of course, all of this is the fault of adults, and none of it is good for society.

My kids still play high school sports, but my involvement with youth athletics is winding down. That's good because I don't have the patience to put up with it the way it is today. Fortunately, I was mostly involved with youth sports when it was still fun for the kids and families alike.

Since I was a teenager, I always wanted to coach my kids in sports. I suppose I thought coaching my kids' sports team was one of those things that made you a man. My dad coached my baseball team when I was a boy. We went 15-0 one year to win the championship. It was an amazing memory for him and me.

My first coaching experience was before I had any kids of my own. Soon after I moved to Harrisburg, I volunteered to coach a Little League baseball team because I thought it would be a good way to help the community. It was an okay experience, but I didn't know any of the kids or the parents, so I wasn't as invested.

T-ball with Will was different. The kids were just learning the game, and I would get to teach them the basics. Plus, I would be coaching my own son! What a great way to spend time with Will while also teaching kids about a game I loved.

I soon learned that the most important thing in T-ball is to protect your testicles, and the next most important thing is to protect your kneecaps. Both sets of appendages were in mortal danger from those flailing urchins. Quickly, I learned to use one hand to protect my lower extremities from bats and balls and the other for everything else. Otherwise, T-ball can be incapacitating to a grown man.

Eventually, I graduated from T-ball and moved up to Grasshopper and then to Biddy Baseball, which was for nine and ten-year-old boys. In Biddy, I got my groove. I coached six seasons as the head Biddy coach, two each for Will, Jake, and Eli. The kids in Biddy were old enough to play something that resembled normal baseball and young enough to be still coachable. Plus, they rarely hit you in the testicles. Coaching Biddy baseball is one of my fondest memories with my kids.

I also coached youth soccer, but that got weird fast. In my hometown, very few people my age played soccer as a kid. We simply didn't have youth soccer in the 1980s. I was on the first varsity soccer team at our high school and was pretty good—a two-time league all-star.

I figured my high school all-star credentials were good enough to teach eight-year-old kids how to kick a soccer ball, but I was incorrect. It seemed you needed to pay a lot of money and be certified by an official soccer organization to coach soccer. Otherwise, you were banned to coach T-ball forever or something like that. The only exception was if you had a foreign accent, especially a British, German, or Spanish one, which meant you automatically were considered a "football" expert.

Anyway, the soccer authorities let me coach kids for a while, but only until they reached the age when my uncredentialed advice might corrupt them. After that, I would have to relinquish my coaching authority to a properly authenticated amateur professional.

Until then, however, I was allowed to teach the eight-year-olds all the important things about soccer. Don't touch the ball with your hands. Don't kick the ball with your big toe. Make sure to fold your hands in front of your private parts when you stand there as somebody blasts a direct kick right at your groin. Honestly, that last thing might be the stupidest play in all of sports.

Love-hate. That describes my relationship with wrestling. I love all the self-discipline it teaches. I love the competitiveness of the sport. I am glad our boys all wrestled for most of their lives.

When they were little, it improved their behavior. They slept better; they wore off some of their seemingly boundless energy. They didn't fight with each other as much.

As they got older, their behavior was mostly self-controlled, aside from being "hangry" when they were watching their weight. And because the boys all wrestled together, they had shared experiences and shared pain, which brought them closer together.

On the other hand, I hate watching them wrestle. I'm sure they're going to be injured while on the mat. A separated shoulder is at the top of my worry list, followed by a broken neck or spine. There have been banged heads, injured knees and ankles, sore hips, and countless scratches and abrasions. But they survived and lived to wrestle another day. I just don't like watching my babies experiencing pain.

The most intense sport I coached was wrestling. I had wrestled since I was about eight years old and was an average wrestler in high school. I earned a varsity letter for three years and finished about .500 for my career. But winning half your high school matches in the Lehigh Valley, Pennsylvania, where wrestling is the best in the country, is like being a state qualifier in most other places. I got to wrestle a lot of really good athletes.

Most people in wrestling have a love-hate relationship with the sport. They love it when it's over. Wrestling is full of tough, physical, and aggressive characters, and that's just the moms. It's the only scholastic sport where it's just you versus them, mano a mano, even when you are four years old.

That's how old Jake was when I took him to his first wrestling practice. Jake was always a great athlete, but he was little, so he always had to compete against much bigger kids. I figured that with wrestling, he'd excel given the chance to demonstrate his athleticism against kids his own size.

I was right. By the time he was in kindergarten, Jake was on the varsity squad. In first grade, he won the league tournament. And he kept winning and winning and winning.

I knew the guys who ran the wrestling program in our hometown, Mike and Josh. Mike was my former practice partner on the high school wrestling team and Josh was an old family friend. Together, they led the squad through many very successful seasons in an extremely tough league, and I was their assistant coach for five years.

All three of my boys wrestled. Jake was the best, but each was very competitive. Will started wrestling later than the others, but he became a bulldog on the mat, beating more experienced kids by his sheer strength. Eli was resilient, perhaps the most intense of the three boys, and you could never count him out even when he was behind. He loved to throw this move called the Peterson, and he could catch even the best wrestlers off guard.

Eli also started wrestling in kindergarten, and he drew a tough match for his first youth varsity bout, against an older and more experienced boy. He was getting beaten badly, and by the end of the second period, he was losing 14-0. One more point in the third period, and he would lose by technical fall.

Coach Mike and Coach Josh surveyed the wrestlers on the mat. Eli was so frustrated he was almost crying. His opponent had hardly broken a sweat. Mike yelled to get Eli's attention.

"Eli," he said.

Eli nodded and listened.

"Put the kid on his back and pin him," said Mike.

"Okay," whimpered Eli.

Pretty good advice, I suppose.

When the whistle blew, Eli put the kid on his back and pinned him. Mike acted like he had it planned the entire time. I wish it were always that simple.

Eventually, Mike and Josh moved on and my friend Rick and I took over. We ran the program together for four years and had a blast. During that time, I routinely spent twenty hours a week planning wrestling, practicing wrestling, and coaching wrestling. It was a great way to stay in shape, teach the kids mental and physical toughness, and most of all, spend time with my boys.

As much as I loved wrestling, Susan wasn't so sure. They didn't have wrestling where she grew up in Beaver, and she didn't know anything about it. When the boys were first starting out, she used to ask if we were going to "play wrestling." Then when she became the team mom and volunteered to wash the uniforms, she called them "onesies" instead of singlets.

When she watched the matches, she engaged in a common behavior among wrestling parents known as "wresticulation." That's when you move your own body into strange positions during your son's wrestling match with the irrational hope that your movements will somehow affect the outcome.

In a way, wrestling became a metaphor for our life. To be successful in such a unique and demanding sport requires persistent hard work, enduring self-discipline, and ongoing self-sacrifice. Indeed, there is no shortcut to avoiding the hardships of wrestling; they are central to its appeal. Surviving the daily pain is what makes wrestlers so resilient. I suppose the same can be said about part-time military service.

There are other similarities. Wrestling tests an individual's ability to violently impose his will upon another human being who is actively trying to resist. Parents generally don't think of it that way when their six-year-old first starts rolling around the practice room. But the first time their kid comes crying off the mat after being slammed to his back in front of hundreds of people, the true nature of the sport is evident. It's brutal.

From the outside looking in, the National Guard is a great way to pay for college, learn a trade, or maybe even get a retirement check down the road. But if you were in the National Guard during the past two decades, you probably went to war. And whether you launched PSYOP missions from an airbase or conducted patrols with an infantry squad, your business while in uniform was death and destruction. I'm not trying to sound like some kind of tough guy, but that's the nature of the armed forces.

People who join the National Guard just for the financial benefits are like guys who join the wrestling team just to get in shape. Eventually, somebody is going to slam you on the mat. If you are not ready, it will be a painful experience.

Our family could handle getting slammed on the mat.

Notes:

The 2nd Brigade Combat Team Facebook page and a 2006 speech by Colonel Gronski (before he became a brigadier general) provide heartfelt tributes to the part-time soldiers of the Iron Brigade. Their first-hand accounts are cited below.

[1] 2/28 BCT Fallen Warrior Memorial Committee, "The 2nd Brigade Combat Team, 28th Infantry Division (2/28 BCT), Pennsylvania Army National Guard was mobilized in January 2005 to support Operation Iraqi Freedom," Facebook, June 29, 2009, https://www.facebook.com/permalink.php?story_fbid=123728606350&id=123723206350.

[2] Colonel John L. Gronski, Captain Kurt Nielsen and Captain Alfred Smith, "2/28 BCT Goes to War," (Speech by Colonel Gronski, July 1, 2006, posted online by the Pennsylvania Department of Military and Veterans Affairs, Public Affairs Office), http://www.milvet.state.pa.us/PAO/pr/2006_07_01.htm.

[3] Ibid.

[4] Ibid.

[5] Ibid.

[6] 2/28 BCT Fallen Warrior Memorial Committee, Facebook, June 29, 2009.

CHAPTER FIFTEEN:
ADVENTURES IN AFGHANISTAN

IN EARLY 2009, NEWLY elected President Barack Obama ordered a troop surge in Afghanistan to reverse a deteriorating security situation. In one of his first acts as commander-in-chief, President Obama sent 17,000 additional soldiers, airmen, and Marines to the country to combat the violence. Like in Iraq two years prior, the 193rd would be part of the surge.

Major Marvin Laing, one of my best friends in the military, was now the chief of intelligence at the 193rd. He knew I was bored at JFHQ. He also needed an experienced intelligence officer to lead the first rotation to Afghanistan and get everything set up for subsequent crews. He asked if I would be willing to deploy again as part of the 193rd.

Well, the whole point of me transferring to JFHQ was to stay home for a while. But even Susan knew I wasn't very happy at JFHQ. She told me she had things under control in the household and reminded me that Christine was doing fine with the business. It would be a short deployment that would help some old friends. Susan encouraged me to go. On March 9, 2009, I left for Afghanistan.

One of the people I went with was Senior Master Sergeant Maria. She was a clerk at JFHQ, where she had spent much of her career. Headquarters clerks rarely get the chance to deploy, so she was excited about the opportunity. It was her very first deployment at the end of a long and productive career.

Senior Master Sergeant Maria and I took the rotator flight from Baltimore to Qatar along with the rest of the deployers and headed to our final destination. Since aircraft were getting targeted by MANPADS and AAA, we got issued flak jackets and helmets to wear while flying over Afghanistan, especially during takeoffs and landings. We were in a C-130 configured for troop transport with mesh nylon seats. Trips like that are loud, cold, and not always super comfortable. I looked at Maria, and she looked nervous. I told her not to worry: "Just do what I do." Then I promptly fell asleep.

Falling asleep in just about any circumstance is a skill I learned in Army infantry school. We always were sleep-deprived, and we would grab any shut-eye any chance we could get. We would doze off in buses to the ranges, while sitting on the toilets and while leaning up against each other standing in line.

For me, sleeping on a bumpy C-130 was like being a baby in a crib. I slept the whole way. Later, Senior Master Sergeant Maria told me that even though she couldn't sleep herself, watching me fall asleep so fast put her at ease. After all, if I was so calm that I could just doze off immediately, then maybe she didn't have anything to worry about.

When we got to Afghanistan, it was noticeably cold. Most of the other places I had been were hot, sandy deserts. This place looked like Denver, with big snowcapped mountains and beautiful scenery all around. I was glad I had packed all my cold-weather gear.

I didn't exactly make a great first impression. As soon as we arrived, one of our supervisory units started assigning additional duties to help with base administration. That very evening, somebody from the 193rd was supposed to report for dreaded "kitchen patrol" (KP) duty at the dining facility. We couldn't get out of it.

Normally, stuff like that gets assigned to junior airmen of the lowest ranks. But all our enlisted aircrew needed rest, the maintenance crews had to work on the airplanes, and we simply didn't have any extra bodies for peeling potatoes. Since I was rolling into an established intelligence shop and could wait a day to take over, I figured I was the most expendable. So I volunteered to do KP duty myself.

In the National Guard, it's not at all unusual for field grade officers to volunteer for manual labor if necessary. But on active duty, it's a whole different culture. Majors don't do KP duty. Fortunately, we were supposed to report in our physical training (PT) uniform, which didn't reveal rank anyway. I just thought I would just show up, do the work, and keep a low profile. How hard could it be?

When I arrived, they didn't make me peel potatoes. Instead, they stationed me at the entrance of the dining facility to scan ID cards for the airmen getting dinner. I made the most of it, greeting all the airmen as they arrived and trying to see if there were any others from Pennsylvania. I was having a good time, standing there smiling in my Air Force shorts and official PT t-shirt.

All of a sudden, some Air Force chief walked in and looked at me like I was the Taliban. Without giving me any chance to respond, he lit into me for wearing the wrong PT uniform pants.

"Who told you to wear shorts in my DFAC?" he bellowed. DFAC is the Air Force acronym for dining facility. "Long pants only! How dare you expose my airmen to those hairy legs!"

Okay, that was kind of funny. But then he told me he was disgusted and I was a disgrace.

It's true, I do have hairy legs. But I'm pretty sure they were not the cause of any gastrointestinal disease that evening among the deployed airmen. I would have worn the long pants if I had known better, but I didn't get the memo. Regardless, there I was on day one, causing a public health crisis at my new base in Afghanistan.

There were a few guys from the 193rd in the dining hall who saw the whole thing, and they made it worse. They were laughing their butts off and catcalling at me the entire time. I couldn't keep a straight face, and that just made the chief even madder. The whole scene was completely ridiculous, and to avoid further embarrassment to both the chief and myself, I just stood there and took the punishment.

The next day, I was at a meeting in my regular uniform when that chief walked in. I just acted like nothing had happened. The look on that chief's face when he saw my major rank made the whole episode worthwhile.

While I had been goofing around in my PT shorts, the rest of the 193rd was getting ready to launch airplanes. The missions started soon after we arrived, and the flights were intense for the aircrew. They observed lots of firefights on the ground and plenty of AAA in the air, albeit mostly from a distance. The Taliban did not have a lot of effective anti-aircraft systems, and they had no command and control, but they had plenty of dangerous weapons. Instead of navigating around known missile batteries or enemy locations, the aircrew had to be on the watch all the time for random potshots. This meant constant vigilance while in flight.

On the ground, the Taliban employed similar random terrorist tactics. They had assorted rockets from various places and would periodically fire them at the base. Typically, some terrorists in a truck would drive somewhere outside the base and launch a volley of rockets during the night, then immediately drive away before we could respond. The Taliban couldn't really aim them effectively, so they would just launch them in the general direction of various points on the base and see what they could hit.

The first time I heard the rockets was soon after we arrived. They sounded like fireworks, except louder and creepier. They would whiz by overhead or wherever they went and explode when they hit the ground. Sometimes, you couldn't hear the rockets, just the boom. Regardless, soon after the attack, the sirens would go off, and everybody would put on their flak jackets and helmets and run into a bunker.

Each bunker was a cargo container, or CONEX as we called them, that was either buried or covered in sandbags. We would sit in these things huddled together with a bunch of other airmen and soldiers, all stinky and crammed together. Then after a while, usually about an hour, we would get the all-clear signal and go back to what we were doing.

After a couple of these rocket attacks, I realized the futility of my response. The sirens went off after the attacks were over. Running to the bunkers only wasted my time, keeping me from either working or sleeping. Unless it seemed like a prolonged volley, I stopped going, figuring that if God wanted to take me with a random rocket attack while I was in bed, then so be it. I added sleeping through rocket attacks to my repertoire of novel ways to snooze.

We soon got into a battle rhythm and settled into a routine. With me from the 193rd was Technical Sergeant Ed Maurice, a friend and colleague I'd known for many years. One of the more cerebral people I met in the Air Force, Technical Sergeant Maurice loved arguing the contrarian position on just about any issue. I don't think he believed half the stuff he said: he just really liked to argue. Regardless, he was an outstanding intelligence analyst and an excellent conversationalist.

He was also a computer whiz, and he configured the laptops in our shop with all the bells and whistles. We used a messaging program called "MIRC Chat," known only to the military. Just about anybody who deployed overseas with the Air Force probably used it at some point. It was this rudimentary program written before they even had cellphones, but we kept using it anyway.

Technical Sergeant Maurice configured our MIRC Chat so that when different people sent messages, the speakers on the computer made different sound effects. That way, we didn't have to stare at the screen and could still know when somebody important was messaging us.

My old friend Hacker from the Romanian Eight was at NATO headquarters in Kabul as our liaison officer. Since headquarters would often send important last-minute changes and urgent requests, Technical Sergeant Maurice set up the system so every time Hacker sent us a message, it made a cartoonish sound like incoming artillery rounds.

One night, after we had launched the airplane, I was catching up on some work. I was alone in the operations center except for two airmen tasked with monitoring aircraft communications. They had just arrived from Harrisburg, and this was their first combat zone tour. I think it might have even been their first shift. They were young and green.

Suddenly, we heard the unmistakable sound of rockets flying overhead and the telltale boom of the explosions. The sirens went off, and we grabbed our battle rattle and headed to the bunker. This was no time to ignore the sirens. Those rockets were too close, and I needed to follow base protocols in the presence of young airmen.

The new guys were understandably apprehensive about what we were experiencing, but they remained calm and cool. We passed the time chatting in the bunker about life on the airbase in Afghanistan. I told them where to eat, where to work out, and where to get a haircut. I told them not to worry too much about the rocket launches unless there were multiple volleys because that would be something new and different from the random terror attacks. Eventually, we got the all-clear, took off our flak jackets, and got back to work.

But only minutes later, the sounds of streaking missiles and exploding ordinance filled the tent again.

"Major Dellicker," the young airman yelled as he grabbed his gear and dashed toward the bunker. "We gotta take cover! It's another attack!"

Actually, Hacker had been following the developments from Kabul and was checking to see if we were okay—via MIRC Chat. Technical Sergeant Maurice had forgotten to turn down the volume on the system, and Hacker was particularly chatty that evening. Every time Hacker sent us a message to see if we were okay, it sounded like more incoming rounds through the computer speakers.

When I see those guys today, I still tease them about diving in the bunker to escape Hacker's text messages.

We tried to find humor in just about everything, but the

deployment was no joke. Afghanistan was the most dangerous place I had been.

As Technical Sergeant Maurice settled in to provide support to our flying operations, I made it my mission to improve base security against these random rocket attacks and other terrorist incursions. Stateside, I had gained experience as the intelligence support to force protection officer and had gone to multiple training programs for this very purpose. I put my training to good use.

Rockets aren't like mortars. They fly straight toward their targets instead of in a big arc. Think of it as a pass versus a punt. We were defending against the pass.

Fortunately, Americans had lots of experience with rockets from our time in Iraq. For years, the Air Force had to defend its bases in places like Balad and Baghdad from rocket attacks similar to what we were experiencing in Afghanistan. The Air Force figured out it was cheaper and more effective to erect concrete barriers around important buildings than to install expensive, questionable structural improvements on the roofs. The rockets would hit the sides of the barriers instead of the buildings.

So I became a construction manager. First, my team would use various intelligence tools to determine the most likely flight paths and detonation patterns of enemy rockets. Then we would analyze the places from where the Taliban was most likely to launch the attacks. Next, we would use web-based applications and engineering manuals to design customized concrete barriers. After a brief approval process, we would order them through base contracting.

From there, a team of American contractors would pour the concrete right on base with a crew of Afghan laborers. The contractors were usually interesting characters, mostly retired military guys, willing to put themselves in harm's way to earn six figures tax-free doing the same construction work they would otherwise be doing at home for one-quarter the pay.

Within a few days, the barriers would arrive at the desired location with a crane and a front-end loader and drop the barriers into place. The whole process would only take a couple of weeks, and it was extremely effective. Over time, these barriers rendered the random rocket attacks less and less effective, and it was very rewarding to complete tangible projects that made our soldiers and airmen safer.

The presence of local Afghans on base was a constant source of anxiety. The whole purpose of our mission was to prepare the national government to defend itself, so we were in regular contact with local Afghans. Air Force security forces were responsible for base security, but they had to manage hundreds of Afghan soldiers and civilians working "inside the wire."

A favorite tactic of the Taliban was to identify residents who worked on American bases and threaten them with a stark choice: either attack Americans from inside or come home to a murdered family. Also, sometimes an Afghan just flipped loyalties or planned an infiltration from the beginning. Regardless of the reason, the threat from native Afghans was a constant reality.

Sometimes, they would just try to ram a truck full of explosives through the gate. Usually, that ended badly for the terrorists. Another method was shooting unarmed servicemen and -women when they didn't expect it. While I was in Afghanistan, two Naval officers went for a run along the perimeter road at their FOB. A member of the Afghanistan army, whom they were there to assist, opened fire, and killed the two men, wounding another.

Soldiers and Marines who routinely go outside the wire have a combat zone experience to which I cannot fully relate. I spent most of my four deployments inside the wire of various airbases and never faced the same danger as many of my fellow combat zone veterans. Dodging random rockets and avoiding chance attacks does not compare to being behind the trigger of an M-4 carbine rifle confronting enemy troops or behind the wheel of a vehicle navigating incendiary explosive devices (IEDs, or truck bombs).

I suppose my infantry background gives me better insight

than most airmen into the nature of close combat. Still, without experiencing it directly, I always found it prudent to avoid commenting about it at all. Those who fired their weapons and lived to tell about it deserve to tell their stories as they see fit without foolish speculation from the rest of us.

Those who do not make it back depend on others to tell their stories. Often, fallen US servicemen and -women would come through our base as their final stop in Afghanistan before going home. Whenever this occurred, and it happened regularly, the entire airfield would stop to pay their respects as they slowly passed.

Saluting flag-draped coffins on foreign soil is something I will never forget. I cannot adequately describe the mix of pride, anger, honor, and loss you feel when as you stand there at attention watching the procession go by. Just trust me when I say it is impossible to view warfare the same way after you experience it.

By early May, a new rotation of airmen from the 193rd had arrived to take our place, and Technical Sergeant Maurice and I got our relief up to speed within a few days. One of the last things we did was see a Toby Keith concert on base, sponsored by the United Service Organizations (USO). Toby Keith and his band are great Americans, flying to all sorts of dangerous places to entertain the troops, even visiting FOBs in remote locations. We enjoyed the show and appreciated his gesture. Then we packed up to go home.

When it was time to depart Afghanistan, we put on our battle gear and boarded the C-130 for the first hop home. I remember looking at Senior Master Sergeant Maria, now a veteran, and wondering what she thought. Then I promptly fell asleep.

We left Afghanistan on May 3 and spent three days in Qatar before catching the rotator home. After being in Afghanistan, the US base in Qatar was like being in Disneyland. They have a big white tent that people call "the bra" because of the way it looks suspended from its poles. You can hang out and have three beers a day—that's the limit—as you wait for transportation.

I got home on late Thursday, May 7, and had the weekend off. Then I had to go back to the unit the following Monday and Tuesday to out-process and turn in all my gear. By Wednesday, I was back to work on broadband projects.

CHAPTER SIXTEEN:
EVERYTHING IS GOING RIGHT

THIS TIME AROUND, I tried to do a better job coming home. After the fiasco of two years prior, when Susan and I yelled at each other while we put the kids on the bus during the first day of school, I knew I needed to do better. Mostly, I needed to stay out of Susan's way and refrain from intervening in her family systems and processes.

I had missed Easter but was home in time for Eli's fifth birthday. Over the past couple of years, Susan had developed a whole network of friends, mostly the moms of the boys' friends. A lot of these women took their kids to the local preschool at our church, Sunshine Center.

These days, the Sunshine Center seems like a relic of a distant, better age. Wonderful teachers would look out for our kids and teach them about God, manners, and good behavior. Thanks to Sunshine Center, all our kids knew how to read, at least somewhat, before they went to kindergarten. The moms volunteered and hung out together, and we enjoyed the Halloween parties that gave out real candy, Christmas shows that actually mentioned Jesus, and egg hunts that still kept "Easter" in the name.

From time to time, Susan would arrange dates with her new friends and their husbands, so we could meet and hang out and get together. Even though I'd heard her talking about "Tracy" and "Marci" and "Suzy," I had never met them. Then we would get together, and I would learn all sorts of interesting things about her new friends.

Tracy was a classmate of mine and one of the very first people I ever danced with in junior high. Marci was the minister's daughter, and once I had gotten in trouble for hitting her in the eye with a spitball at a pizza restaurant. Suzy was married to Joe, who was one of my best friends in kindergarten. That's what you get when you move back to your hometown.

Susan didn't know about my connections with these women when she met them, and it was nice for her that she made these friends without my introductions. For me, it was a great way to get reacquainted with long-lost pals from high school. We made lots of good friends in Kutztown.

The Ledeboers would become our closest friends. Susan met Fran as a volunteer for track and field day at the elementary school. Fran and Susan each had a mom crush on the elementary school gym teacher, Mr. T. They didn't know Mr. T. had been my high school wrestling coach. He secretly told me about all their antics.

Fran's husband, Ted, is a nerd like me who likes to watch birds and loves to go camping. Their son Hayden was best buddies with Will, and their twins Tess and Wyatt were about the same ages as Jake and Eli. We went on vacations together to all kinds of interesting places, like Lake George, New York; Bar Harbor, Maine; and the mountains of rural North Carolina, to visit Fran's hometown.

With encouragement from Fran and me, Will and Hayden decided to enroll in an environmental camp for elementary school students at the local community college. They weren't too keen on taking a "class" during the summer, but it looked like they would get to spend a lot of time outside, and a few of their other friends were going too. We all figured they would be able to play in the woods, slosh around the creek, and collect crayfish and other creatures that little boys think are cool.

After the first day, however, we realized that the program wasn't quite what we had expected. It was mostly indoors, and the boys were disappointed about being stuck inside. The instructor, a nice man I'll call Mr. B., seemed to be taking the program a little more seriously than the boys would allow. I'm sure they were a bit rambunctious and not on their best behavior.

Fran and the other moms and I would take turns driving to and from the college with the boys. After a couple of days, it was my turn to pick them up, so I went to the classroom to collect them from Mr. B. I was hoping the boys would be in a better mood because I knew they had been outside most of the day.

When I introduced myself to Mr. B., his facial expression changed instantly, and his new face was not a pleasant one. He sternly said to me that while they were outside, my son was showing his friends how to eat grasshoppers.

"Oh, I see," I said to Mr. B without changing my expression. "Did Will at least show them how to take the back legs off first? Otherwise, the bugs might scratch their throats."

Mr. B. stared in horror. He had nothing more to say. I just took the boys home.

That evening, I had to apologize one-by-one to all the other moms for the grasshopper-eating incident. I explained that Kevin had returned from survival school and taught us which plants and bugs around the yard were edible and which had to be avoided. Our boys were the only kids in the neighborhood who had a rule that before they ate a new bug, they had to check with Dad first. Will was clearly trying to impress his friends, and shocking Mr. B. was just a bonus.

Thankfully, all my girlfriends just laughed and chalked it up to boys being boys. None of the boys got worms, and no grasshopper legs got stuck in their throats. We did, however, decide that Mr. B. had probably had enough. So the next day Fran and I decided to take all the boys swimming instead of to class.

At some point, Susan decided that she would like to get back in the classroom. She was still working for Dellicker Strategies, but she missed being with the students and speaking German. Our boys were getting older and more independent, so she decided to start teaching again.

First, she took a part-time job teaching German at the local community college. Then a few years later, she got a half-time position teaching at the nearby high school. These jobs helped Susan earn some extra money, get out of the house and, most importantly, get back into her academic field.

While our roots in the community were getting stronger, Susan was making new friends, and the business continued to grow. We already had branched out into other industries with our broadband work, and we soon launched a new practice around online learning and digital instruction. It was a logical progression. Once schools had better internet access, we could show them how to apply that technology to improve academic outcomes.

We hired instructional specialists, data analysts, and trainers that could put all these pieces together. Wherever possible, we hired veterans. Mike was a former Marine Corps radio operator who helped with technical designs. Carl was a former paratrooper with the 82nd Airborne. John was a retired Navy chief. Brian was an Army National Guard intelligence analyst. Another Brian was an Air Force strategic planner.

Over the next few years, we compiled a team of some of the best educational technology professionals on the East Coast to develop and deliver these innovative services. I hired one of my friends who was very talented, out of work, and needed a job. I hired Jake's third-grade teacher, who had retired after a thirty-year career and could help train other teachers in our system. I even hired my brother-in-law Jim, a business teacher with a master's degree in education. He could help me sell the program and serve as an account manager for western Pennsylvania. By 2015, Dellicker Strategies had ten full-time employees and was helping more than 100 schools use technology to improve student performance.

The business was snowballing, and lots of schools were signing up for the company's new digital learning services. Kevin and his team were driving all around Pennsylvania and New Jersey, setting up new programs, and they could hardly keep up with all the work.

One day, Kevin told me that he had messed up and double-booked one of his team members for a school visit. Would I help him conduct the meeting?

At first, I said no. I didn't feel qualified to offer advice to school administrators about digital learning and was content to stay in the background and keep the books. Besides, I thought the company would look small and unprofessional, having a husband-and-wife team walk around a school together.

But when Christine called to ask if I would reconsider, I figured this was more than Kevin just messing around. They needed the help. Christine assured me that with my master's degree and teaching experience, I had more than enough credentials for the role. And all I had to do was walk around, be pleasant and take good notes.

"Okay," I said, but I was still concerned about how it would look to have Mr. and Mrs. Dellicker show up together. Christine agreed, so she suggested I use my maiden name and go as Susan Frank instead of Susan Dellicker. That wasn't really lying, and people wouldn't know we were married. I agreed.

On the day of the meeting, I was relaxed and enjoying my new role as "digital learning consultant." Kevin was having a bit too much fun pretending we were business colleagues instead of husband and wife. We arrived early and sat down in a conference room, waiting for the group of school administrators to arrive. Nobody would have guessed we were anything but a pair of professional colleagues.

Then Kevin looked over and noticed that a button on my blouse had popped open. My shirt was wide open for all the world to see. I fumbled to fix it but was having trouble, and the administrators were due in the room any minute.

In a last-ditch effort to save my modesty, Kevin reached over to assist. Of course, right at that moment, one of the school administrators walked into the room and caught Mr. Dellicker adjusting Ms. Frank's blouse. The lady just smiled at us awkwardly and sat down like nothing had happened, as Kevin and I both turned a bright shade of red. Before we could explain, the rest of the group walked into the room, and we got caught up in the meeting. We never did reveal our secret.

I always wondered what that lady must have said about us after we left.

After returning from Afghanistan, I went back to JFHQ at Indiantown Gap with some trepidation. But after my rough start, the work at JFHQ was better. Colonel X. had retired, and I had completed all the domestic operations training requirements. Then I got involved with a new real-world mission. It was not quite as exciting as my deployments overseas but still very interesting, nonetheless.

I was selected to be the military liaison to the FBI in their Intelligence and Operations Center (IOC) during the G-20 Summit of World Leaders in Pittsburgh. In the fall of 2009, the world was still recovering from the collapse of the global financial system, and we were witnessing the early emergence of the "Occupy Wall Street" protests and the "Antifa" movements of recent times. The National Guard deployed hundreds of troops to maintain law and order in the city of Pittsburgh during this important meeting to ensure that any protests remained peaceful and the environment was safe for world leaders.

The IOC was just east of downtown Pittsburgh near the Steelers practice complex. I sat next to representatives from the Secret Service, the State Police, and the Pittsburgh police inside the FBI facility. My primary job was to ensure adequate cross-communications among the National Guard and all these other responsible agencies, so it was mostly a lot of talk and emails. But in doing the job, I got to see a little bit how the FBI synthesized information and how the Secret Service protected the President. It only lasted a week, but it was quite a rewarding experience, the capstone event of my time at JFHQ.

During this period, I also completed Air Command and Staff College (ACSC), which is a lengthy course required for promotion to lieutenant colonel. If you are a decent officer on active duty, the Air Force generally sends you and your whole family to Alabama for an entire year, where you can complete the course in a low-stress, high-leisure academic setting. It's a nice break from deployments and offers outstanding pay and benefits for mid-level Air Force officers and their families.

The Guard only gets a handful of seats for officers to go to Alabama, and most Guardsmen cannot just uproot themselves and their families for a year to complete ACSC. But the Air Force makes officers complete the same course anyway, so they offer an online curriculum. Guardsmen have two options for online ACSC: the normal version that includes all the classes without the research, and a longer version that results in a master's degree. My friend Marv told me the master's program was easier because you get to write papers instead of taking tests, and I believed him. He was wrong.

For two full years, I spent between four to eight hours a week working on my ACSC classes. Assignments were due each Sunday, so usually, I would start working on Friday afternoons after I finished my regular work. Then I would try to finish early Saturday mornings before the rest of the family got out of bed. Sometimes, I couldn't avoid spilling into our family time, which wasn't fair to them or me. The low point was when I had to work on an assignment while we were on vacation in New England. The whole family went out to breakfast in downtown Boston while I stayed in the hotel to work on my class. That was awful.

I persevered, and eventually, I finished the course. I learned a few important things and read a couple of good books, but mostly, this was checking a box. I would have been a more productive officer and better human being if I could have used those 600 hours I spent on ACSC doing just about anything else, especially spending time with my family. Someday, the active Air Force is going to figure out a way to recognize civilian work experience and academic credentials as viable alternatives to box-checking military courses designed for active duty. I didn't regret completing the program, but I was sure glad when it was over.

Fortunately, the payoff came quickly. The Air National Guard unit at State College needed an intelligence officer to lead its analysis, correlation, and fusion (ACF) cell, and the job required a lieutenant colonel. Since I had completed ACSC, I qualified to compete for the position. And even though my work at JFHQ had improved, I was still excited to do something different.

There were some downsides to taking the job at State College. I would have to leave for a month of training, which I didn't want to do. I also would have to drive three hours each way to attend weekend drills, which meant I would stay overnight every Saturday. That was placing another burden on my family.

There were plenty of good things about the job, however. I would get another chance to work for Sharon Hedges, who was now a full-bird colonel in charge of the State College intelligence squadron. I would gain valuable leadership experience and would learn more about military strategy and operational assessment. And even though I had to leave for a month of training, the school was in Hurlburt Field, Florida, one of the prettiest places on earth.

Susan and I talked it over. While she acknowledged the difficulties of being overnight once a month, she also pointed out that I usually got home from Saturday drills in Harrisburg drills late anyway and just went to bed. She also said she felt better about me staying put than driving ninety miles after a long day at drill. Finally, she said that if I got the job, she would come and visit me in Florida during my month of training. That sealed the deal for me.

The only question had to do with deployments. The State College unit did not deploy as often as Harrisburg, but when they went overseas, they usually went for longer periods. Unless we had to fight World War III, I didn't want to disappear for six to twelve months while my kids were entering high school.

I talked to Colonel Hedges about it. She assured me that up to that point, State College deployments were all volunteer. She acknowledged that I had deployed enough for a while and was supportive of me taking a break. Overall, the likelihood of a long, unwanted deployment seemed to be slim. I applied for the job, got accepted, and said goodbye to JFHQ.

The Air and Space Operations Squadron in State College was still part of the 193rd Special Operations Wing, but it was not part of AFSOC. Instead, it supported the United States Pacific Command (PACOM) and focused on Asia. Since almost all my overseas experience had been with Central Command (CENTCOM), which encompassed the Middle East, this was a welcome change of scenery. I could count on training exercises to South Korea or Alaska instead of regular deployments to the desert.

The ACF cell consisted of some very smart and experienced intelligence analysts. They prepared operational-level support to air defense units and provided up-to-date information about enemy air forces, from Russian bombers off the coast of Canada to Chinese fighters in the straits of Taiwan. They provided reserve support to Air Force operations from California to India and everywhere in between. I was excited to get to work.

After Kevin accepted the assignment at State College, I saw an advertisement for a beautiful farmette for sale in our school district. It was surrounded by woods and fields with an old farmhouse, a barn, and a pond. The land was adjacent to state game lands, which meant nobody could build behind us. It was an idyllic property, a perfect setting for three high school boys.

We called our realtor friend Patrick and asked for a showing, but he delivered bad news. The person who listed the house had gotten cold feet and decided not to sell. It was off the market.

We persisted. We asked Patrick to explain that we were a local family with young boys in no hurry to buy. That we grew up in the area and would be great caretakers of this beautiful farm. Eventually, the owner relented and agreed to show the property to us, but it still wasn't back on the market.

Kevin and I arrived on a snowy day with Patrick. At the property was the homeowner, a woman who looked vaguely familiar. After an awkward hello and some clumsy small talk, she asked about our family. We talked about Will, Jake, and Eli.

"Your son is Will Dellicker?" she said.

"Yes, why?" I replied.

It turned out that the owner of the property was a retired special education aide at the Northwestern Middle School, where Will was in eighth grade. Unbeknownst to us, Will had repeatedly volunteered to help her with her special education students, and she had grown fond of him. When she found out Will was our son, she agreed to sell the farm to us.

The purchase of that property capped an unbelievably fortunate stretch for the Dellicker family. Business was booming. Kevin's military career was advancing. I was happy and teaching again. The kids were doing well. We had good friends. Everybody was healthy. We were incredibly blessed, and everything seemed to be going our way.

What could possibly go wrong?

CHAPTER SEVENTEEN:
EVERYTHING IS GOING WRONG

IN EARLY 2014, OUR dear friend Fran Ledeboer passed away after a long bout with cancer. Fran was very well-liked, so it was tragic news for the entire community. Of course, it was devastating for the Ledeboer family. Ted was a hero for holding his family together.

Fran's passing affected Susan more deeply than I initially perceived. They were very close, and Fran was perhaps the friend whose company Susan enjoyed the most. But Fran was more than somebody to hang out with. She was a counselor, a comforter, and an inspiration to those around her. Being without Fran left a big void in Susan's heart.

Shortly thereafter, Susan's father ended up in the hospital with blood clots in his leg. It was very serious. For a while, we thought they might have to amputate. He recovered, but Susan felt terrible that she was in eastern Pennsylvania while he was in Erie. She drove out to sit by his side and thought about him when she was home.

Then in June of 2015, our next-door neighbor, Eric the Dad, died in a motorcycle crash. This tragic accident occurred right after we sold our house in Kutztown. We both felt awful that just when his family needed us the most, we were moving out of the neighborhood. We knew there was nothing we could do about this unpredictable sequence of events. Still, it added more sadness to the bittersweet feelings we already had about the move.

Yes, the farm was the fulfillment of a dream. But it seemed that we were leaving behind something more than just our friends and neighbors. We were leaving behind those innocent childhood years. Kutztown was where we had raised our babies, and our boys were becoming teenagers. We hadn't prepared for those types of feelings when we decided to move, but they were upon us, nonetheless. The boys were growing up, and life was changing fast.

So was my military situation. Colonel Hedges left to take a new job at the Pentagon, so there was a leadership gap in the squadron. It was great for her career, but I was going to miss her in State College.

About that time, the unit received a notice of realignment from PACOM to CENTCOM. That could only mean one thing. The Air Force needed more help fighting the ongoing wars in the Middle East.

Sure enough, I got asked to deploy just a few months later. The unit was being mobilized to fight the Islamic State of Iraq and Syria (ISIS) and needed "volunteers." The only good news was that it was just for three months. But now, on top of everything else, we had to prepare for another deployment.

Meanwhile, the business was getting harder to handle. We had achieved tremendous success with our digital learning platform, and our services were in demand. But as the number of clients grew, so did our expenses. I had to hire a salesperson. We were long overdue for a new website. We needed to diversify our client base and automate some of our processes. Dellicker Strategies was no longer a basement-based business, and we were now supporting ten families with our work.

Around this time, Susan decided that she didn't want to work for Dellicker Strategies anymore. She transitioned out of administrative operations, and for the first time in a decade, she was not involved with day-to-day business affairs. Susan had done a ton of work for the company over the years. She knew the employees, managed the finances, and ran the home office. I respected her decision, but she was going to be irreplaceable.

Susan said it was because the finances had become too

complicated and that the company had outgrown her part-time role. That was a reasonable explanation, but I didn't believe that was the main reason. Maybe she just got bored. Perhaps she was stressed about the upcoming deployment. Regardless, with no little kids at home anymore and a part-time teaching schedule, I was concerned she was getting too isolated in the new house. She had started to look sad again, like when we were in Texas. I was worried about her.

The military added to her anxiety. At some point in the middle of all this, I got a call from the State College unit about my upcoming deployment. The timeframes had changed. Instead of being three months, it had been extended to almost nine months. And since I had previously volunteered, I was still on the list to go.

I couldn't believe it. I felt like the victim of a bait-and-switch. I told them to forget it. I simply couldn't go for that long. I couldn't do that to Susan.

They said it was too late to change the plan. There was nothing they could do.

I considered resigning my commission on the spot. But even that probably wouldn't have gotten me out of the deployment. You can't just cancel orders if they're already in the system.

Then I thought for a minute. *I've heard that line before, "There's nothing we can do."* That was the same thing they had told me in Texas when they had wanted to send me home from intel school. We had fixed that problem then. We could fix this one now. I needed to calm down.

I talked to a few people and made a couple of phone calls. It didn't take long until I found two qualified officers who could go instead. Perhaps they were doing me a favor, or maybe they felt bad for my wife. It's possible they just really wanted to go. Regardless, they agreed to take my place on the deployment. And after some wrangling with the unit and paperwork exercises, I got off the list. Whew.

That was a wake-up call for me and my relationship with the National Guard. Although I had declined to participate in exercises and schools over the years, this was the first time I had ever gotten out of a real-world mission. I didn't like the way it made me feel. I knew that it was an impossible situation and that I might have lost everything with Susan had I deployed. But I still felt I had let down my peers by asking them to bail me out. I couldn't put myself, my family, or my fellow airmen in that position again.

I resolved to get out.

I started to plan an orderly exit leading to retirement. I knew that JFHQ had two major DOMOPS events coming up, and I was already trained in the job. One was the Democratic National Convention in Philadelphia, and the other was the Presidential Inauguration in Washington, D.C. They needed help, and I needed to make a change.

I wasn't thrilled to be going back to JFHQ, even for a short period. I still had memories of Colonel X barking at me fresh in my mind. I wondered what new set of spankings I might receive this time for stepping out and trying to do my job. Honestly, I was just hoping to finish my career on a positive note and then retire. I never expected it to end with me bitterly limping to the finish line.

The business was no reprieve. We got caught up in an unforeseen political firestorm that became a bona fide crisis for Dellicker Strategies. The inauguration of a new governor had exposed sharp policy disagreements between Democrats in the executive branch and Republicans in the state legislature. Politicians in Harrisburg could not agree on funding priorities, and the June deadline to pass a budget came and went with no resolution. Without money from the state, schools started hoarding their cash. Districts had to borrow money to pay for essential expenses, and hardly any were spending money on new initiatives. Right after we ramped up our team, our customers couldn't purchase our services.

This posed quite a conundrum for me. On the one hand, the underlying appeal of our programming remained, and the schools still liked what we were selling. Since the budget impasse couldn't last forever, I could just wait for a few months and pick up where I left off.

On the other hand, the business was hemorrhaging cash, and I was going into debt just to make payroll. If I kept everybody working without getting paid, I might not be able to recover. Ever the optimist, I chose the optimistic route. We kept working.

The impasse persisted: one month, three months, six months. Every time it seemed like the politicians were on the brink of an agreement, the talks would suddenly unravel. Eight months passed with no resolution. We couldn't hang on anymore, waiting for this to end. We needed to end this high-stakes gamble now. I announced layoffs.

Jake's teacher quit before I had to fire her. Thank goodness.

Next was my old friend, the talented guy who needed a job.

Then came my brother-in-law. Jim said he understood the circumstances, had no regrets, and knew I was doing the best I could. What a class act. The truth is, I was terrified to lay off Jim. I didn't know if it would estrange me from my in-laws forever or trigger something worse, like a crisis in my marriage. Anytime somebody snidely remarks about how great I have it owning my own business, I remember how I felt when I laid off my brother-in-law.

Unfortunately, we weren't out of the woods yet. After it became clear that the state was not coming through, I needed a Plan B for Dellicker Strategies. I vowed never again to let the whims of politicians impact my business the way we had just experienced. We had three fundamental problems. First, we were overly dependent on Pennsylvania schools as a client base. Second, we were too constrained by geography. We could only serve customers within a six-hour radius of Harrisburg. Third, we were spending far too much time on the sales process relative to the size of the deals. We had to fix all three of these problems right away if we were going to survive.

Our old business model was services-based. Consultants would go on-site to conduct planning, deliver training, and track outcomes. It had worked well, but it was too labor-intensive. Our new model had to be solutions-based. We would use technology tools, online training, and specialty software to automate the process and cut costs. If we were successful, our new product would be much cheaper, more accessible, and easier to sell. Now we just had to convince somebody to help us pay for all the development.

That was easier than we expected. Christine called an old friend Tom in the venture capital business and explained our situation. He was eager to help. Tom gave me a crash course in raising capital and helped me prepare a basic funding pitch. He sent it to a few venture capital firms, and within a few days, we already got a meeting. "It never happens that fast," said Tom. We were encouraged.

We had a series of meetings with this guy from Philadelphia, a big-shot financier. He was a founding partner in one of the biggest tech financing firms on the East Coast. Now he was semi-retired and investing money on smaller projects. He liked our team, agreed with our mission, and thought we had a good business model.

Within a couple of weeks, I had a term sheet for a sizeable investment that would pay for software development, production of online training modules, a new website, and a sales and marketing infrastructure. In return, the venture capitalist would take part ownership of my company. I thought it was a fantastic deal, and my entire team was excited about the prospects.

Things were on track. The lawyers were negotiating the fine points of the agreement, the accountants were taking care of the taxes, and I was filing new paperwork with state and local agencies. Then on the day of closing, our VC backed out.

He gave no notice and no reasonable explanation. Officially, he said he wanted to see if some of our sales projections played out as expected, but that didn't make any sense. He knew everything about our sales pipeline from dozens of pages of documents. Unofficially, my lawyer thinks he had a limited amount of money to invest and simply found a better deal. That's certainly possible. But it didn't make me feel any better.

When we counted all the money lost on this failed transaction, the costs were staggering. We had wasted $32,000 in legal fees,

$11,000 on accountants, and $9,000 for an aborted website. I had made a job offer to a salesperson that I couldn't honor and had to lay off another one of my most productive employees. For three months, I had spent almost all my time on this deal at the expense of everything else, including sales, marketing, and service delivery. So much for Plan B. What a waste.

How did everything get so messed up so fast?

At one point in the middle of all this, Susan shut down. She called in sick to work, laid on the bed, and cried. I took her to the doctor, but I didn't need a professional to tell me what was going on. The stress of the past year had finally pushed her over her limit. It would take her two full weeks before she felt comfortable enough to go outside and several more months before she was fully recovered.

I had those same feelings of responsibility that I had from our time in Texas, only worse. Susan had been riding a rollercoaster with me for sixteen years and had made plenty of sacrifices to support the children and me. Now I was second-guessing everything. Maybe I had stayed in the military too long. Maybe I needed to quit my stressful business and get a normal job. Maybe the farm was a bad idea. Yes, definitely, the farm was a terrible idea. Or maybe not?

I don't know what else to write about this whole episode. I just hope others never have to experience anything similar.

CHAPTER EIGHTEEN: ANOTHER CHANCE

I WAS READY TO quit. The military. My business. Whatever.

I did my fair share of feeling sorry for myself during that time. Susan was depressed. The business was in the tank. My military career was going nowhere. I even started to need reading glasses.

I had purchased a pair of readers as part of a costume to roast my friend John, who had just turned fifty. He was a retired state trooper who had used to go undercover as a drug dealer. So I dressed up to look like a caricature of him, with a long-hair wig, fake earrings, oversized jacket. The glasses completed the outfit. To my dismay, when I put the reading glasses on to make fun of him, I realized they worked. Now I didn't just feel like a loser. I felt like an old loser.

My kids could see that I wasn't myself. I was grumpy and routinely was making mountains out of molehills. One day, Will, who was about sixteen at the time, pulled me aside.

"Dad, worrying is a type of sin. You taught me that, and it says so in the Bible." He was right. Jesus addressed worry head-on in his Sermon on the Mount. "When you obsess about things and try to solve your problems by yourself, you are telling God you don't trust Him. You need to change your ways and trust in God."

Then he apologized for being disrespectful. Will always apologized about everything, especially when he told a truth that was painful to hear. He got that from me. We always joked that together we would make a great skit on *Saturday Night Live* called the "Apologize Guys."

But Will was right.

Plenty of people had given me the same advice: Susan, her dad, my parents. Yet hearing the same message in plain language from my son was exactly what I needed.

While I had been feeling sorry for myself over all these setbacks, I had forgotten about the three priorities Susan and I always said were most important: God, Family, and Country.

I had to start with God.

Isn't it interesting that when things are going well, we give ourselves the credit, but when things are going poorly, we blame others? I had forgotten that my success was not the result of my own brilliant planning and flawless execution, but God's gracious providence. I didn't need to buck up and work harder to solve my mounting problems; I needed to step back and get down on my knees.

Maybe all those trials were simply God's way of reminding me who is in charge. All good things come from Him, but nowhere does He promise to protect his followers from earthly suffering. In fact, sometimes, God *uses* suffering to discipline his children and prepare them for future challenges.

But God does promise his followers that He will be with each of them through all their trials. And He assures us that in the end, goodness will prevail. As Paul writes, "I consider that our present sufferings are not worth comparing with the glory that will be revealed in us" (Romans 8:18).

Sometimes, perspective is exactly what we need. With the help of God, I laid more of my burdens on the shoulders of Jesus.

I can't report some instant fix to all my problems or sudden transformation into some kind of super-Christian. But I do know that the Holy Spirit is working in my life. And it is making a difference, especially in my relationship with my family.

I don't know what I would have done without my friends and family. I am blessed to have supportive parents and in-laws and many gracious friends and neighbors who got me through some truly difficult times. Their loving attention helped me muddle through those four deployments, survive those long military schools, and handle all those short missions and weekends away. I couldn't have done it without them.

I wish all Guardsmen and their families had such a wonderful network of friends and family to get through the stress and uncertainty of part-time military service. Unfortunately, I know that is not the case. As our country continues to rely on the Guard and Reserve to defend our freedoms and fight our nation's wars, it continues to deliver underfunded family support services and inaccessible resources. Our part-time military families deserve better.

Besides recommitting to God, I had to recommit to my wife. Susan always says, "When marriage is good, it is really, really good. But when it is bad, it is awful." I think one of her girlfriends gave her that quote. It should be on a greeting card or something. Honestly, if Susan and I hadn't been so committed to the institution of marriage, our relationship, and God, our marriage might have been a casualty of the Global War on Terrorism.

There *were* times in our marriage that were downright awful. Screaming fights. Unreasonable demands. Petty manipulations. Both of us were guilty parties. I repeatedly asked Susan to do things that added to the pressure and kept her on the rollercoaster. She routinely assigned ulterior motives to my words and actions and filtered me through a lens of anxiety and prior bad experiences. Often, our kids got to witness our terrible behavior firsthand. It's amazing they still talk to us.

But we never gave up.

When we first met, our love was a noun, a romantic feeling like in a Hollywood movie. Today, our love is more like a verb, a deliberate action that we do for each other. I think it's a more mature and truthful version of the real thing.

Susan and I still fight, and we still behave poorly. But it seems that the fights are fewer, less intense, less hurtful.

A few weeks ago, Susan told me I was as mean as Joseph Stalin. Jake heard the exchange and reminded her that Stalin killed seventy million people. A few years ago, that sassy retort might have made driven Susan into a fit. This time, she just laughed. Argument over.

I am so fortunate to have Susan as my wife.

Together, our kids are our biggest blessing. Through all the turmoil in our lives, they have been a constant source of joy.

In many ways, Will is more emotionally mature than both Susan and me. He is a natural leader, a friend, and an example to his peers.

Jake is conscientious and empathetic with the best belly laugh in the world. He surprises Susan and me almost daily. Of all three boys, Jake gets in trouble the most, but usually not in a bad way. Mostly he is just so curious and resourceful.

Jake cannot tell a lie.

Not long ago, Kevin attended a school board meeting when the district adopted a new anti-substance abuse policy. They made vaping equivalent to smoking and added vaping paraphernalia to the list of prohibited items in school. Kevin and I realized we never really talked about vaping with the boys, so we made a point to bring it up.

The next night at the dinner table, Kevin told the boys about the change in school policy and made it clear he and I would not allow vaping in our household. I asked each boy if they knew people who vaped, and they all said tons of kids. Then I asked each of them if they ever tried it, and they all said no. We had no reason to doubt them.

The very next day, I went up to Jake's room to put something away and couldn't believe what I found. Half-exposed in a drawer near his bed was this battery-powered plastic thing with a long cylindrical tube and a screw-in attachment. It looked exactly like the vaping paraphernalia pictures from the school board meeting.

We were livid. It's not like vaping is equivalent to smoking pot or smuggling booze, but we had just talked to them about vaping the day before. Jake had looked us in the eyes and gave us an emphatic denial. It was so unlike Jake. We couldn't believe he would lie to us like that.

I stewed all day while we waited for Jake to come home. We met him at the door. Kevin pulled the device out of his pocket and handed it to Jake.

"Can you please explain how this works, Jake?" he scowled.

Jake scratched his head for a moment and looked genuinely puzzled. Then he answered. "Oh yeah, Dad," Jake recalled. "If you screw that little end into the stem of your bicycle tire, it lights up when you pedal. Grandma Phoebe gave it to me in my Christmas stocking a couple of years ago."

Jake never even suspected we thought it was something nefarious.

Eli is the king of the quip, an expert zinger. He is a master of the one-liner, able to silence the most confident showoff with a single phrase. He's also somewhat of a math wizard.

When Eli was a toddler, he used to ask us to give him math problems to do while we were driving in the car. In elementary school, the kids had a "fun day" and could choose among various activities like tag, basketball, or foursquare. He asked if he could do number puzzles. By the time he turned ten, he said he wanted to go to MIT and become an actuary. I had to google "actuary" to know what he was talking about.

But Eli is not just into academics. He wrestles, plays baseball, and golfs. Of all three boys, Eli may be the most competitive. I kind of knew that by watching the three boys play growing up, but Mr. T. confirmed it after having all of them in gym class. Eli wants to win, and he works very hard to achieve success on the athletic field and in the classroom.

When Eli was eight years old, he gave me one of my most memorable gifts of fatherhood to date. It was just before Christmas, and I was going through a Bible study with him about Jesus and the cross. Eli is so smart and discerning that sometimes I wonder if he believes what I am saying without scientific proof. I wasn't sure if I was getting through.

The next day, Christmas Eve, Eli approached me sincerely and said he wanted to talk. He said he had thought a lot about what we read and talked about the day before and had made a decision. He said he understood what I was saying and wanted to follow Jesus. He asked if I would help him say a prayer offering his life to the Lord. I was floored.

The point of all this chatter about marriage and the kids is this. If the business fails, if the military career ends, if we lose the farm, we still have our family. We could end up a complete failure in all those other endeavors, but because of that Christmas Eve exchange with Eli and similar conversations with Will and Jake, our lives would still be a success. That's both true and liberating. Our family is the fruit of our labor.

But this story does not end there. Success in adjusting your attitude tends to enable success in other things.

Susan got back to normal and is doing great. She took a new job with a different school district and is teaching German full-time again. She enjoys the productive days and new relationships with students and colleagues. And with all three boys in high school, she doesn't miss a thing in their schedules.

Dellicker Strategies also recovered and is thriving again. After the mess with the venture capitalist, my employees and I pushed hard to get some important new sales and renewals. We continued to develop our software and online learning components according to plan, albeit with a lot fewer bells and whistles. By the end of 2017, Dellicker Strategies found a buyer for the entire digital learning practice. I was able to shed most of my debt, provide jobs for all my employees, and get back to basics doing the broadband projects like I used to do.

It was amazing what we had accomplished. Our digital learning services had improved the quality of classroom instruction in dozens of schools. More than 90 percent of our customers reported better academic performance, with hundreds of students earning higher scores on standardized tests. Our small company had an outsized impact on helping students learn.

After the sale, I started an entirely new branch of the business focused on cybersecurity. I found some retired military veterans who were experts in the field and asked them to help me develop a new product line. By the beginning of 2019, we rolled out a suite of services focused on helping schools and municipalities protect their data from cybercriminals. It was invigorating to launch something so important in an exciting field with a new group of great people.

Even my military career turned around. After the near fiasco in State College and my reluctant return to JFHQ, I expected to put in my time until I retired in a year or two. But my experience at Fort Indiantown Gap was completely different the second time around. Nobody hollered at me, nobody played silly games, and everybody seemed to appreciate my contributions. Things were much better.

Maybe it was because of my rank. The last time through, I was a captain among colonels.

Perhaps it was due to my training. I was much better prepared for the job.

It could have been my new boss, Colonel K., the same Air Force navigator who had sat on my initial interview board and hired me as an Air Force officer in 1998. He was an outstanding leader who looked out for his people.

Or maybe it was my colleagues. They all seemed much more professional this time around, especially the Army officers.

All those things were probably contributing factors, but the main reason was something completely different. It was my attitude. I was no longer a know-it-all hotshot with a chip on my shoulder. I was older, wiser, humbler.

While I was at JFHQ, an unforeseen opportunity opened at my old unit in Harrisburg. My longtime friend and colleague, Marv

Laing, was still the chief of intelligence at the 193rd. He took a new job at the wing and needed a replacement. He asked if I could interview to fill the role.

I told him yes but was honest about my timeframe. I told him I intended to retire in two years when I hit twenty-three years of service. He didn't seem to mind. He and his boss selected me for the job (I think I was the only applicant).

When I arrived back at the 193rd, I found the people and the work just as exciting as I remembered from ten years ago. There were still a few old guys around. Hacker was there, along with a handful of pilots and navigators I had known. Most of the intelligence section was brand new. It was a fresh start in an old familiar place: it felt like coming home.

Susan could see the change in my attitude. I wasn't complaining about going to drill anymore. I was excited about the mission and the people. And the people are truly extraordinary. Consider some of the twenty-percent soldiers and their families who serve with me part-time:

Tim is my senior NCO, a purchasing manager at a federal agency in his civilian job. He spent a year in Iraq as an Army truck driver and returned to the combat zone four times as an Air Force intelligence analyst. He is a semi-professional sportscaster and an amateur religious scholar. His wife Erinn was nominated for "Pennsylvania National Guard Spouse of the Year" for her tireless work supporting military families, including her own, especially while Tim was deployed.

Tom is a four-time combat-zone veteran and a teacher at a local school for troubled youth. He and his wife Colleen spend their summers taking their kids around the country in a recreational vehicle. Tom and his family traveled together to Alabama for a year to complete in-residence ACSC with the active duty. He has spent about one-third of his life in uniform since joining the Air National Guard.

Brandon is a civilian contractor. He's arguably the smartest guy in the group on the Commando Solo weapon system. He's deployed about eight different times, first as an enlisted electronic communications specialist and later as an intelligence analyst. Most recently, he did an exercise in Lithuania with the Army National Guard. His wife Megan is also a military veteran, juggling her work as a teacher, a wife, and a mom while supporting Brandon's ongoing military adventures.

Ed (Technical Sergeant Maurice) is a security expert in the civilian world. He has held a whole bunch of other interesting jobs since I've known him, from insurance salesman to bartender. He is an expert on all kinds of relevant and irrelevant subjects and may be the most informed briefer in the wing. He was recently selected to become an officer after a long career as an NCO. His wife Andrea is an accomplished nurse, and she took a one-year sabbatical to travel with Ed to Texas for his officer intelligence school. While he was there, Ed taught several classes because he was more qualified than the instructors.

Mike is a manager for the state Department of Welfare. He was an Army infantry soldier and chemical weapons specialist before becoming an Air Force Intelligence Officer. He has deployed four times to the combat zone as a part-time airman, traveling across Europe and the Middle East. Once, he got detained in China when his civilian airline made an unforeseen landing.

AJ is an information technology manager. He runs cybersecurity operations for a major insurance company. He's also deployed four times as an intelligence analyst since 9/11. In his free time, he serves on the alumni board of Penn State Harrisburg, where he leads an annual charity event for the Four Diamonds Fund, which benefits children with cancer. He juggles work, military, and single-dad responsibilities as a with class and humor, one of the most accomplished officers in the squadron.

Scott is a banker. He lives with his wife Shannon and their daughters almost two hours away from the unit. For the past year, Scott has been doing a special tour at Fort Meade to assist with information warfare.

He is one of our most prolific deployers, volunteering for just about every opportunity there is. That's a good thing because we need his expertise. Plus, he can hook you up with a credit card.

Heath is another guy with an interesting civilian resume. He joined the Guard in his late thirties after 9/11 because he wanted to fight terrorists. Heath has a master's degree in biology and works as an emergency medical technician in civilian life. He lives with his wife Alicia in Philadelphia and drives his motorcycle to drill each weekend, even in the middle of winter. Heath is a closet snake-eater and wants to go to Ranger School if he gets the chance.

I don't even know how to categorize Rene. His family owns a bakery in Reading that he helps run. He's also a building inspector for the city and rents houses on the side. He aspires to be a *Flip or Flop* entrepreneur. Rene is in his early thirties, but he already owns several properties and is working on his MBA. His wife Yesenia put her career on hold to take over family responsibilities and business duties while Rene deployed to the combat zone.

April is a college student. She just turned twenty-one but is mature beyond her years. Fresh out of intelligence school where she earned distinguished graduate honors, April is already an accomplished analyst and excellent briefer. She was tested this summer on her first deployment to the Middle East. She is currently attending Penn State on the GI bill and probably will be an officer someday.

Courtney will be too. For many years, she worked as an enlisted technician in the intelligence shop, doing the job of about three officers. Recently, she took a position as a business systems analyst for the Navy. Her husband Kenny is also in the Air Force. She recently completed her college degree, juggling all these responsibilities with her small children. An experienced deployer, Courtney is our go-to person for getting things done. Last year, she talked her younger sister into enlisting in the Air Guard.

Kurtis is our newest officer. He has a degree in microbiology and an interest in woodworking. He makes all kinds of cool stuff out of wood for the intel shop. Another experienced deployer, Kurtis spent six months in Africa supporting a secret special operations mission that sent him to multiple countries. Recently married to Marisa, he unearthed a 100-year old wall with her while planting a garden in their backyard. Now they both are amateur archaeologists.

Bryanne is a nineteen-year-old student, just finishing intelligence school. She is attending college this fall, but she spent most of the summer helping our deployers prepare for the Middle East. Next year, we expect her to have a chance to go on her own combat deployment. By the time she starts her sophomore year, she will have visited multiple states, traveled to several countries, and gained combat zone experience.

My squadron commander owns a hardware store. He collects tractors and has deployed ten different times.

My former group commander is a stay-at-home mom. She is a C-130 test pilot who deployed four different times.

Backed by their families, these National Guardsmen plan and execute special operations missions around the world. They launch Commando Solo aircraft from all kinds of nasty places to deliver combat airpower for American strategic priorities. They support special forces raids of Taliban strongholds in Afghanistan. They convince civilians to expose ISIS positions in Syria. They warn Iranian terrorists to stay away from Kurds in Iraq.

And when they are done, these twenty-percent soldiers go home to their families and return to their offices, schools, banks, and bakeries, where their colleagues say, "Thank you for your service," and wonder which airport they were guarding for the past three months.

So it goes with twenty-percent soldiers.

EPILOGUE: COMMITMENT REVISED

IN OCTOBER OF 2017, our oldest son Will raised his right hand and swore an oath to defend the United States Constitution as a member of the Pennsylvania Army National Guard. If you count Kevin's middle name (it's Willard too), that's four generations of Willard Dellickers in the US military with seventy-seven years of uninterrupted service.

Our son was a junior in high school and seventeen years old at the time of his enlistment, so we had to sign waivers to let him in. He chose the infantry, arguably the most dangerous job in today's military for new enlistees.

As his mom, I wish he would have been a clerk or something.

As his dad, I was proud of his choice but had no delusions about what he might experience if deployed. No parents want to see their son in harm's way.

Will immediately began attending drill weekends at the local armory, and just after Memorial Day, he left for Fort Benning, Georgia, where he spent the entire summer. While his friends were practicing football, hanging around, and going on vacation, he was completing Army basic training. He got back on a Friday, reported to the armory the next Tuesday, and started his senior year the following Monday. It was Will's first experience with Guardsman whiplash.

When he got home, Will was super excited to tell everyone about his training. For the most part, his friends obliged, serving as avid listeners who were happy for him and eager to share his experiences. But soon, Will realized that despite his best efforts, most people couldn't relate to what he went through. It was strange for us to see the same emotions in Will that we had felt so many times. Mostly, we just wanted to reassure him that he wasn't alone. He was a Guardsman now too.

Having a son in the military affects your perspective.

Kevin delivered a briefing last summer on the topic of Russia, and somebody said we should be sending US troops to defend Ukraine. He asked him if Ukraine was important enough to send his own son to fight against the Russians. That kind of ended the debate. He probably never would have said that before. But isn't that the question we all should be asking?

Too many Americans are disconnected from the reality of life in the military, whether active duty, Guard, or Reserve. And the gap is getting wider. We've often heard people say that soldiers and their families know what they are getting into. That they are all volunteers. That their job is to train and fight. Therefore, we shouldn't be reluctant to use them when required to advance our national interests at home or abroad.

In a sense, that's all true. It's also true that their volunteer service means that the people who say such things can do so safely and comfortably from their own homes.

The fact is, we've been at war now for eighteen years, longer than the War of 1812, the Civil War, World War I, World War II, and the Korean War combined. Maybe it's time we figure out how to bring our troops home.

It's also time we fix a broken family support system for the Guard and Reserves. To their credit, the military is trying. Both the Department of Defense and the National Guard Bureau seem to acknowledge the problem, launching several new initiatives in the past few years.

But despite their good intentions, none of these efforts are hitting the target. That's because they remain base-focused instead of family-centered. And they don't provide nearly enough resources to meet the demand. As a result, thousands of Guard and Reserve families are left behind.

The solution is straightforward. Family support services should be fully funded and delivered where the families live, not where they report for duty. These simple changes would go a long way toward helping these extraordinary families bear the heavy loads we ask them to carry.

Our life in the Guard certainly has been difficult. Spending 20 percent of your life doing anything is quite a commitment. We chose to be in the Guard.

Sometimes we wonder what our lives would have been like if we had that 20 percent back. Perhaps we could have earned 20 percent more money. We might have had 20 percent more time as a family or been together for 20 percent more birthdays, holidays, and special occasions. Maybe we could have had a 20 percent better marriage, whatever that means.

Playing "what if" is a silly exercise. The truth is, given the chance, we would do it all again. The National Guard gave Kevin a life of adventure, sending him to sixteen countries and thirty states to train and fight our nation's wars. And it gave Susan a sense of purpose, knowing that her strong family stewardship guided three boys to manhood while their father was away. Together, we served our country while honoring God, building a marriage, raising a family, and growing a business. We would never trade that for 20 percent of anything.

The National Guard is part of who we are.

To the thousands of other Guardsmen and their families who are just like us, thank you for your service.

And to a nation that invented the concept of the citizen-soldier, we remain grateful for the opportunity to serve in such a unique and rewarding capacity. It is a humbling and satisfying experience that's worth preserving.

Thank you and God bless,

Kevin and Susan

The End

MILITARY ACRONYMS AND ABBREVIATIONS

11-B	Army Military Occupational Special Code for Infantryman
14N	Air Force Specialty Code for Intelligence Officer
AAA	Air Defense Artillery
ADVON	Advanced Echelon
AFSC	Air Force Specialty Code
AFSOC	Air Force Special Operations Command
AG	Adjutant General
AGR	Active Guard Reserve
AMS	Academy of Military Science
APC	Armored Personnel Carrier
BCT	Brigade Combat Team (Army)
CENTCOM	Central Command
CIA	Central Intelligence Agency
CJSOTF-W	Combined Joint Special Operations Task Force- West
CQ	Charge of Quarters
DFAC	Dining Facility (Air Force)
DIA	Defense Intelligence Agency
DOMOPS	Domestic Operations
DSG	Drill Status Guardsman
ECS	Electronic Communications Systems

FBI	Federal Bureau of Investigations
FOB	Forward Operating Base
HRF	Homeland Response Force
HUMINT	Human Intelligence
ICS	Incident Command System
IED	Incendiary Explosive Device
IMINT	Imagery Intelligence
INF	Infantry
ID	Infantry Division (Army)
INTREP	Intelligence Report
IOC	Information Operations Center
ISIS	Islamic State of Iraq and Syria
JEOC	Joint Emergency Operations Center
JFHQ	Joint Force Headquarters
KP	Kitchen Patrol
MANPAD	Man Portable Air Defense
MILES	Multiple Integrated Laser Engagement System
MISO	Military Information Support Operations
MISREP	Mission Report
MOS	Military Occupational Specialty
M-DAY	Mobility Day
MRE	Meal- Ready to Eat
NATO	North Atlantic Treaty Organization